VISUAL QUICKSTART GUIDE

MACROMEDIA SITESPRING

FOR WINDOWS AND MACINTOSH

Paul Devine

 Peachpit Press

Visual QuickStart Guide
Macromedia Sitespring for Windows and Macintosh
Paul Devine

Peachpit Press
1249 Eighth Street
Berkeley, CA 94710
510/524-2178
800/283-9444
510/524-2221 (fax)

Find us on the World Wide Web at: www.peachpit.com
To report errors, please send anote to errata@peachpit.com
Peachpit Press is a division of Pearson Education

Copyright © 2002 Paul Devine

Editor: Jacqueline Aaron
Copyeditor: Hon Walker
Production Coordinator: Kate Reber
Compositor: Owen Wolfson
Cover design: The Visual Group

Notice of Rights
All rights reserved. No part of this book may be reproduced or transmitted in any form by any means, electronic, mechanical, photocopying, recording, or otherwise, without the prior written permission of the publisher. For information on getting permission for reprints and excerpts, contact Gary-Paul Prince at Peachpit Press.

Notice of Liability
The information in this book is distributed on an "As Is" basis, without warranty. While every precaution has been taken in the preparation of the book, neither the author nor Peachpit Press, shall have any liability to any person or entity with respect to any loss or damage caused or alleged to be caused directly or indirectly by the instructions contained in this book or by the computer software and hardware products described in it.

Trademarks
Macromedia is a registered trademark and Macromedia Sitespring is a trademark of Macromedia. Visual QuickStart Guide is a trademark of Peachpit Press, a division of Pearson Education.

Throughout this book, trademarked names are used. Rather than put a trademark symbol in each occurrence of a trademarked name, we state we are using the names only in an editorial fashion and to the benefit of the trademark owner and with no intention of infringement on the trademark.

ISBN 0-201-77057-1
9 8 7 6 5 4 3 2 1
Printed and bound in the United States of America

Acknowledgements

I cannot thank enough the people who helped me complete this book.

Jacqueline Aaron's editorial acumen and patient guidance helped me find clarity amidst jargon and muddy thoughts. Like a Zamboni machine making old rutted ice anew, Hon Walker removed many scratches and pits from the surface of my manuscript. The Peachpit team, a pleasure to work with, kept the standards high and the encouragement flowing; many thanks to Wendy Sharp and Kate Reber for their experienced direction and to Marjorie Baer for the opportunity.

While I should thank the entire Sitespring team for creating a top-notch product, I owe special thanks to Andrew Strombeck for his cogent manuscript corrections and to Paul Gilbertson for his tireless answers to obscure questions.

Thank you to my friends who encouraged me despite my whining, to my dad for the first computer, to my mom for her tireless energy, to my step-mom for showing me the tinkerer's joy, and to my aunt for being my guide to the world at large.

TABLE OF CONTENTS

Chapter 1: Introduction to Sitespring   **1**
What Web Teams Do 2
Problems with Team-Based Web Development 4
A Case for Sitespring 8
Getting Around in Sitespring 12

Chapter 2: Users and Clients   **19**
Understanding Users 20
Working with User Accounts 22
Modifying A User Account 27
Viewing User Information 30
Working with Client Organization Accounts 33
Working with Client User Accounts............. 37

Chapter 3: Projects and Project Sites   **43**
Creating and Editing Projects................... 44
Managing Projects 47
Completing a Project........................... 51
Linking Users and Projects 54
Managing Project Sites 58
Exporting, Importing, and Taking Snapshots
   of Projects.................................. 64

Chapter 4: Folders and Files   **71**
About Versioning 72
Managing Folders 74
Viewing Files or File Histories 77
Reverting to Earlier Versions of Files............. 81
Publishing Files 83
Removing Files................................. 86
Uploading Files................................. 88
Administering Sitespring Helper................. 90
Configuring Sitespring Helper 96

Chapter 5: Tasks and Reports   **103**
Managing Tasks 104
Viewing Tasks.................................. 117
Linking Files and Folders to Tasks 123
Working with Reports.......................... 128
Using Email Notifications 133

v

Table of Contents

Chapter 6: Discussions — **135**
Working with Discussions........................136
Administering Discussions......................146

Chapter 7: Managing Version Control — **151**
Managing Shared Folders 152
Managing File Versioning 157
Version Control and File Extensions............160
Using the Revision Cleanup Wizard.............163

Chapter 8: Administering Sitespring — **177**
Updating Project and Task Settings.............178
Editing the Server Setup........................184
Editing the Mail Server.........................191
Project-Site Settings............................195
Managing Licenses..............................202
Configuring the Log.............................204
Viewing Detailed System Information 209

Index — **211**

Introduction to Sitespring

Your phone rings. It's your boss. She asks you why you didn't finish the changes the client asked for. You hardly even hear the words; her tone of voice alone gets your heart pumping fast. As she's talking, you start frantically hunting for the request in your email in-box. You promise her you'll get the changes done immediately, as you fess up that you can't find the email that asked for them in the first place.

If you've ever built a Web site, you've probably dealt with a situation like this. These days Web creators don't just need tools to build images and pages; they also need tools to plan, organize, and communicate about the building process and the pages themselves. That's where Sitespring comes in: It helps people on Web teams work together more easily and effectively.

Before diving headfirst into learning how the program manages such an unwieldy task, it makes sense to review what Web teams do and, more importantly, how team members work together. After a quick refresher on the challenges posed by collaborative Web development, the purpose and utility of Sitespring will be all the more apparent.

Chapter 1

What Web Teams Do

Many tasks go into building a Web site or Web project, from creating attention-getting graphics to developing complex e-commerce applications. For this reason, Web teams often involve many people with a variety of skills. First, with even a moderately sized site, the sheer volume of work often requires a number of people just to get the site built in a reasonable amount of time. Second, it's rare to find one person whose skills cross all the disciplines needed to create a good site. When building a house, you wouldn't expect a painter to install the plumbing. By the same token, you wouldn't expect a programmer to come up with award-winning graphics. Web teams can range in size from a few individual contractors (**Figure 1.1**) all the way up to dozens or hundreds of people at some of the larger Web design houses (**Figure 1.2**).

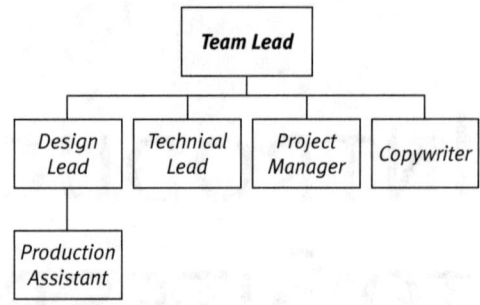

Figure 1.1 In smaller Web teams, people often perform multiple duties and have roles that are less specific.

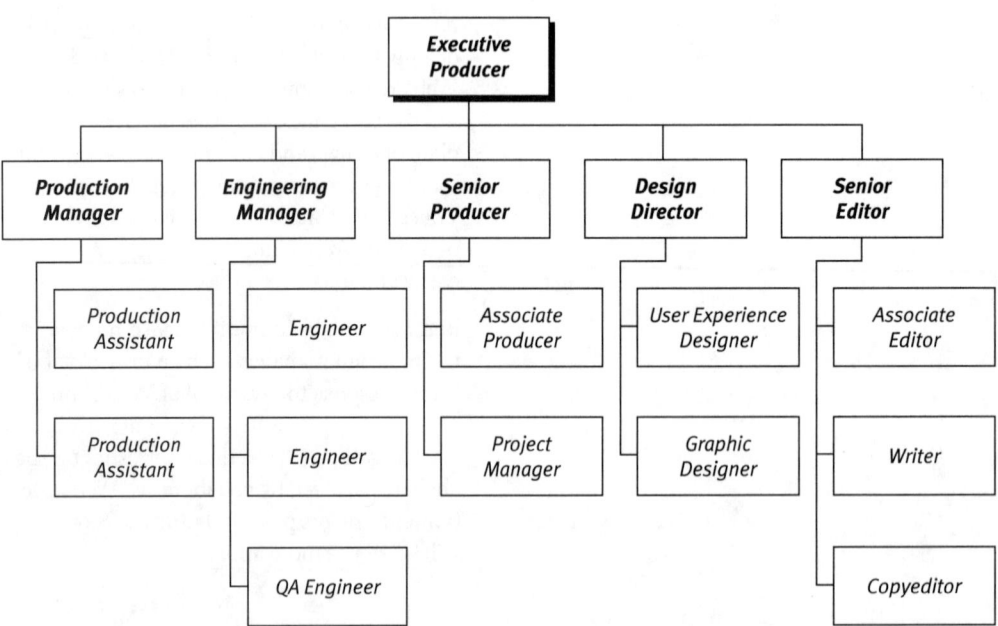

Figure 1.2 In big Web companies, teams can get quite large and are often composed of smaller teams dedicated to various job functions.

Introduction to Sitespring

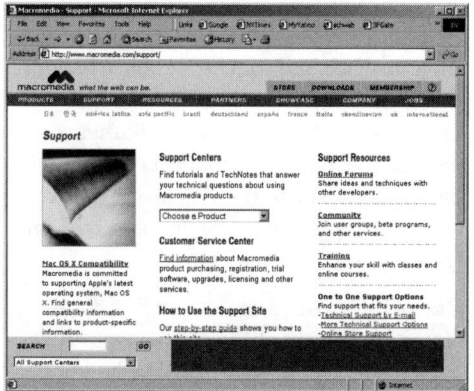

Figure 1.3 A Web page may look like one simple element, but in reality, 36 files make up the page you see here. On this page, some of the elements exist as both Flash files and regular images.

Similarly, the scope of a Web project—as with a construction project—can vary greatly. A construction job could involve moving a wall, making over a few rooms, or demolishing a whole building, while a Web project could consist of building a page, redesigning a discrete area of a site, or rebuilding a large site from the ground up.

How team members work together and what they do on a daily basis can vary dramatically. The bottom line, however, is that they're all building Web pages and sites. The typical Web page isn't really one entity; rather, it contains anywhere from a few to dozens of files. The Macromedia support page shown here (**Figure 1.3**) contains 36 files, which make up the images, buttons, and other elements of the page. Now consider the entire Macromedia site, which comprises thousands of pages. Even if each page contains just 36 images or other elements, that's a total of more than 100,000 file references (assuming the Macromedia site contains 3,000 pages, a highly conservative guess). There wouldn't actually be 100,000 separate files, because many pages would reference the same navigational images, for instance. Nonetheless, you get a sense of how many files can make up a large Web site. Creating all these files requires an endless amount of coordination, planning, and work. Keeping track of all the Web site files in development is every bit as complicated as keeping track of all the parts of a house that's under construction. Often, because of this level of difficulty, the process of modifying a large site is broken down into a series of smaller projects, in which only one section of the site at a time is changed.

WHAT WEB TEAMS DO

3

Problems with Team-Based Web Development

A Web project can run amok for myriad reasons. Building something, be it a steel bridge or a Web page, often leads to overruns in time and cost. With a bridge, you might run into problems if the steel doesn't arrive from the forge on time. With a Web page, the e-commerce software may take longer to deploy than you anticipated. Being able to identify and resolve problems (or avoid them altogether) while building a Web site often makes the difference between launching on time and launching at all. Many of the problems come down to faulty communication, poor planning, and trying to accomplish more than you can handle.

Client Problems

Anyone who's had some experience building Web sites has a client horror story. It doesn't matter whether your client is another company or the marketing manager down the hall; as outsiders to the Web team, clients are not privy to the headaches and problems their requests cause within the team.

One of the most common and frustrating issues arises right at the start of a project. When you discuss what you'll be building for the client, gauge the scope of the work, and plan the time line (**Figure 1.4**), the client naturally doesn't have as clear an understanding of what you're talking about as you do. You're the expert; the client is not. This is the root of many problems. Clients who misunderstand the goals at the beginning of a project will never be happy with what you build.

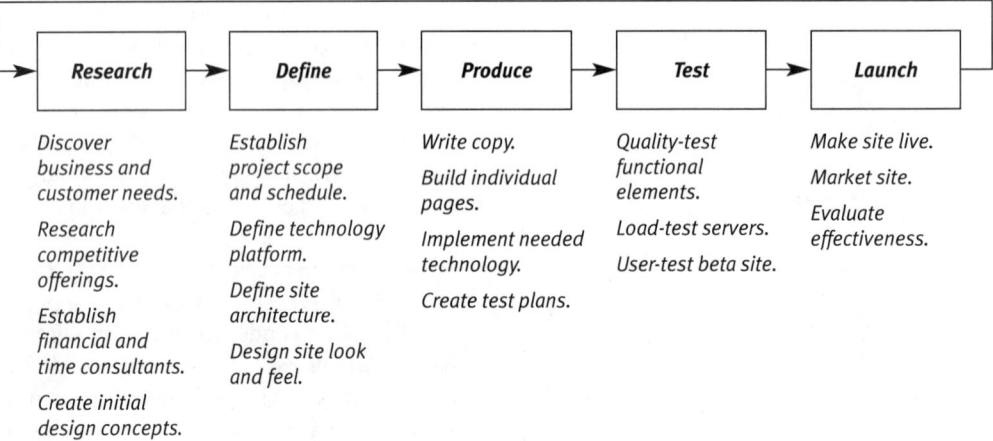

Figure 1.4 A simplified Web development process involves researching what you need, defining what you'll build, producing what you define, testing what you produce, and launching the final site.

This brings up another problem: clients who change their mind midstream. Often what the client needs the site to do evolves after construction is already under way. Other times clients realize, after they see what you've done, that it's not what they're looking for. Another frustrating difficulty arises when a client says one thing one day and something different the next. Whatever the reason, it's very costly and time consuming to go back and change work that's already been done.

Finally, clients rarely understand the scope of work that a project requires. It's not uncommon for them to ask for something that falls outside of the agreed-upon parameters. A related problem is that clients can be surprised by how long it takes to get certain tasks done. This is particularly true of some of the more technical tasks if the client has no experience with software development.

Team Member Problems

As if client problems weren't enough, our own worst enemy can be ourselves—especially when it comes to large Web teams. The various tasks that go into building a Web site require different personalities. A programmer or database designer needs a near-fanatically obsessive nature to develop flawless code. A graphic designer must be creative and able to think in terms of color and composition. A project manager pores over schedules, prods folks on deliverables, and makes sure nothing's forgotten.

continues on next page

Besides the different approaches to the Web site, the jobs themselves often come with different sets of jargon. This can be especially difficult when one term has different meanings. I once worked on a Web team whose members had backgrounds in different worlds: The producers came from print publishing, where *in production* means in the process of being built, while the technical team came from software development, where *in production* means being used by customers. Such language differences can lead to people thinking they're agreeing when actually they're saying opposite things.

Complicating matters further, you often run into a chicken-and-egg problem wherein, say, the person producing the HTML layout needs the programmer to complete his task first, while the programmer needs the HTML code finished before she can do her work. As a result, each person gives half-completed work to the other, or one of them throws a placeholder into his work and waits for his counterpart's work to be completed (**Figure 1.5**). Confusion often arises over which version of a file is the current one, or whether something is considered the final version. For example, keeping track of the fact that the page is complete but the picture of the woman in the middle needs to be replaced can create confusion.

In this muddle, there's usually a trail of emails a mile long discussing the minutiae and what's left to be done. Sometimes a crucial email doesn't reach the one person on the team who has the needed information. Other times people simply forget a line from last Friday's email in which somebody mentioned they needed a new background image for the home page. All of this communication and coordination leads to many of the small but all too frequent problems.

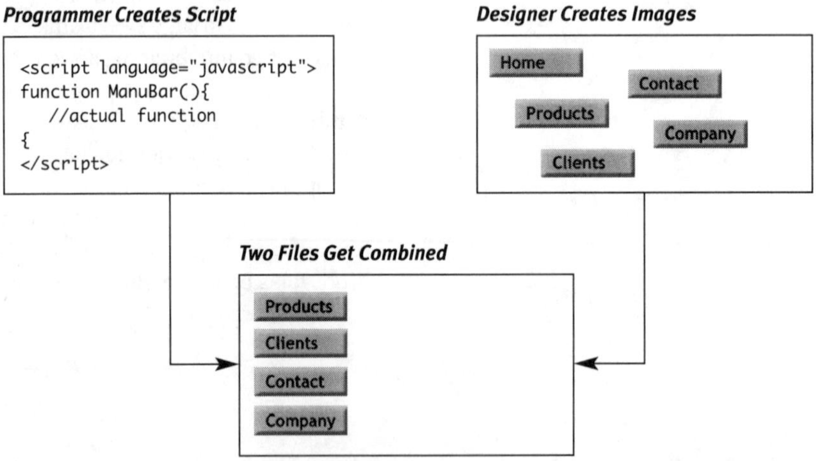

Programmer Creates Script

```
<script language="javascript">
function ManuBar(){
    //actual function
{
</script>
```

Designer Creates Images

Two Files Get Combined

Figure 1.5 To create the final Web page, the programmer needs to create the JavaScript (which doesn't work without the images), and the graphic designer needs to create the buttons (which don't work without the JavaScript). Each needs to work with an understanding of what the other is producing.

Introduction to Sitespring

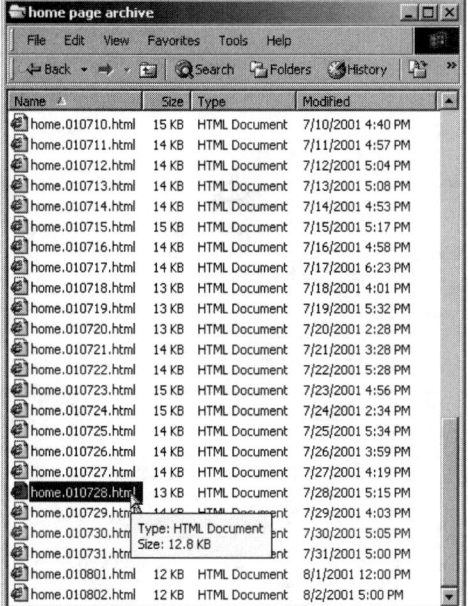

Figure 1.6 This folder contains many versions of a site's home page. A different version for each day adds up to 365 versions for just one year.

Files Get Lost

Each day Web team members create new files. Maybe the file is a navigation button, or maybe the file handles what the shopping cart does after the Process My Order button is clicked. Most files going into a Web site aren't complete upon their creation; rather, many versions of the same file get created over time. Each file can change slightly, such as when a new font is tried for the navigation bar, for instance. Or it can change quite a bit if you've decided, say, to reorganize how each page is structured. Whatever the reason, keeping track of an endlessly growing set of files can overwhelm even the most organized folks (**Figure 1.6**). One of the most heartbreaking situations is when the client asks for major changes to a set of files, which you carry out, saving over the original files. You meet with the client, excitedly showing your new work, and the client opts for the earlier version of the file after all. Now you have to go back and re-create a file that already existed. Equally frustrating is when a graphic designer spends all day tweaking an image, and an HTML coder needs to make a small change to the same image to make it work on the page. The coder pulls the image from the server down to his hard drive to start making changes, while the designer uploads his completely reworked graphic to the server—but then the HTML coder places his slightly changed version of the old file back on the server. All of a sudden the designer's updates have been for naught, as visitors to the site will still see the old file. This happens almost daily in Web production when people don't take steps to prevent it.

Chapter 1

Projects Go Off Track

Every Web team has worked on a project that's gone off track. Sometimes the project strays just a bit; sometimes the team loses sight of the track altogether. Any of the situations discussed so far can lead to problems. The most common problems, however—and the most serious—have to do with project planning. Problems related to individual files and communication pale in comparison with problems stemming from bad project planning. Ultimately in a poorly planned project, dates get missed, priorities get ignored, and projects get finished late if at all. With so many things that can go wrong, what's one to do? That's what the next section is all about.

A Case for Sitespring

Now that you've been reminded of the nasty things that crop up in your job from time to time, let's talk about what Sitespring is and how it can help you overcome these problems. To begin with, Sitespring is a Web-based application. To get the Sitespring server running, your network administrator installs the software on your production server (the machine that hosts the Web sites in development). Then you access Sitespring using a Web browser either within your company network or—depending on how your network administrator has set things up—from any browser connected to the Web (**Figure 1.7**).

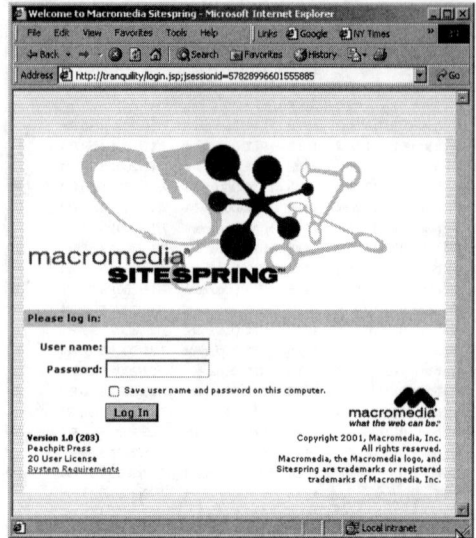

Figure 1.7 You access the Sitespring application from within a Web browser.

Sitespring simplifies the following:

◆ Team communication and coordination

◆ Client communication

◆ File management

◆ Task and project management

Introduction to Sitespring

1. *The Web team creates files in design applications and enters information about the project using a Web browser.*

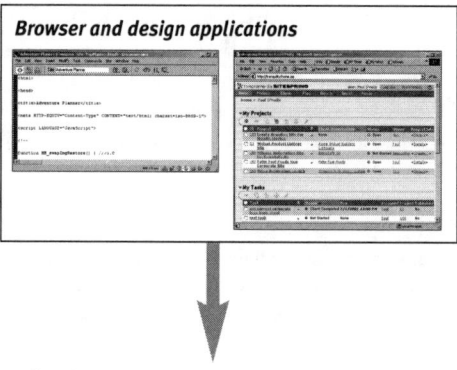

2. *The Sitespring server tracks HTML files, images, dates, and other data about the project.*

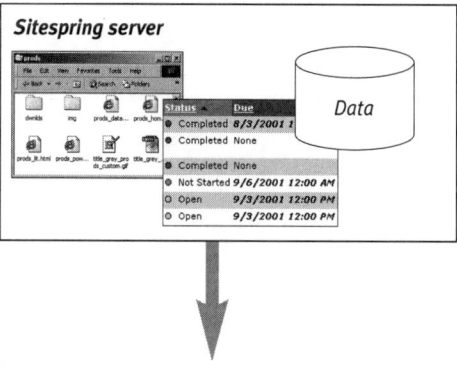

3. *Clients view the project status and approve work at project sites.*

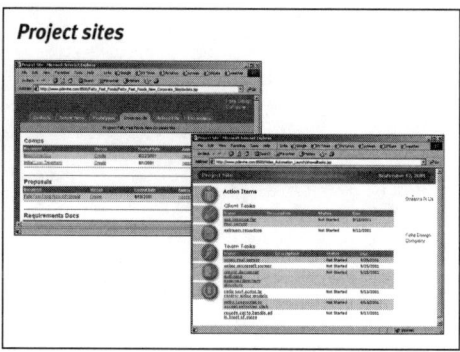

Figure 1.8 Using a browser, the Web team enters information about the project and files. The server stores and organizes that information. Clients access the information through project sites that Sitespring creates.

What Sitespring Can Do

Naturally, Sitespring won't solve all the problems that arise while building a Web site, but it will help with many of them. First, by giving you a central location where all information about the project resides, it helps you resolve or prevent many communication problems. Because both the Web team and the client go to the same source for checking the status of a project, you're much more likely to have a similar understanding of where things stand (**Figure 1.8**). Also, because you're using Sitespring every day to build the site, you're much more likely to keep the information in it up-to-date.

Sitespring lets you create a record of client communication, including the all-important client sign-off, on works in progress. Sitespring also maintains the discussion history for various issues and tasks in its messaging system.

Another important benefit of Sitespring is the automatic file versioning it does for you. Each time you save a file, Sitespring saves a copy of the version immediately preceding it. It stores the last several versions in case you need to go back to an earlier one. You can also save a snapshot of all the files in a project at critical points in development, such as client sign-off.

If you've been overwhelmed by version control systems before, don't worry; Sitespring hides the complexity of more formal schemes by saving versions behind the scenes without your needing to do anything. You can even save versions of files from the programs you use every day without specifically saving or labeling them.

continues on next page

Finally, Sitespring helps you keep track of the status of each task, as well as which tasks each team member needs to do. Nothing is more important during site production than knowing which tasks have been completed and which remain to be done. A file, say a graphic, usually follows a certain path when it moves through a Web team. First, the graphic designer creates the file, then the production person optimizes it for the Web. This ordered process is often called *workflow*. Sitespring helps you structure your team's workflow and keep tabs on how well the process is working.

Sitespring's email notification feature allows team members and clients who don't have daily assignments to be notified when they have something they need to do (**Figure 1.9**). This is particularly important when you want to let your clients know they have tasks that they still need to accomplish. You wouldn't expect them to check their task list every day, so it's handy to have them notified when it's their turn to perform a task—and even handier to have an email trail if they fall a week behind in completing their task and wonder why you haven't finished yours. Most important, if the task is related to a file, the task notification includes a link to the latest version of the file, thus helping you avoid confusion about which version to use.

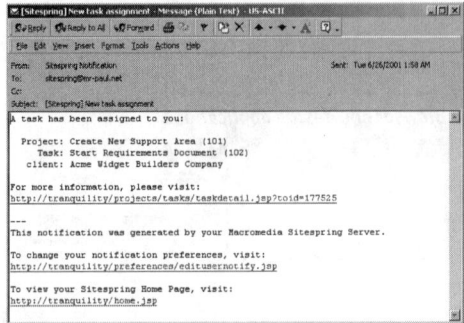

Figure 1.9 You can configure Sitespring to send you an email notice when a new task has been assigned to you.

What Sitespring Can't Do

While Sitespring will make communication easier among team members and with clients, it would be foolish to expect it to solve all of your communication problems. You'll still need to keep on top of the client to give you what you need. You'll still need regular team meetings to go over outstanding items and make sure things are on track.

If you're familiar with a programmer's version control system, you'll notice that Sitespring provides a smaller set of versioning features. Version-management systems like CVS and SourceSafe provide a rich set of features that let programmers track changes to a code base, keep track of release histories, and compare differences between individual documents. Fully-functional version-control systems are complex beasts that require a technical understanding of how to manage the system. Sitespring is not designed to replace such critical tools for more technical developers. It will, however, maintain recent versions of files—be they graphics, code, or HTML— and let you save snapshots of entire projects. Sitespring's simplified implementation provides a useful set of features without overwhelming Web team members with a bunch of extra tools.

Sitespring Will Change Your Work Habits

Nothing can replace wise project management, excellent execution strategy, and good old-fashioned teamwork, but Sitespring can help you produce top-quality Web sites in a timely manner. Right when you start using Sitespring, you'll notice that it changes how your team gets things done. Like any new tool, it will change your work style. Give yourself some time to adapt to a new way of doing things, and don't get frustrated if in the first few weeks you encounter some resistance from the team as well as some glitches in the way the system works and how people use it. Also, be prepared to give a short tutorial to clients as they start to work with the system.

Chapter 1

Getting Around in Sitespring

The first time you log into Sitespring, you'll find yourself on your own Sitespring home page. Each user who logs in will see a custom-tailored page. At first glance it can seem confusing—there's a lot of information and numerous buttons that take you to other places within the application. Let's walk through the highlights so you can get your bearings.

The Home Page

The home page contains an overview of projects, tasks, discussions, and reports that relate to your work (**Figure 1.10**). At the top of the page are standard navigation buttons that appear on every page throughout the Sitespring application. Under each section heading you'll find items that relate specifically to you and your work. Under the section My Projects, for example, you'll see a list of projects you're currently working on. Under My Tasks, you'll find items that have been assigned to you by other members of the team. The My Discussions area lists topics in a messaging system related to the projects and tasks. Finally, the My Reports section lists any custom reports you have saved.

The Navigation Bar

The navigation bar sits on top of each page and lets you reach frequently used parts of the application quickly (**Figure 1.11**). Just below the buttons that take you to the major areas of the application, you can see what's called a bread crumb trail, which identifies your current location (**Figure 1.12**). The "bread crumbs" let you trace back through a complex navigation path in the manner of Hansel and Gretel making their way through the forest. The rightmost element of the bread crumb, in gray, is the current page, while the pages to the left, in blue, are those farther up

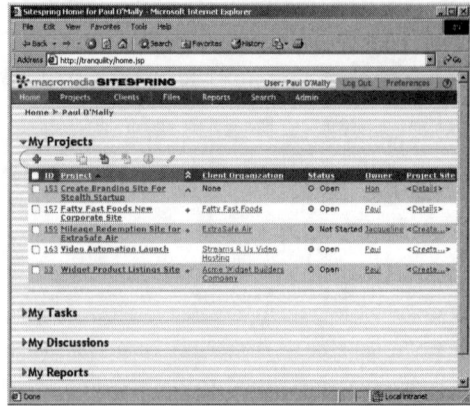

Figure 1.10 Your Sitespring home page contains a wealth of information about your projects and tasks.

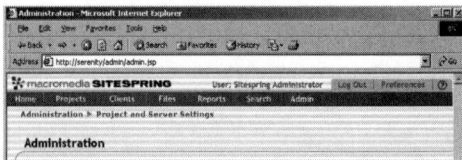

Figure 1.11 The navigation bar provides one-click access to often-used pages of the application.

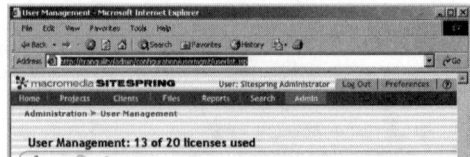

Figure 1.12 The bread crumb trail identifies your current location within Sitespring and allows quick navigation to screens farther up in the hierarchy.

in the hierarchy. You can click any of the names in blue to go directly back to that page. The bread crumbs represent the primary navigation path to each page, since some pages have more than one way of getting to them.

Home—The Home button takes you back to your home page. This page, which you see when you first log in, gives an overview of your current tasks and projects. It also lets you delve into discussions and view your reports.

Projects—The Projects button takes you to the Projects page, which lists all the projects in the system. You can quickly view their status and drill deeper into particular projects for more detailed information.

Clients—The Clients button takes you to the Client Organizations page, which lists all the clients in the system. The page also functions as a handy client phone and URL list. You can view, add, edit, and delete client information on this page.

Files—The Files button takes you to the File Explorer, which lets you manage and control file versions, and open and edit files. Users with permission can publish files to the project site.

Reports—The Reports button takes you to the Create Report page, where you can create and view reports about project tasks. You can set up reports by a variety of parameters, such as viewing only overdue tasks or only those tasks that have been completed.

Search—The Search button takes you to the Search page, where you can search for tasks, projects, clients, discussion messages, and users within the system. This can be useful when you know a keyword or phrase about an item but can't remember where to find it.

continues on next page

Admin—The Admin button appears only to the administrator and users with project-manager permissions. It takes you to the Administration page, where you can configure Sitespring, add new users, and accomplish other administrative tasks.

Log Out—The Log Out button logs you out of the application. Normally you won't use this button much, as you're automatically logged out of Sitespring every time you close your Web browser. This is a useful feature, however, if you're at a client's office and just want to check something in Sitespring from a shared computer. You don't want the client to see your private information, so you can log out without closing the browser. You would also use the Log Out button if you wanted to log back in as another user, say, the administrator.

Preferences—The Preferences button takes you to your preferences, where you can configure or update your contact information such as name, email address, email notification settings and phone number.

Help—The Help button, a question mark icon ⓘ, takes you to the help area, where you can get more information about the part of Sitespring you're currently using. The help information opens in a new browser window, so clicking it doesn't disturb what you're doing.

✔ Tip

- Be careful not to click a navigation button or link when you're in the middle of updating an item. If you click a navigation element without saving your work in progress, you'll lose the changes you've made. But if you want to abandon a change and haven't clicked Save, here's a handy trick: Simply click a navigation link and your updates will be canceled.

Introduction to Sitespring

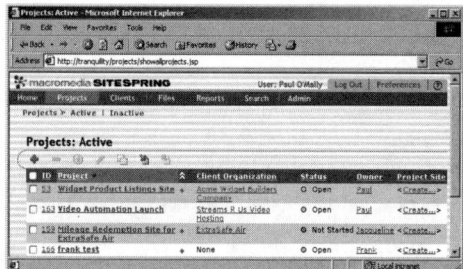

Figure 1.13 The Projects page presents a high-level overview of current projects and their status.

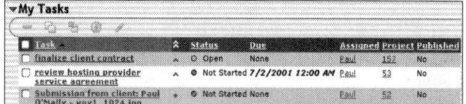

Figure 1.14 The task list on the home page shows tasks that need to be completed, their due dates, and their priority level (the symbols to the left of the Status column).

The Projects Page

The Projects page gives you a quick overview of currently open projects (**Figure 1.13**). Under the Status heading, you can see whether the project has been started; under Owner, who owns the project; and under Client Organization, who the client is. Clicking any of these items—or any item listed in blue and underlined—brings you to a more detailed page about the item. You can also access inactive or completed and closed projects by clicking the inactive link in the bread crumb section of the navigation bar.

✔ Tips

- From the Projects page you can sort the project list by name, priority, status, or any of the other column names simply by clicking the column heading.

- The currently selected sort order has a triangle next to the heading, which points up or down depending on whether the sort is ascending or descending.

- Clicking the selected heading a second time reverses the order of the sort. For example, if you've sorted the projects by priority with the highest-priority projects at the top of the list, clicking the Priority heading again will put the lowest-priority projects at the top.

The Task List

Most team members will spend a great deal of time interacting with their task list (**Figure 1.14**). Each person's task list shows the items that the team member needs to accomplish. Generally a Web team member juggles more than one project at a time, and in a hectic work environment it's hard to stay on top of what you need to do next. Losing track of a task's status can be especially irksome to other team members when they need you to finish your task before they can do theirs.

continues on next page

Chapter 1

The task list on the home page shows your tasks that have yet to be completed, their priority, status, due date, and whether a linked file has been published. By clicking the Projects button and then on a particular project, you get to a task list that has not only your own tasks but also other people's tasks. It also displays tasks that have been completed and those that are outstanding. This way the team member who's waiting for you to finish your task can check whether you're done.

Working with Modules

Throughout Sitespring, modules organize related pieces of information into logical groups. On your home page are four modules: My Projects, My Tasks, My Discussions, and My Reports (**Figure 1.15**). Modules can be expanded or collapsed. When you expand a module, it shows the first ten items in the module list. To see the rest of the items, you need to click the Show All link or page through the list (see below). When you collapse a module, only the module's title and the expand icon ▶ are displayed.

When a module contains more than ten items, you can page down or scroll through the module. Modules with ten items or less display their entire list on a single page.

To collapse or expand a module:

1. Find the module you would like to expand or collapse.

2. Click the expand icon ▶ or collapse icon ▼ to the left of the module name (**Figure 1.16**).

3. The page reloads with the module expanded or collapsed (**Figure 1.17**).

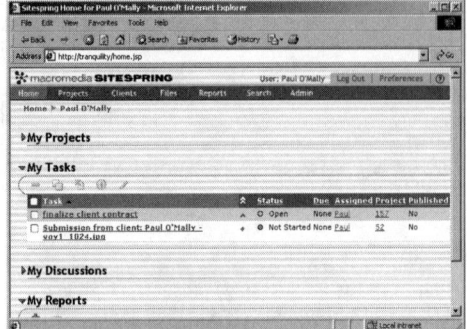

Figure 1.15 The modules on your home page organize the information into logical groups.

Figure 1.16 Click the triangle next to a module's title to expand the module.

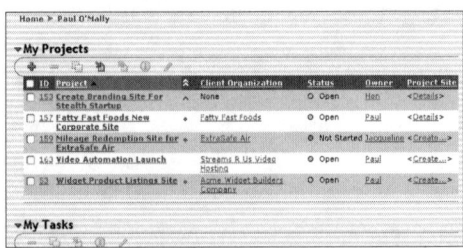

Figure 1.17 The module expands.

Introduction to Sitespring

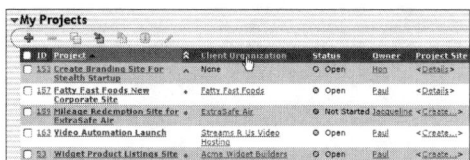

Figure 1.18 Click a column heading to sort the items in that module by that heading.

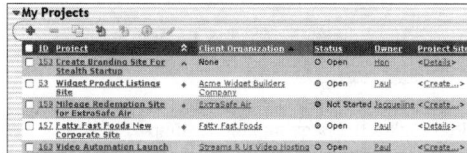

Figure 1.19 The module sorts according to the column heading clicked.

Figure 1.20 Click the Select All check box next to the leftmost column heading to select all the items.

Figure 1.21 All the items are selected.

To sort a module by heading:

1. Find the module you would like to sort.

2. Click the column heading by which you would like to sort the module (**Figure 1.18**).

3. The page reloads with the module list sorted by that column (**Figure 1.19**).

To select all items in a module:

1. Find the module that contains the list of items you'd like to select.

2. Click the Select All check box next to the leftmost column heading (**Figure 1.20**).

3. The check boxes for each item in the module are selected (**Figure 1.21**).

17

Chapter 1

To page through a module list:

1. Find the module you'd like to page through.
2. Click the page number you'd like to go to (**Figure 1.22**).
3. The new page of the module opens (**Figure 1.23**).

To show all items in a module:

1. Find the module for which you'd like to display all items.
2. Click the Show All link in the lower-right corner of the module (**Figure 1.24**).
3. A new page loads with all the items of that module displayed (**Figure 1.25**).

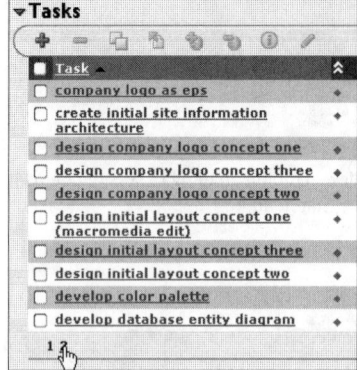

Figure 1.22 For a list of more than ten items, click the page number to jump to additional items.

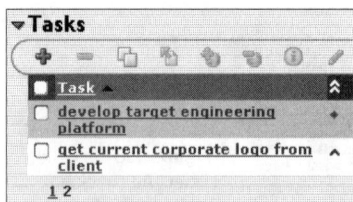

Figure 1.23 The page reloads with the new list in the module opened.

Figure 1.24 Click the Show All link to display every item in a module list.

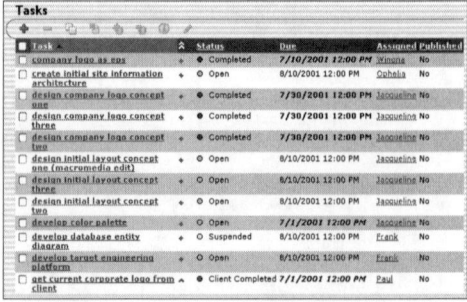

Figure 1.25 All the items in the module are displayed

Users and Clients

Sitespring's job is to facilitate work among team members and communication with clients. To get started, you need to let Sitespring know who these people and companies are. You do this by adding accounts that identify and describe users and clients.

This chapter defines the different types of users in Sitespring and explains how to create, edit, and remove accounts for them. It also walks you through the steps involved in administrative tasks such as changing your password or user profile. Finally, the chapter covers how to grant or revoke project-site permission and how to add and remove names in a project-site contact list.

Chapter 2

Understanding Users

Sitespring recognizes three types of users. The first is normal users. These are members of the team who are actively working on the Web project or site. Throughout this book the word *user* by itself refers to normal users. Among these users are those who have project manager permissions and those who don't. Project managers can add, edit, or delete accounts for users and clients; create and update the project site; and do other advanced tasks (**Figures 2.1** and **2.2**).

Second, there are client users—the clients of the team that's building the Web site. Client users can log into an external project site that lets them check the status of the project and—depending on what modules you make available to them—respond to tasks, participate in certain discussion threads, and approve documents submitted for review. They can't, however, log into the main Sitespring site. While client users can be assigned tasks and can approve a site that's been submitted for review, they can't edit files or do many of the tasks normal users can (**Figure 2.3**).

Third, there is one administrator. The Sitespring administrator, whose user name is admin, has special permission to edit the server configuration and run the Revision Cleanup Wizard. No other users can be given administrator permissions, and the admin account cannot be renamed or deleted (**Figure 2.4**).

Normal User
Can
◆ View projects, tasks, and project sites.
◆ Be assigned, create, and edit tasks.
◆ Delete user-created tasks.
◆ Create, edit, and delete files.
Cannot
◆ Add, edit, or delete projects, user accounts, or project snapshots.
◆ See the Admin button.
Can Be Permitted to
◆ Log into a project site.
◆ Appear in a contact list.
◆ Engage in discussions.

Figure 2.1 This chart depicts what normal users can do in Sitespring.

Normal User with Project Manager Permissions
Can
◆ Add, edit, and delete normal user accounts.
◆ Add and edit projects and project sites.
◆ Delete any user-created projects and project sites.
◆ Add, edit, and delete accounts for client users and client organizations.
◆ Add, edit, and delete project snapshots.
◆ Update a project-team list.
◆ Publish files to a project site.
◆ Associate folders with a project.
◆ Do everything a normal user can.
Cannot
◆ Set users' notification preferences.
◆ Edit system configuration.
Can Be Permitted to
◆ Log into a project site.
◆ Appear in contact list.
◆ Engage in discussions.

Figure 2.2 This chart depicts what users with project manager permissions are allowed to do.

Users and Clients

Client User

Can
- Be assigned tasks.
- Approve documents.

Cannot
- Log into main site.

Can Be Permitted to
- Log into a project site.
- Appear in contact list.
- Engage in discussions.
- Upload files through project site.

Figure 2.3 Client users can do less than normal users can.

Administrator

Can
- Edit system preferences.
- Receive system event notices.
- Add, edit, and delete projects.
- Add, edit, and delete accounts for client users and client organizations.
- Add, edit, and delete normal user accounts.
- Add, edit, and delete project snapshots.
- Update a project-team list.
- Associate folders with a project.

Cannot
- Be assigned tasks.
- Own a project.
- Appear in contact list.
- Engage in discussions.

Figure 2.4 Only one person, the administrator, can configure the system.

Sitespring limits the quantity of accounts to the number of normal users you license plus the administrator account (which does not count as one of the normal user accounts). Sitespring does not limit the quantity of client user accounts; you may have as many of those as you'd like. The basic Sitespring server comes with a license for three users; if you need more, you can purchase licenses in one- or five-user increments. You might squeeze in an additional user by letting someone use the administrator account as his or her regular login. Think twice before you do this, though. With the administrator account, you can do many of the tasks a user can, but you can't be assigned tasks or own projects.

Client users are not to be confused with client organizations. A client organization is generally the company that uses your services. In a large corporation, a client organization could be another department in the company. A client user is a person who works for a client organization, and it's the client user who will be given access to your projects. Suppose Bob is a client user who works for Ford Motor Company, the client organization. When creating accounts, you should create the client organization account before creating client user accounts for that organization. You can then associate the client user, Bob, with the client organization, Ford, when you create the client user account.

Many of the tasks explained in this chapter can be performed only by users with project manager permissions or by the administrator; such requirements are noted in the task descriptions.

Chapter 2

Working with User Accounts

Only the administrator and users with project manager permissions can add, edit, or delete user information. Other types of users cannot access the Administration page.

The following directions apply to adding, editing or deleting normal user accounts (those that are used by members of the Web development team). To add, edit or delete a client user account, see the following section, "Working With Client User Accounts."

To add a user account:

1. Log in as the admin user or as a user with project manager permissions.

2. Click the Admin button in the main navigation bar at the top of the screen (**Figure 2.5**).

3. The Administration page opens. Click the User Management link (**Figure 2.6**).

4. The User Management page opens. Click the Add icon ✚.

5. The Add User page opens. Enter the person's user name, password, and contact information. Note that user names and passwords are case-sensitive and limited to sixteen characters. The fields you're required to fill in are marked with an asterisk. (For more information, see descriptions of each field in the following sidebar.) If the team member gets added to a project-site contact list, the corresponding Name, Title, Company, and Email fields will be viewable by the client, so use discretion (**Figure 2.7**).

Figure 2.5 The Admin button appears only to the administrator or users with project manager permissions.

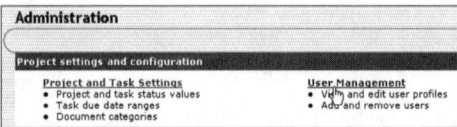

Figure 2.6 The User Management section allows you to add, edit, and delete user accounts.

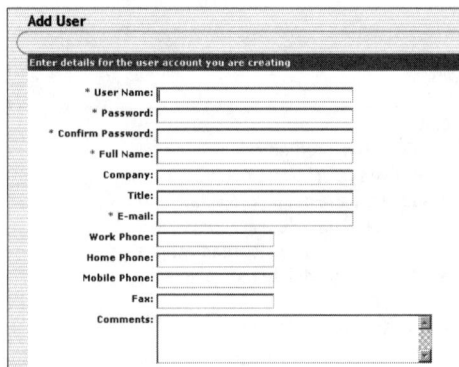

Figure 2.7 Enter the user's contact information. The email address will be used for task notification, and the contact information may be viewed by clients.

Users and Clients

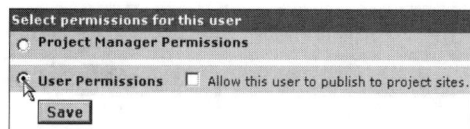

Figure 2.8 Assign permissions that are appropriate to the user's role.

6. Select user permissions. Users with basic permissions can create and edit tasks, view information about projects and clients, and do other essential tasks. If you give users permission to publish to project sites, they can also move files to the project site for a client to see.

Users with project manager permissions have additional abilities. While normal users can view information about projects, clients, and users, project managers can add, edit, and delete that information. See "Understanding Users, earlier in this chapter for more information about permissions (**Figure 2.8**).

continues on next page

The Add User Fields

User Name—User names are unique and are used for identification throughout the application.

Password—Unlike client users, normal users can change their own passwords. Assign normal users an initial password, and for security reasons ask them to change it when they first log in (see "To change your password" later in this chapter). Passwords will not appear on a contact list, of course.

Confirm Password—Retype the password you just entered to make sure you input it correctly.

Full Name—Enter the full name of the user. You can sort lists of team-member names alphabetically; if you'd like the lists to be sorted by last name, type the last names before the first names in this field. Otherwise, team-member lists will be sorted by first name.

Company—Enter the name of the company the team member works for. In most cases this will be your company.

Title—Enter the team member's job title.

E-mail—Enter the team member's email address. Clients may see this address and Sitespring will send notices about task and project status here; if the user has multiple addresses, choose the one that's most applicable.

Work Phone—Unless you configure the program otherwise, only normal users will be able to see this field. If there's a chance you might set up a project-site contact list so that clients can see work phone numbers, be sure to furnish a complete number rather than an internal extension.

Home Phone—Unless you configure the program otherwise, only normal users will be able to see this field.

Mobile Phone—See "Home Phone."

Fax—See "Work Phone."

Comments—Only normal users will be able to see this field.

23

Chapter 2

7. Click Save to add the new user, or click any navigation link to cancel the operation.

✔ **Tip**

- Don't navigate from the page without first clicking Save, or you'll lose your work. If you're on the Add User page and you need to use your browser to find out some information, create a new browser window by going to the File menu and selecting the option to create a new window. In the new window, find the information you need, then go back to the Add User window to finish entering the information and click Save.

To edit user information:

1. Click the Admin button in the main navigation bar at the top of the screen (**Figure 2.9**).

2. The Administration page opens. Click the User Management link.

3. The User Management page opens. Click the check box next to the name of the user whose profile you would like to edit.

4. Click the Edit icon 🖉 at the top of the User Management module (**Figure 2.10**).

5. Edit the user information (**Figure 2.11**). (See "To add a user account" earlier in this chapter for detailed information about the fields in this form.)

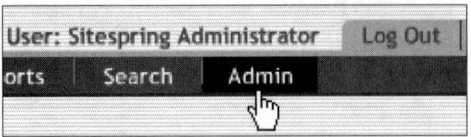

Figure 2.9 Click the Admin button to go to the Administration page.

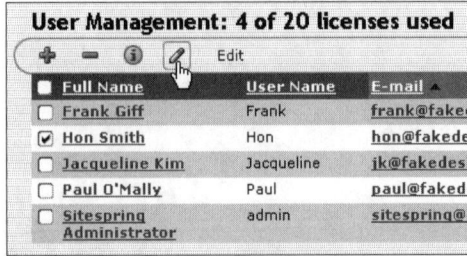

Figure 2.10 Select a user account to edit by clicking the appropriate check box and then clicking the Edit icon.

Figure 2.11 Edit the user information you'd like to change.

Users and Clients

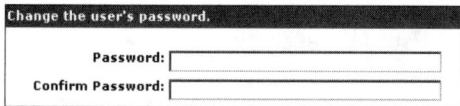

Figure 2.12 Leaving the fields blank will leave the password untouched; entering a new value in the fields will update the password.

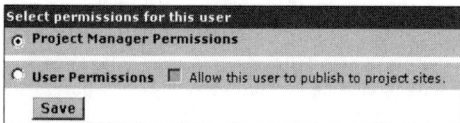

Figure 2.13 Update a user's permissions to fit the user's role on the team.

Figure 2.14 Click the Admin link to go to the Administration page.

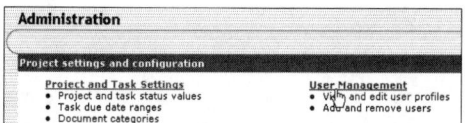

Figure 2.15 Click the User Management link to open the User Management page.

6. Enter a new password only if you'd like to change the user's existing password. If you leave these fields blank, the user's password will remain unchanged (**Figure 2.12**).

7. Update the user's permissions (**Figure 2.13**). See "Understanding Users," earlier in this chapter for more information about what these permissions mean.

8. Click Save to keep the information, or click any navigation link to discard the changes.

✔ **Tip**

- Normal users cannot edit their access privileges, but they can edit their contact information. See "To change your user profile" later in this chapter for more details.

To delete a user account:

1. Log in as the admin user or as a user with project manager permissions.

2. Open the Administration page by clicking the Admin button in the main navigation bar at the top of the screen (**Figure 2.14**).

3. Click the User Management link on the Administration page (**Figure 2.15**).

continues on next page

WORKING WITH USER ACCOUNTS

25

Chapter 2

4. Check the selection box next to the name of the accounts you would like to delete (**Figure 2.16**).

5. Click the Delete icon ▬ at the top of the module (**Figure 2.17**).

   The Delete User Accounts confirmation page appears. Click the Delete button to carry out the deletion; click the Cancel button to leave it alone (**Figure 2.18**).

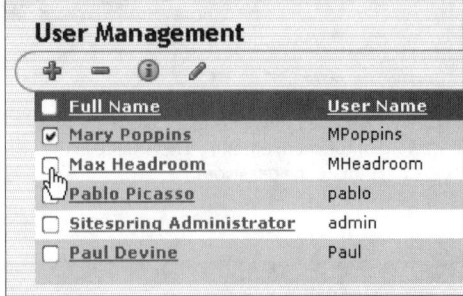

Figure 2.16 Select the accounts you would like to delete by clicking the corresponding check boxes.

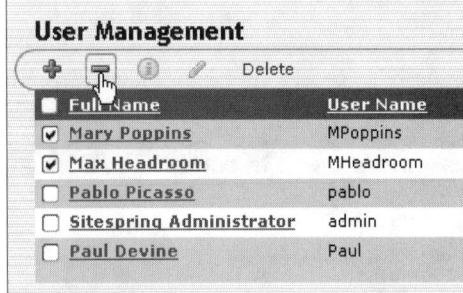

Figure 2.17 Delete accounts for a user or a group of users.

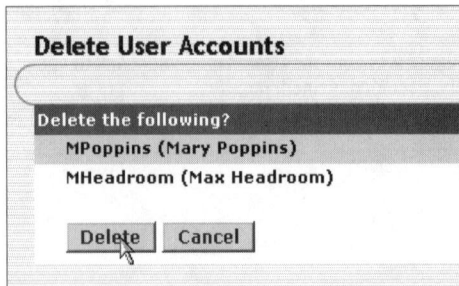

Figure 2.18 Click the Delete button to confirm the deletion of the selected accounts, or click Cancel to leave them intact.

26

Users and Clients

Figure 2.19 The Preferences area lets you change your contact information, email options, and password.

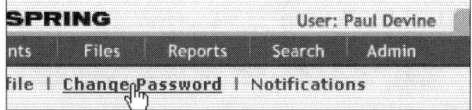

Figure 2.20 Click the Change Password link to change your own password.

Figure 2.21 After typing in your old and new passwords, retype your new password and click Save.

Modifying A User Account

Normal users can't modify their own access privileges, or add and delete accounts unless they have project manager or administrator permissions. However, any normal user can change his or her password, edit his or her user profile, and change his or her email notifications.

The user profile stores information such as the user's name, email address, phone numbers, company name, and job title. As a normal user, you can update your own information through the Preferences area.

You can also change your email notification preferences. Sitespring automatically sends email notices to keep users informed about projects and tasks. You can tell Sitespring what types of actions or situations should trigger the sending of email notices. You might want to receive an email anytime something about a project changes, or you might simply want to know only when a task of yours is overdue. Unlike the information in the user profile and even your password, only you can change your email notification preferences. Neither your project manager nor the system administrator can change the email notification preferences you set.

To change your password:

1. Click the Preferences button in the main navigation bar (**Figure 2.19**).
2. Click the Change Password link just below the main navigation bar (**Figure 2.20**).
3. Type your existing password in the Old Password field (**Figure 2.21**).

continues on next page

Chapter 2

4. Type your new password in the New Password field.

5. Retype your new password in the Confirm Password field, to confirm that you typed it correctly.

6. Click Save to keep your new password, or click any navigation link to discard the change.

To change your user profile:

1. Click the Preferences button in the main navigation bar (**Figure 2.22**).

2. Edit the fields containing your name, email address, phone numbers, company, and title (**Figure 2.23**).

   Note that the email address you list here will be the one that notifications are sent to, so you should use an address that's appropriate. If you'd like to change the event parameters around which an email notice is triggered, see "To change your email notification preferences" later in this chapter.

   Also be aware that the information listed here can be viewed by clients if you're listed on a project-site contact list.

3. Click Save to keep your changes, or click a navigation link to discard them.

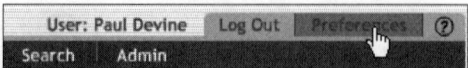

Figure 2.22 The Preferences area is where you change your contact information, including your email address.

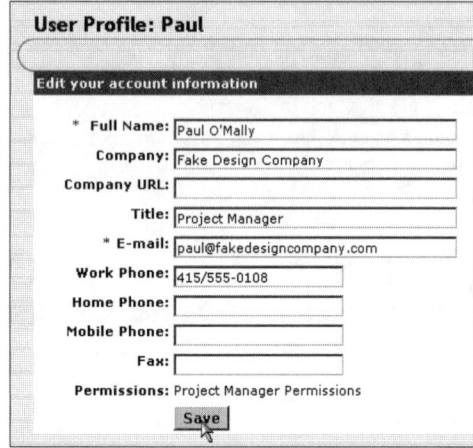

Figure 2.23 Update your user preferences, then click Save.

Users and Clients

Figure 2.24 Click the Preferences button.

Figure 2.25 Click the Notifications link.

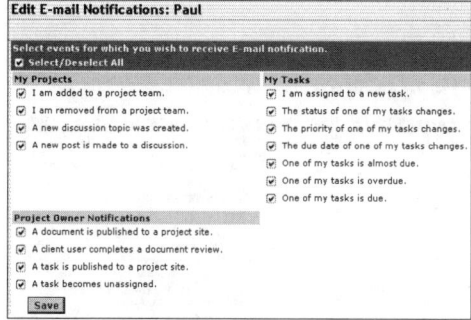

Figure 2.26 Select the events for which you would like to receive email notices. These settings apply to all projects and tasks.

To change your email notification preferences:

1. Click the Preferences tab in the main navigation bar (**Figure 2.24**).

2. Your User Profile page opens. Click the Notifications link just under the main navigation bar (**Figure 2.25**).

3. Check the boxes next to the events or actions for which you'd like to receive an email notice (**Figure 2.26**).

    Remember that these are global settings, so they apply to all projects and files. Users who do not have project manager permissions will not see the Project Owner Notifications list.

4. Click Save to update your information, or click on a navigation link to discard your changes.

✔ Tips

- To select or deselect all of the events or actions for which you'd like to receive an email notice, check the Select/Deselect All checkbox.

- Before any user can receive email notices, the administrator must configure the mail server preferences. For more, see Chapter 8.

MODIFYING A USER ACCOUNT

29

Viewing User Information

When you're part of a large team or company that's building Web sites or projects, keeping track of who's working on what project can be quite confusing. Think Abbott and Costello's "Who's on first?" routine without the humor.

To avoid confusion, you can view lists of all the users. You can also view a list that contains only the members of a particular project team.

In addition, you can create project-site contact lists, which allow the client to see selected members of the team. Only administrators or users with project manager permissions can include team members on the project-site contact list, but any user can view the list. Note that users must be added to the project in order to be added to the project-site contact list.

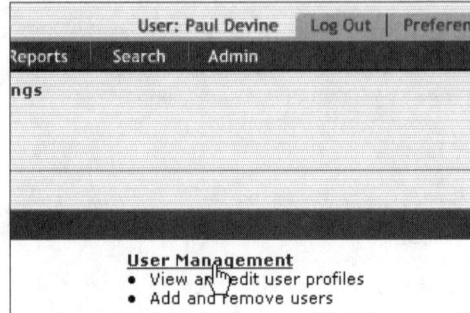

Figure 2.27 To open the User Management page, click the User Management link.

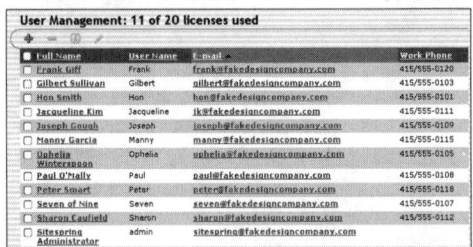

Figure 2.28 The User Management page lists all normal users.

To view a list of all normal users:

1. Click the Admin button in the main navigation bar.
2. The Administration page opens. Click the User Management link (**Figure 2.27**).
3. The User Management page opens; a list of all normal users is displayed (**Figure 2.28**). See the appropriate sections of this chapter to add, edit, or delete user accounts.

✔ Tip

- By default, the user list sorts alphabetically by name. If you'd like to sort the list by another category, click the heading of the column by which you'd like to sort the list. For example, if you'd like to sort the list by email address, click the E-mail link that heads the top of that column.

Users and Clients

Figure 2.29 To view the Team module, click the expand icon next to the Team module heading.

Figure 2.30 The Team module lists the normal users involved in the project.

Figure 2.31 The Show All link appears only if the team has more than ten members.

Figure 2.32 The Team Members page lists all 11 members of the team.

To view a list of normal users involved in a project:

1. Navigate to the Project page for the project whose team members you'd like to see listed. To do that, *do either of the following:*

   ▼ If the page you're on has a Client Projects module or a My Projects module that lists the project you'd like to work with, click the project name link in the Project column.

   or

   ▼ Click the Projects button in the main navigation bar. The main Projects page opens. Find the project you'd like to work with in the list, and click the project name link in the Project column.

2. The Project page opens. If the Team module isn't expanded, click the expand icon ▶ to the left of the Team heading (**Figure 2.29**).

   The first ten project-team members are listed in the Team module (**Figure 2.30**).

3. If more than ten people comprise the project team, click the Show All link in the lower-right corner of the module (**Figure 2.31**).

   If fewer than ten people comprise the team, you're already seeing a complete list, and this link will not appear.

   The Team Members page opens and displays the entire project-team list (**Figure 2.32**).

VIEWING USER INFORMATION

Chapter 2

To add or remove normal user names in the project-site contact list:

1. Navigate to the Project page. To do that, *do either of the following:*

    ▼ If the page you're on has a Client Projects module or a My Projects module that lists the project you'd like to work with, click the project name link in the Project column (**Figure 2.33**).

    or

    ▼ Click the Projects button in the main navigation bar. The main Projects page opens. Find the project you want in the Project column list, then click the project name link.

2. The page for that project opens. If the Team module isn't expanded, click the expand icon ▶ next to the Team heading.

3. To add or remove user names in the project-site contact list, *do either of the following:*

    ▼ To add user names to the contact list, click the check box next to the name or names you want to add. Then click the Add to Project Site icon 🐝 in the Team module (**Figure 2.34**). The corresponding contact information will then appear on the project-site contact list (**Figure 2.35**).

    or

    ▼ To remove users from the contact list, click the check box next to the name or names you want to remove. Then click the Remove from Project Site icon 🐝 in the Team module.

    The Project page reloads with a green success notice at top.

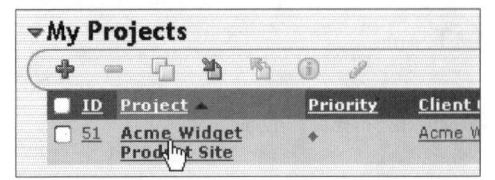

Figure 2.33 You can access a project page by clicking on the project name on your Sitespring home page.

Figure 2.34 To select user names to add to the contact list, click the check boxes next to them.

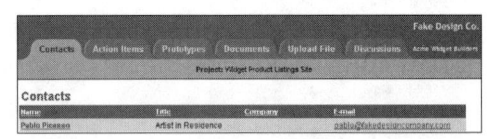

Figure 2.35 Names of team members who have been added to the contact list appear on the project-site page.

VIEWING USER INFORMATION

32

Figure 2.36 Click the Clients button in the main navigation bar to bring up the Add Client Organization page.

Figure 2.37 Enter as many details about a client organization as you'd like; the only required field is the name.

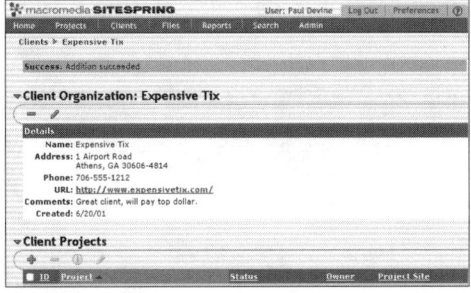

Figure 2.38 After you've successfully added a client organization account, the Client Organization module for that client opens.

Working with Client Organization Accounts

In Sitespring, client organizations represent the company, department, or group for which the Web site or project is being built. If the Web team works for another company, that company is the client organization. If the team is part of a large company and building a site for another department, that department is the client organization.

The purpose of establishing a client organization account is to group client users belonging to the same organization. Sitespring stores certain information about the client—the URL, for instance—in one location; if the information changes, you need to update it only once.

Only the administrator and users with project manager permissions can add, edit, or delete a client organization account.

To add a client organization account:

1. Click the Clients button in the main navigation bar (**Figure 2.36**).

2. Click the Add icon ✚ at the top of the Clients module.

3. Enter the client organization's name and contact information.

    The only field required here is the name field; however, it's a good idea to include as much information as you can. Inevitably a team member will need to look up a client's URL or phone number at some point (**Figure 2.37**).

4. Click Save to add the new client, or click a navigation link to cancel.

    The Client Organization page for the new client opens (**Figure 2.38**).

continues on next page

Chapter 2

✔ Tips

- You may want to add a client organization for contractors, such as photographers or artists, who you add as client users, so that they can upload files through project sites.

- You can link projects and client user names to a client organization immediately after adding the account. Simply click the Add icons in the respective modules under the Client Projects heading at the bottom of the Client Organization page that appears in step 5 (**Figure 2.38**).

- It's a good idea to create the client organization account before creating any accounts for client users belonging to that organization. That way when you create the client user accounts, you can associate them with the client organization at that time rather than having to go back and do it later.

To edit client organization information:

1. Click the Clients button in the main navigation bar.

2. From the list displayed, click the name of the client organization you wish to edit (**Figure 2.39**).

3. Click the Edit icon ✎ at the top of the Client Organization module (**Figure 2.40**).

4. Update the name or contact information.

5. Click Save to retain your changes, or click a navigation link to discard them (**Figure 2.41**).

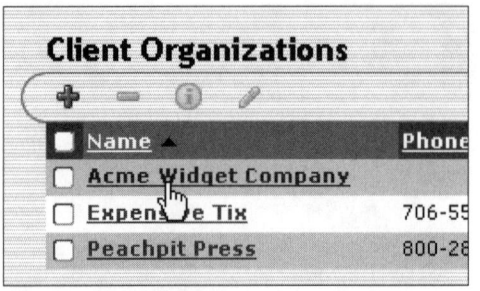

Figure 2.39 Click the name of the client organization whose information you would like to edit.

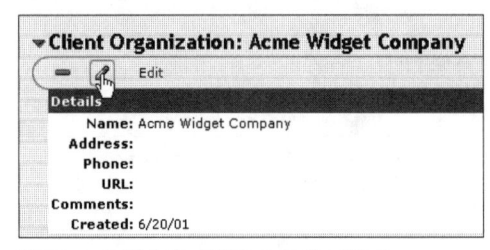

Figure 2.40 Click the Edit icon on the Client Organization module to make changes.

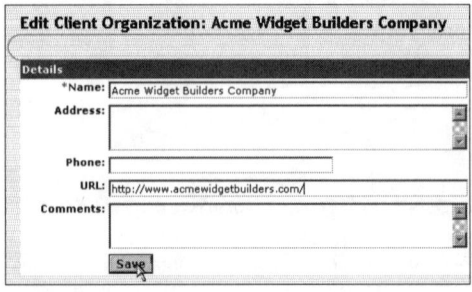

Figure 2.41 Save the changes you've made to a client organization's information.

Users and Clients

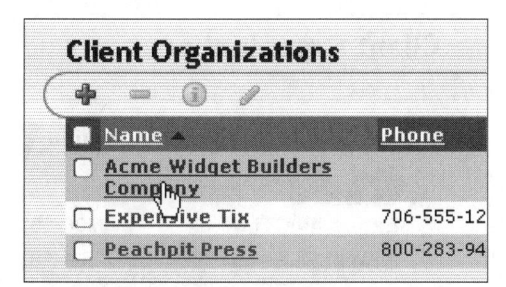

Figure 2.42 Click the name of the client organization whose account you would like to delete.

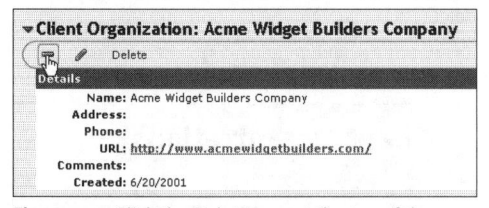

Figure 2.43 Click the Delete icon at the top of the Client Organization module to remove the client.

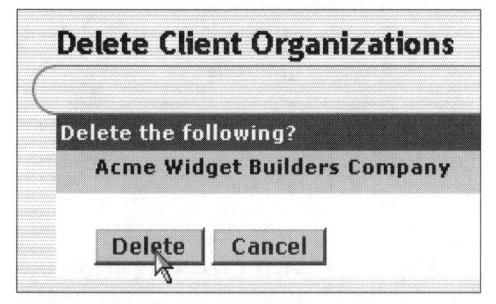

Figure 2.44 Confirm the deletion by clicking the Delete button.

To delete a client organization account:

1. Click the Clients button in the main navigation bar.

2. Click the name of the client organization whose account you would like to delete (**Figure 2.42**).

3. Click the Delete icon at the top of the Client Organization module (**Figure 2.43**).

4. Confirm the deletion by clicking the Delete button, or click Cancel to leave it alone (**Figure 2.44**).

WORKING WITH CLIENT ORGANIZATION ACCOUNTS

35

Chapter 2

To delete multiple client organization accounts:

1. Click the Clients button in the main navigation bar.

2. Click the check box to the left of the names of the client organizations whose accounts you would like to delete (**Figure 2.45**).

3. Click the Delete icon — at the top of the Client Organizations module (**Figure 2.46**).

4. Confirm the deletion by clicking the Delete button, or click Cancel to leave it alone (**Figure 2.47**).

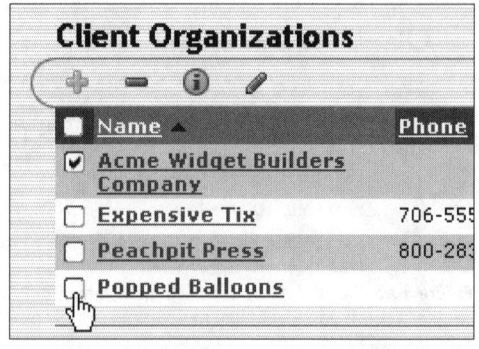

Figure 2.45 Click the check boxes to select the client organizations whose accounts you would like to delete.

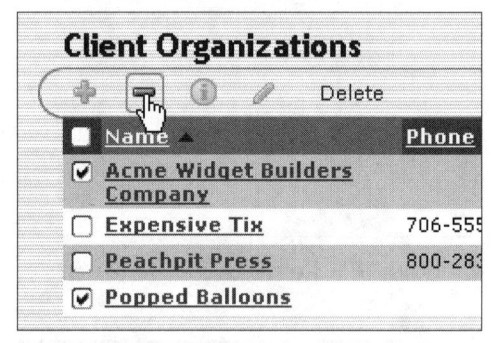

Figure 2.46 Click the Delete icon to delete the client organization accounts.

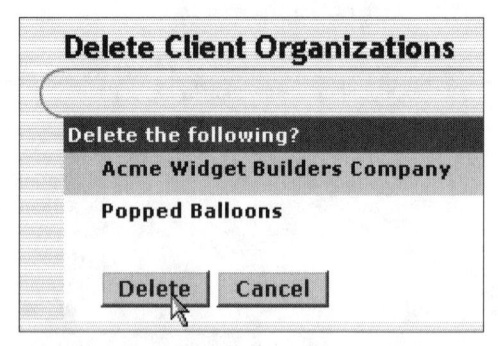

Figure 2.47 Click the Delete button to confirm the deletion.

Working with Client User Accounts

Web teams don't often think of their clients as members of the team. Yet clients frequently need to provide information, files, or decisions so that the project can proceed. In many ways, you can consider the people in the client organization part of the extended Web team.

Sitespring does just that by offering client user accounts. Client users can't log into the main Sitespring interface—where Web team members spend most of their time working—but they can log into a project site, if they're given permission to do so, and be assigned tasks. Read on to learn how to add, edit, and delete client user accounts.

Only the administrator and users with project manager permissions can add, edit, or delete a client user account.

New User Fields

User Name—Assign a user name. This is the person's identity within Sitespring and must be unique to distinguish individual users.

Password—Assign a password. Unlike normal users, client users cannot change their own password. For security reasons, you should use different passwords for each client user. Make note of the passwords you assign, as there's no way to retrieve a lost password; you'll have to assign a new one.

Confirm Password—Retype the password to confirm you entered it correctly.

Full Name—Enter the full name of the user.

Title—Enter the user's job title.

Client Organization—Enter the name of the company, department, or organization to which the client user belongs.

E-mail—Enter the email address of the user. Note that Sitespring automatically sends the client user an email notice if the person has a task assigned to them.

Work Phone—Enter the user's work phone number.

Home Phone—Enter the user's home phone number.

Mobile Phone—Enter the user's mobile or cell number.

Fax—Enter the user's fax number.

Comments—Write any details you'd like to record about the user. The client user cannot see these comments.

To add a client user account:

1. Click the Clients button in the main navigation bar.

2. In the list of clients, find the name of the client organization to which the new user belongs (**Figure 2.48**). This is usually the company or department for which the user works. (If the appropriate client organization doesn't exist, see "To add a client organization account" earlier in this chapter.) Click the name of the client.

3. In the Client Users module, click the Add icon (**Figure 2.49**).

4. Enter the information about the new user. The fields that must be filled in are marked with an asterisk. See the sidebar about each field for more information (**Figure 2.50**).

5. Click Save to save the information, or click a navigation link to cancel.

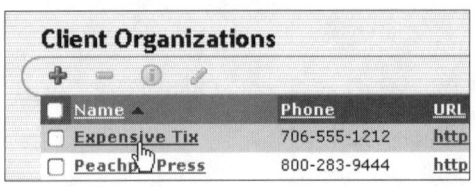

Figure 2.48 Click the name of the client organization to which you'd like to add the client user account.

Figure 2.49 Click the Add icon in the Client Users module.

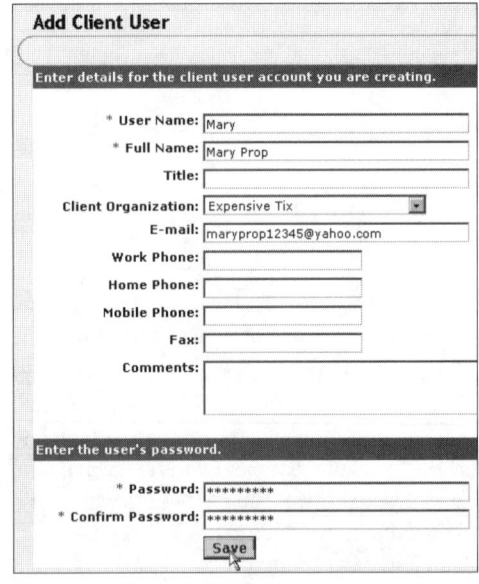

Figure 2.50 After entering the client user's information, click Save to add the user account.

Users and Clients

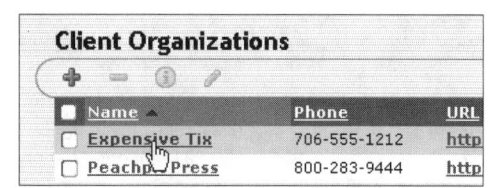

Figure 2.51 Click the name of the user's client organization.

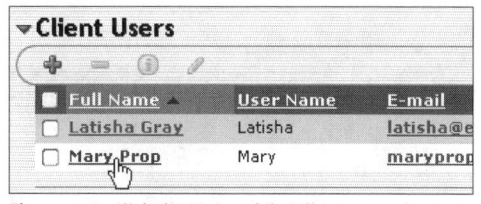

Figure 2.52 Click the name of the client user whose information or password you'd like to edit.

Figure 2.53 Leave the password fields blank if you don't want to change the client user's password.

To edit client user information and passwords:

1. Click the Clients button in the main navigation bar.

2. Click the name of the client organization to which the client user belongs (**Figure 2.51**).

3. Under the Full Name column, click the name of the client user whose information or password you would like to edit (**Figure 2.52**).

4. Edit the fields that you would like to change. See "To add a client user account" earlier in this chapter for more information about the fields. The password fields will come up blank when you edit a user's information.

    ▼ To keep the password unchanged, leave the Password and the Confirm Password fields blank (**Figure 2.53**).

    or

    ▼ To change the user's password, enter a new password in both the Password and the Confirm Password fields.

5. Click Save to save your changes, or click a navigational link to discard them.

WORKING WITH CLIENT USER ACCOUNTS

39

To delete a client user account:

1. If the page you're on has a link to the client user's client organization, click the client organization's link (**Figure 2.54**).

   Otherwise, click the Clients button in the main navigation bar. The Client Organizations page opens. Click the name of the user's client organization.

   The Client Organizations page opens.

2. To select accounts for deletion, *do either of the following*:

   ▼ To review a client user's information, click the user's name. The user's account details page will open. Then in the Client User module, click the Delete icon ━.

   or

   ▼ To delete one or more client user accounts without reviewing user information, click the check box next to the names of the users whose accounts you would like to delete. Then in the Client User module, click the Delete icon ━ (**Figure 2.55**).

   The Delete Client Users confirmation page opens.

3. If you're sure you want to delete the client user accounts, click the Delete button; if not, click Cancel (**Figure 2.56**).

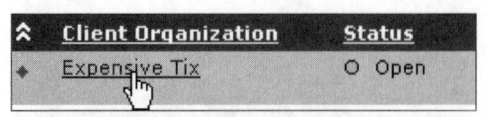

Figure 2.54 In the My Projects module on your home page, you can navigate directly to a client organization page by clicking the organization's name.

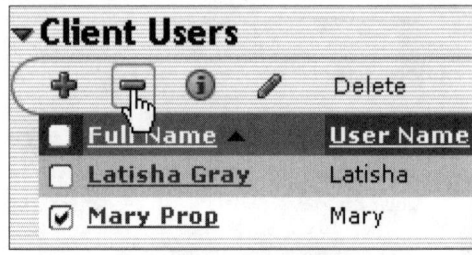

Figure 2.55 Select the user account you'd like to delete in the Client Users module, and click the Delete icon.

Figure 2.56 Confirm the deletion by clicking the Delete button.

To grant or revoke project-site permission:

1. Navigate to the Project Site page of the project site. This is not the project site itself, but rather the page in Sitespring from which you can configure the project site. To get there, *do either of the following*:

   ▼ If the page you're on has a Client Projects module that lists the project you'd like to work with, in the Project

Users and Clients

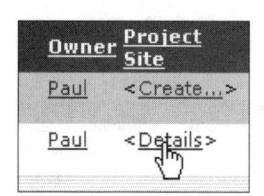

Figure 2.57 The My Projects module on your Sitespring home page has links to each project site in the last column.

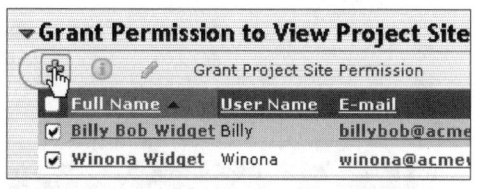

Figure 2.58 Select the users for whom you'd like to grant permission to view the project site, and click the plus-sign icon.

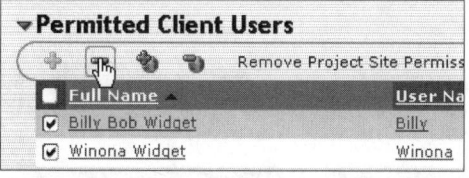

Figure 2.59 You can revoke certain users' permission to view the project site by selecting their names and clicking the minus-sign icon.

Site column click the <Details> link for that project (**Figure 2.57**).

or

▼ Click the Projects button in the main navigation bar. The main Projects page opens. Find the project you'd like to work with in the list. In the Project Site column, click the <Details> link for that project.

2. The Project Site page opens. If the Permitted Client Users module isn't open, click the expand icon ▶ next to the Permitted Client Users heading.

3. To grant or revoke permissions, *do either of the following*:

   ▼ To grant permissions, click the Add icon ✜ in the Permitted Client Users module. The Grant Permission to View Project Site page opens. Select the users to whom you'd like to grant project-site permission, and click the check box to the left of their names. Then click the Add icon 🐾 (**Figure 2.58**).

   or

   ▼ To revoke project-site viewing permission, click the check box next to the names of the users for whom you'd like to revoke permissions. Then click the Remove Project Site Permission icon ▬ in the Permitted Client Users module (**Figure 2.59**). The Remove Permission to View Project Site confirmation page opens. Click Remove to revoke the permissions, or click Cancel to leave them intact.

The Project Site page reloads.

WORKING WITH CLIENT USER ACCOUNTS

41

To add or remove client user names in the project-site contact list:

1. Navigate to the Project Site page for the project site that contains the contact list you'd like to change. (This is not the project site itself, but the page in Sitespring that lets you configure the project site.) To do that, *do either of the following:*

   ▼ If the page you're on has a Client Projects module that lists the project you'd like to work with, click the <Details> link for that project in the Project Site column.

   or

   ▼ Click the Projects button in the main navigation bar. The main Projects page opens. Find the project you want in the list. In the Project Site column, click the <Details> link for that project.

2. The Project Site page opens. If the Permitted Client Users module isn't open, click the expand icon ▶ next to the Permitted Client Users heading.

3. To add or remove users in the project-site contact list, *do either of the following:*

   ▼ To add users to the project-site contact list, click the check box next to the names of the users you would like to add. Then click the Add to Project Site icon 🐾 in the Permitted Client Users module (**Figure 2.60**).

   or

   ▼ To remove client users from the project-site contact list, click the check box next to the names of the users you would like to remove. Then click the Remove from Project Site icon 🐾 in the Permitted Client Users module (**Figure 2.61**).

   Names of client users added to the contact list show up on the client-viewable project site on the Contacts page, while those of removed users do not (**Figure 2.62**).

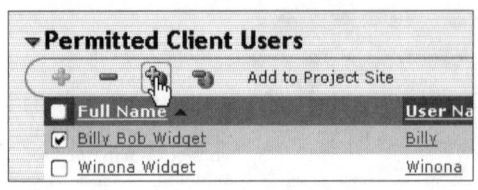

Figure 2.60 To add client users to the contact list, click the check box next to their names, then click the Add to Project Site icon.

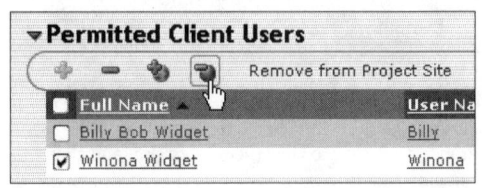

Figure 2.61 To remove client users from the contact list, select their names and click the Remove from Project Site icon.

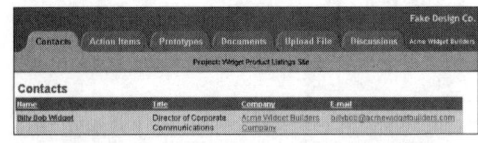

Figure 2.62 Names of client users you have added to the site contact list appear on the project-site Contacts page.

Projects and Project Sites

You wouldn't be a member of a Web team without a project to work on. In Sitespring, a project is a Web site or section of a Web site that your team has been assigned to build. Sitespring organizes tasks and files according to project. Each project is associated with one client organization and has one project owner, who's usually the project team lead or project manager. You can also create a project site—a small Web site where a client user can log in and communicate with the project team and view project status.

All the tasks presented in this chapter can be performed only by users whose accounts have project manager permissions. Depending on your role on a project team and how your organization chooses to divide responsibility, you may or may not have permission to create or change a project's information.

This chapter explains how to create and modify projects, create and modify project sites, import and export projects to and from Microsoft Project, and, finally, save a snapshot of an entire project.

Chapter 3

Creating and Editing Projects

In order to manage projects successfully, you need to come up with a project management strategy. Should all users have the ability to alter project information, or should that be restricted? Should each client have only one large project, or should the projects be broken down? Only you can determine how best to organize your work and information. Be sure to start out with a strategy and stick with it, or even the best project-organizing tool won't help you.

In this section you'll learn how to create and edit projects.

To create a project:

1. Navigate to a page that contains a projects module or to the main Projects page itself. To do that, *do either of the following*:

   ▼ If you're already on a page in Sitespring that has a projects module, locate the module. It will be called My Projects on your home page, or Client Projects on the Clients page.

   or

   ▼ To navigate to the main Projects page, click the Projects button in the main navigation bar. The main Projects page opens.

2. Click the Add icon ✚ at the top of the projects module (**Figure 3.1**).

3. The Add Project page opens. Enter the information for the project you are creating. Fields marked with an asterisk are required (**Figure 3.2**). See the notes about each field in the sidebar.

4. Click Save to update your information, or click a navigation link to discard your changes.

   The Project page opens.

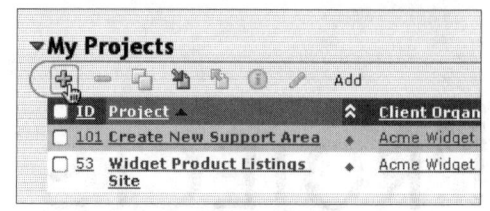

Figure 3.1 Click the Add icon to create a new project.

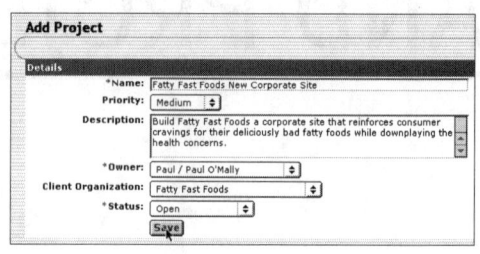

Figure 3.2 Enter details about the project, then click Save.

44

Projects and Project Sites

✔ Tips

- If there's already a project in Sitespring that's similar to the project you're about to create, you might want to clone the existing project rather than create a new one. When you clone a project, Sitespring creates a new project containing the same team list and tasks as those of the original project. This saves you valuable data entry time. See "To clone a project" later in this chapter for more information.

- If you need to create entries for both a new client organization and a new project, generally it's a good idea to create the client first; you can then associate the client with the project as you create the project. If you've already created the project entry, don't worry. Just leave the Client Organization field as None. After creating the client entry, go back and edit the project to associate it with the new client.

- Sitespring's requirement that each project name be unique can actually help your team keep track of the various projects—if you create descriptive names for them. You might wind up searching the system for a project long after it's been completed, so pick a name that will mean something down the line.

- The name of the project always appears alongside the name of the client, so you don't need to enter the client's name as part of the project name.

- Try not to mark all projects with a priority of High, because then the field will lose its significance and project-team members won't be able to prioritize their work. If you really take an honest assessment, you'll find that some projects are not as important as others. Use the High priority mark sparingly so folks will know when it's truly time to jump on a project's tasks.

Add Project Fields

Name—Use a unique name for the project. In Sitespring, two projects cannot have the same name.

Priority—Choose a priority level from the pull-down menu.

Description—Enter a project description that will be meaningful to the team and the client. Also make sure the description will make sense later, in case you ever want to refer to an archived project.

Owner—Assign a project owner from the pull-down list of user names; usually this is the project team lead. The project owner's name and email address appear throughout Sitespring in project references. (When accounts are created for new users, the program adds the users' names to the pull-down choices.)

Client Organization—Choose a name from the client pull-down list. (When accounts are created for new clients, Sitespring adds the clients' names to the pull-down choices.)

Status—Enter the status of the project. For new projects this is generally Not Started or (if the project has truly begun) Open.

CREATING AND EDITING PROJECTS

45

Chapter 3

To edit a project:

1. Navigate to a page that contains a projects module or to the main Projects page itself. To do that, *do either of the following:*

    ▼ If you're already on a page in Sitespring that has a projects module, locate the module. It will be called My Projects on your home page, or Client Projects on the Clients page.

    or

    ▼ To navigate to the main Projects page, click the Projects button in the main navigation bar. The main Projects page opens (**Figure 3.3**).

2. Among the projects listed, find the name of the one you would like to edit. To open the project's page, *do either of the following:*

    ▼ To go straight to the edit page, click the check box to the left of the project name (**Figure 3.4**), then click the Edit icon ✎ (**Figure 3.5**).

    or

    ▼ To get to the edit page through the Project page, click the name of the project you would like to edit. The Project page opens. Click the Edit icon ✎ at the top of the Project page.

3. Change the desired information (**Figure 3.6**). See the notes under "To create a project" earlier in this chapter for more information about each field and tips about project information.

4. Click Save to update your information, or click a navigation link to discard your changes.

    The Project page opens.

Figure 3.3 Click the Projects button to get to the main Projects page.

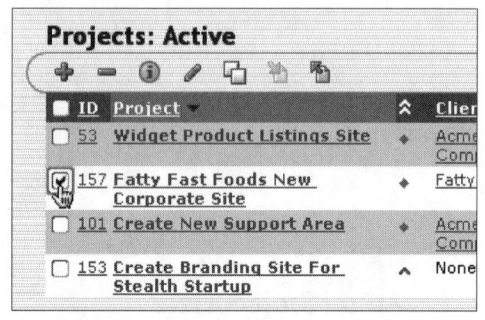

Figure 3.4 Click the check box to select a project to edit.

Figure 3.5 Click the Edit icon to edit the project.

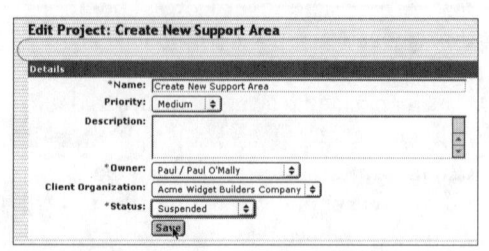

Figure 3.6 Update the project information, then click Save.

Managing Projects

If you need to create a project that's similar to a project already in progress, you can save valuable time by cloning—or making a copy of—the project, with all tasks set to Not Started. When you clone an existing project, Sitespring makes a new project that duplicates the original project's team list and tasks, with each task's status reset to Not Started. This saves you the time of reentering duplicate information.

You can also add a folder to a project in order to associate the folder and its contents with the project. Once you've done this, the items in the folder will become part of any project snapshots you take. A project may have one or more folders linked to it.

You associate folders not on your hard drive, but rather on the Sitespring server's hard drive. The entire project team will access the folders from the server. You can access the folders and files from outside of Sitespring using the normal applications that you would use for any file. Adding a folder to a project merely allows you to link tasks and take snapshots; it doesn't prevent any normal interaction with the folder outside of Sitespring.

Chapter 3

To clone a project:

1. Navigate to a page that contains a project module or to the main Projects page itself. To do that, *do either of the following*:

   ▼ If you're already on a page in Sitespring that has a projects module, locate the module. It will be called My Projects on your home page, or Client Projects on the Clients page.

   or

   ▼ To navigate to the main Projects page, click the Projects button in the main navigation bar. The main Projects page opens.

2. To clone the project, *do any of the following*:

   ▼ If you are on your home page or the main Projects page, find the project that you would like to clone in the projects module. To select the project, click the check box in the leftmost column next to the project's name. Now click the Clone icon at the top of the module (**Figure 3.7**).

   or

   ▼ If you're already on a Project page, you don't need to select the project. Click the Clone icon at the top of the projects module.

3. The Clone Project page opens. Update the project information in the fields on the form (**Figure 3.8**). For more information about what to enter, see "To create a project" earlier in this chapter.

4. Click Save to update your information, or click a navigation link to discard your changes.

   The new project opens with the status of the project's tasks reset to Not Started (**Figure 3.9**).

Figure 3.7 Click the Clone icon to make a copy of the project.

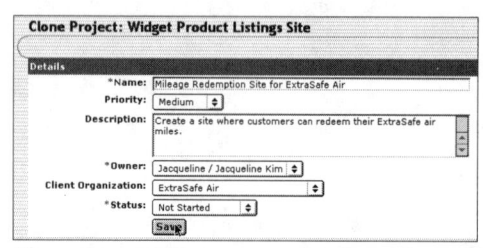

Figure 3.8 Change the information to reflect the new project you're creating.

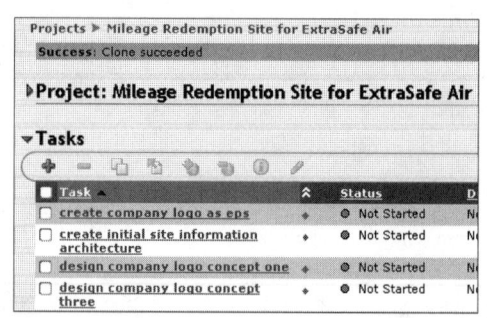

Figure 3.9 The cloned project opens with all the tasks from the original project reset to Not Started.

MANAGING PROJECTS

48

Projects and Project Sites

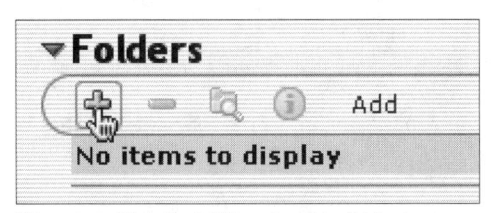

Figure 3.10 Click the Add icon to add a folder to the project.

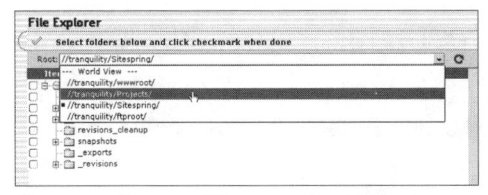

Figure 3.11 Choose a different top-level folder from the pull-down menu.

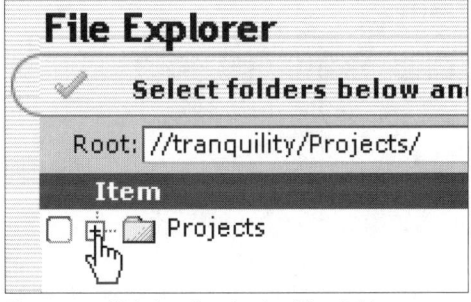

Figure 3.12 Click the plus sign beside a folder to expand it and show the subfolders it contains.

To add a folder to a project:

1. Navigate to a page that contains a project module or to the main Projects page itself. To do that, *do either of the following:*

   ▼ If you're already on a page in Sitespring that has a projects module, locate the module. It will be called My Projects on your home page, or Client Projects on the Clients page.

   or

   ▼ To navigate to the main Projects page, click the Projects button in the main navigation bar. The main Projects page opens.

2. Among the projects listed, find the name of the one you would like to edit. To open the project's page, click the name of the project you want to edit.

3. The Project page opens. If the Folders module isn't already expanded, expand the module by clicking the triangle next to the Folders heading.

4. Click the Add icon ✥ at the top of the folders module (**Figure 3.10**).

5. The File Explorer opens. In the list of folders, find the folder you'd like to add to the project. If the server running Sitespring is sharing more than one top-level (or Root) folder, you can choose another top-level folder from the pull-down menu at the top of the File Explorer (**Figure 3.11**). You can expand a folder by clicking the plus-sign icon ⊞ that appears to the left of folders containing subfolders (**Figure 3.12**).

   continues on next page

MANAGING PROJECTS

49

Chapter 3

6. When you've found the folder you'd like to add to the project, click the check box next to it (**Figure 3.13**). You may add more than one folder; just click the corresponding check boxes.

7. Click the Add icon ✔ at the top of the File Explorer to add the folder to the project (**Figure 3.14**), or click any navigation link to cancel the operation.

   The Project page reopens with a green success notice at the top; additionally, the folder is added to the Folders module (**Figure 3.15**).

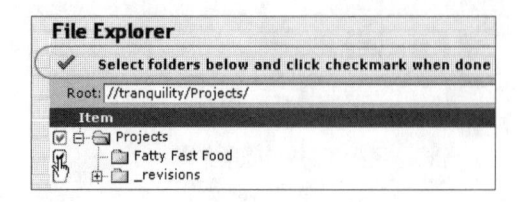

Figure 3.13 Select a folder to add by clicking the check box to the left of the folder.

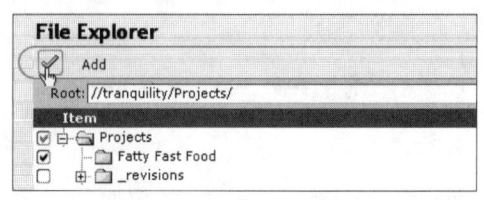

Figure 3.14 Click the Add icon at the top of the module.

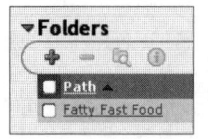

Figure 3.15 The Project page reloads with the folder added.

Completing a Project

As part of the normal life cycle of a project, you change a project's status to Complete when all work associated with the project has ended and the project is finished. Alternatively, you mark a project's status as Suspended if the project needs to be put on hold. Changing the project status to Complete or Suspended removes references to the project and its associated items throughout the application. For example, tasks associated with the project will not appear in users' task lists. You can still gain access to a closed project by going to the Inactive Projects page from the main Projects page. When you are truly done with a project, you can delete it. But before you do so, think carefully.

Deleting a project removes all references to the project, deletes the project site if there is one, and removes all project-related tasks. If you want to remove all references to the project but retain access to the project information, you should change the project's status to Suspended or Closed. This has the same effect as deleting a project, except you can still access it through the Inactive Projects link on the main Projects page.

If you're confident that you and, more importantly, your client won't need access to any of the information about the project again, you can permanently delete the project and its related information.

Chapter 3

To complete or suspend a project:

1. Navigate to the Edit Project page to change the project's status. You can get there from your home page, from the main Projects page, or from the Project page for the project. To do that, *do either of the following*:

    ▼ To navigate to your home page, click the Home button in the main navigation bar. Your home page opens.

    or

    ▼ To navigate to the Projects Page, click the Projects button in the main navigation bar. The main Projects page opens.

2. Among the projects listed, find the name of the one you would like to edit. To open the project's page, *do either of the following*:

    ▼ To go straight to the Edit Project page, click the check box to the left of the project name, then click the Edit icon ✏ (**Figure 3.16**).

    or

    ▼ To get to the Edit Project page from the Project page, click the name of the project you would like to edit. The Project page opens. Click the Edit icon ✏ at the top of the Project page.

3. The Edit Project page opens. From the Status pull-down menu, select Suspended or Completed, as appropriate.

4. Click Save to update your information, or click a navigation link to discard your changes (**Figure 3.17**).

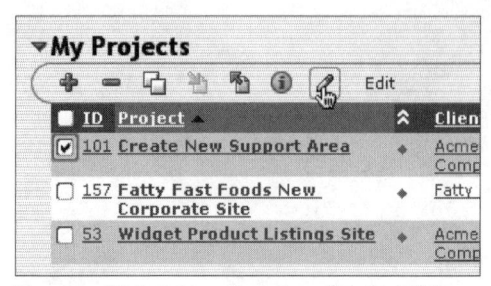

Figure 3.16 Select the project, then click the Edit icon.

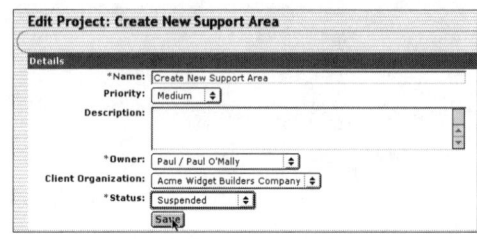

Figure 3.17 Click Save after you've assigned the project a new status.

Figure 3.18 Click the Projects navigation button to go to the main Projects page.

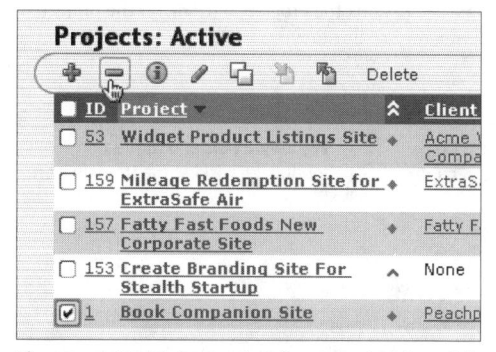

Figure 3.19 To delete a project from a project list, click the check box next to the name of the project you'd like to delete, then click the Delete icon.

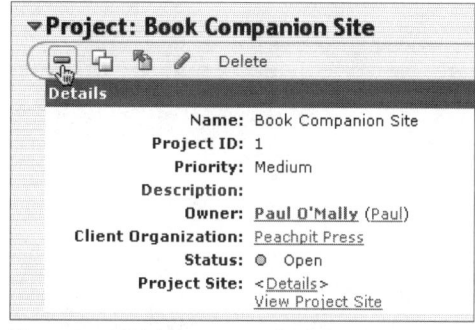

Figure 3.20 To delete a project from the Project page, click the Delete icon at the top of the Project module.

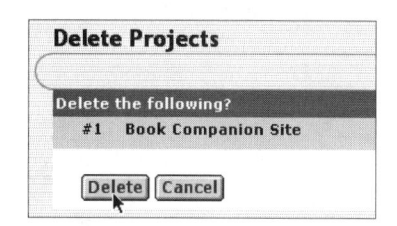

Figure 3.21 Think carefully before confirming a project deletion, as you can't undo it.

To delete a project:

1. Navigate to a page that contains a project module, or to the main Projects page itself. To do that, *do either of the following*:

    ▼ If you're already on a page in Sitespring that has a projects module, locate the module. It will be called My Projects on your home page, or Client Projects on the Clients page.

    or

    ▼ To navigate to the main Projects page, click the Projects button in the main navigation bar (**Figure 3.18**). The main Projects page opens.

2. Now you're ready to delete the project. To do that, *do either of the following*:

    ▼ If you're on your home page or the main Projects page, find the project that you would like to delete in the Projects module. To select the project, click the check box in the leftmost column next to the project's name. Now click the Delete icon ▬ at the top of the module (**Figure 3.19**).

    or

    ▼ If you're already on a Project page, you don't need to select the project. Click the Delete icon ▬ at the top of the Project module (**Figure 3.20**).

    The Delete Projects confirmation page opens. You cannot undo a project deletion.

3. Click the Delete button to delete the project, or click the Cancel button to leave it alone (**Figure 3.21**).

Chapter 3

Linking Users and Projects

Users linked to a project appear on the Project page in the Team module. You can quickly see who's working on a project by looking at the Team module. Assigning a task to a user on a project automatically links the user to the project. You can also link and unlink team members manually. If there's a project site for the project, you can publish contact information for members of the project team on the project site.

Adding a user to a project team does not automatically add the user's name to the external project-site's contact list. You should add a team-member user name to the contact list if you'd like client users to have access to the user on the site, since the user's contact information will appear alongside his or her name.

To link a user to a project:

1. Navigate to the Project page for the project to which you'd like to link the user. To do that, *do either of the following*:

    ▼ If you're on a page that has a link to the Project page you want, click the link (**Figure 3.22**).

    or

    ▼ In the main navigation bar on any page, click the Projects button. The main Projects page opens. In the Project column, click the name of the project to which you'd like to link a user.

2. The Project page opens. If the Team module isn't expanded, expand the module by clicking the triangle next to the Team heading (**Figure 3.23**). Click the Add icon ✚ (**Figure 3.24**).

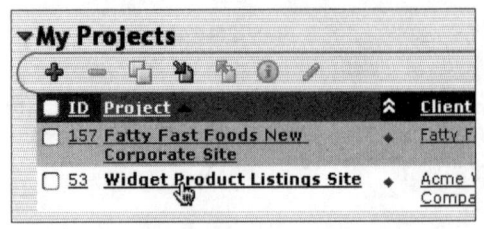

Figure 3.22 Clink the Project page link for the project to which you'd like to link a user.

Figure 3.23 Expand the Team module by clicking the triangle icon.

Figure 3.24 Click the Add icon to add a team member to the project.

Projects and Project Sites

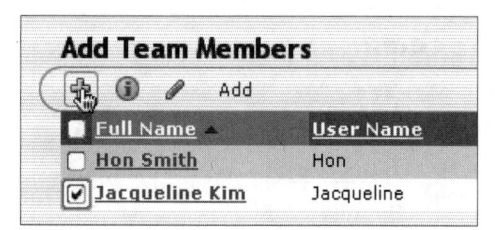

Figure 3.25 Select the team member or members you'd like to add to the project, then click the Add icon.

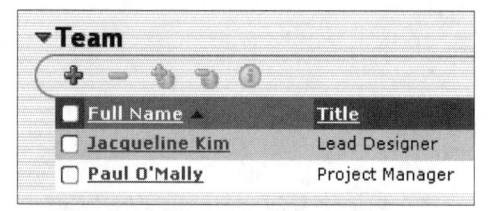

Figure 3.26 The Project page opens, listing the new member of the project team.

Figure 3.27 Click the Projects navigation button to open the main Projects page.

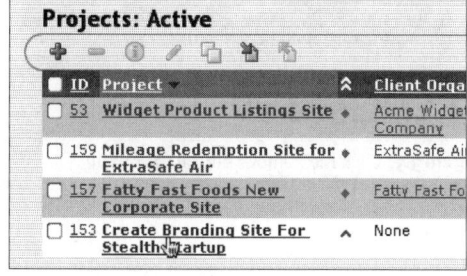

Figure 3.28 Click the link to the project from which you'd like to remove a user.

3. The Add Team Members page opens. Select the user you'd like to add to the project by clicking the check box to the left of his or her name.

4. Click the Add icon ✥ to add the team member to the project (**Figure 3.25**), or click a navigation link to leave the page and cancel the operation.

   The Project page opens with the updated team-member list (**Figure 3.26**).

✔ **Tips**

- If you assign a user a task on a project, that user will automatically be added to the project team. There's no need to add a user to a project separately unless the user doesn't have any project tasks assigned.

- Some users may have set their email notification preferences so that they receive a notice when they are added to a project team. These users will get an email after you add them to the project. Users who do not have this preference will not. See "Using Email Notifications" in Chapter 5 for more information.

To unlink a user from a project:

1. Navigate to the Project page for the project from which you'd like to remove the user. To do that, *do either of the following:*

   ▼ If you're on a page that has a link to the Project page you want, click the link.

   or

   ▼ In the main navigation bar on any page, click the Projects button (**Figure 3.27**). The main Projects page opens. In the Project column, click the name of the project from which you'd like to unlink a user (**Figure 3.28**).

   continues on next page

LINKING USERS AND PROJECTS

55

Chapter 3

2. The main Projects page opens. If the Team module isn't expanded, expand the module by clicking the triangle next to the Team heading.

3. Select the user you'd like to remove from the project by clicking the check box to the left of his or her name (**Figure 3.29**).

4. Click the Remove icon — to remove the user from the project (**Figure 3.30**).

5. The Remove Team Members page opens. Click the Remove button to confirm your decision, or click Cancel to abandon the operation (**Figure 3.31**).

   The main Projects page opens with the updated team member list.

✔ Tips

- Removing a user from the project team does not remove any of the user's assigned tasks from the project task list. The user merely no longer shows up as a member of the project team. To delete or reassign tasks for a removed user, see "Managing Tasks" in Chapter 5.

- Removing a user from the project team also removes the user from the project-team list on the project site.

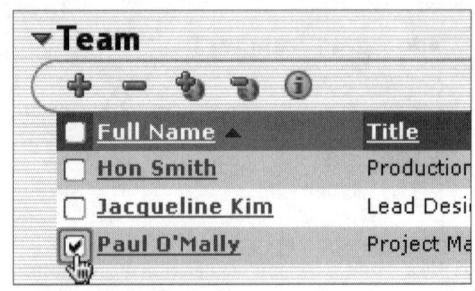

Figure 3.29 Select the user you'd like to remove from the project by checking the check box next to his or her name.

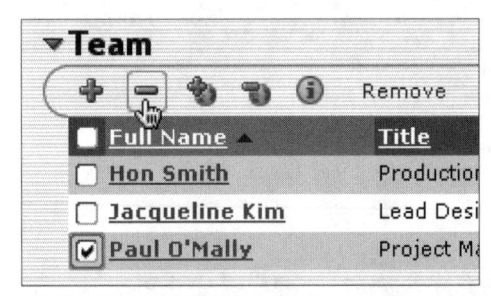

Figure 3.30 Click the Remove icon to remove the selected team members from the project.

Figure 3.31 Click the Remove button to confirm the change.

Projects and Project Sites

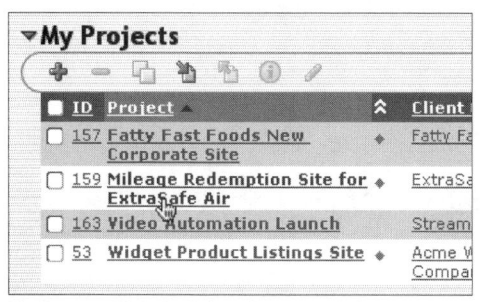

Figure 3.32 Click the link to the project whose project-site contact list you'd like to update.

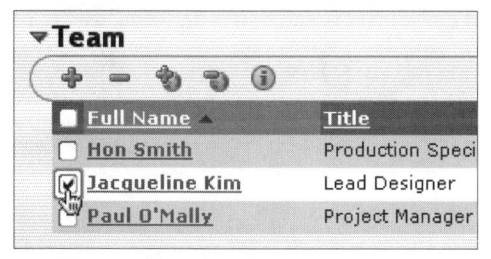

Figure 3.33 Click the check box next to the team-member names you'd like to add or remove.

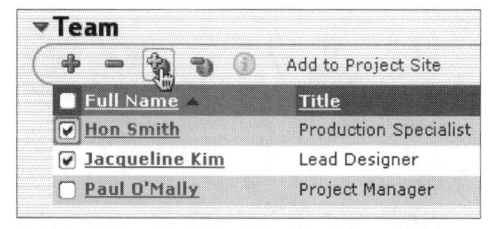

Figure 3.34 To add the names of the selected users to the contact list, click the Add to Project Site icon.

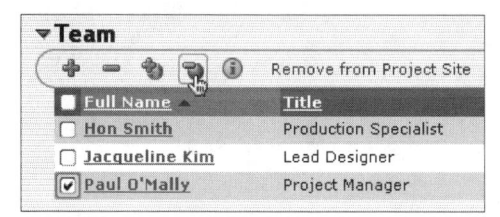

Figure 3.35 To remove the selected names from the contact list, click the Remove from Project Site icon.

To add or remove user names in the project-site contact list:

1. Navigate to the Project page for the project whose contact list you'd like to update. To do that, *do either of the following*:

   ▼ If you're on a page that has a link to the Project page whose contact list you want, click the link (**Figure 3.32**).

   or

   ▼ In the main navigation bar on any page, click the Projects button. The main Projects page opens. In the Project column, click the name of the project whose contact list you'd like to update.

2. The Project page opens. If the Team module isn't expanded, open the module by clicking the triangle next to the Team heading. If you're adding a user who is already a member of the project team, proceed to step 3. Otherwise, before continuing, add the user to the team by following "To link a user to a project" earlier in this chapter.

3. Click the check box to the left of the team-member names you'd like to add to or remove from the project site's contact list (**Figure 3.33**).

4. To add or remove user names in the project site's contact list, *do either of the following*:

   ▼ To add the names of the selected members to the contact list, click the Add to Project Site icon (**Figure 3.34**).

   ▼ To remove the names from the contact list, click the Remove from Project Site icon (**Figure 3.35**).

   The Project page reloads with a green success notice at the top. If you view the project site, you'll see that the contact list has been updated.

57

Managing Project Sites

A project site is a small Web site that gives the client a view into the project. Each project site is tied to a project in Sitespring and is separate from the Project page that your team uses to keep track of a project's status. The project site facilitates communication between the team and the client users who have permission to log into the site. Depending on the modules you choose to make visible, clients can see the status of their project, sign off on work in progress, use the messaging tool to communicate with the team, upload files if they have permission to do so, and view the project contact list. As you update the status of tasks and projects in Sitespring, the project site is updated automatically.

Because project sites reflect the status of and information about a particular project, the project must exist before you can create a project site for it. You can choose the look and feel of the project site when you create it by using one of Sitespring's eight project-site templates, or you can create your own template if you feel comfortable editing a page that uses JavaServer Pages (JSP) tags to place dynamic information. (Note, however, that once you've created a project site you cannot choose a new design template for the project site. If you want to change a project site's graphical look and feel, you need to either edit the actual JSP templates for the project site or delete the project site and re-create it with a new template.)

Finally, you can customize each project site to fit the needs of a particular project. A small project with clearly defined boundaries, for instance, may not require a discussion thread. For that project site you could disable the discussion module so it would not appear on the project site. Once you create a project site, you can change the information clients see and the features they have access to by

Projects and Project Sites

making modules visible or hidden. Hiding a module does not delete the information it contains; it merely prevents clients from accessing the information.

In this book, the Project Site details page is the name given to the page within the main application where you configure the project site's parameters. Don't confuse the Project Site details page with the actual project site itself, which displays information for the client.

Figure 3.36 In the My Projects module, the <Create...> link is on the right-hand side.

Figure 3.37 On the Project page, the <Create...> link is at the bottom of the Project module.

To create a project site:

1. Navigate to a place that has a <Create...> link for the project for which you'd like to create a project site. If a project site has not yet been created, such links exist in the lists of projects on your home page, on the main Projects page, and in the Project module on the Project page. Each project can have only one project site, and once the site has been created, the links to create the site are replaced with <Details> links that take you to the Project Site details page. Find the <Create...> link in *any of the following locations:*

   ▼ If you're on your home page, you'll find the link in the Project Site column on the right in the My Projects module (**Figure 3.36**).

   or

   ▼ If you're on the main Projects page, you'll find the link in the Project Site column on the right in the list of projects.

   or

   ▼ If you're on the Project page, you'll find the link at the bottom of the Project module at the top of the page (**Figure 3.37**).

2. Click the <Create...> link.

continues on next page

MANAGING PROJECT SITES

59

Chapter 3

3. The Create Project Site page opens. Choose a design template for the project site from the pull-down menu (**Figure 3.38**). The design template will not affect the information that appears on the project site, only how the pages are presented. Click the Preview Template Designs link if you'd like to see samples of the different designs (**Figures 3.39** and **3.40**).

4. Update the project path if necessary. The URL for the project site is the project path combined with a base URL for all of the project sites. The base URL is the name of the server plus the project site port number. The project path defaults to a path structure of *the name of your client/the name of the project*. You can update this path to anything you wish, although most users will probably not need to do this. You need to update the path only if you'd like the files for the project site stored in a different location from the default location.

5. Click the Save button to keep your changes, or click a navigation link to cancel them (**Figure 3.41**).

6. The Project page opens, with a green success notice at the top of the page indicating that the project site has been created. The project site defaults to showing all modules and preventing client-user access (**Figure 3.42**). To change the modules that the project site displays, see "To edit a project site and set visible modules" below. To give client users access to the project site, see "To grant or revoke project-site permission" in Chapter 2.

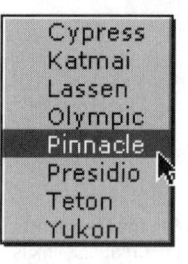

Figure 3.38 To choose a design for the project site, choose a template from the pull-down menu.

Figure 3.39 Click the Preview Template Designs link to see the sample templates.

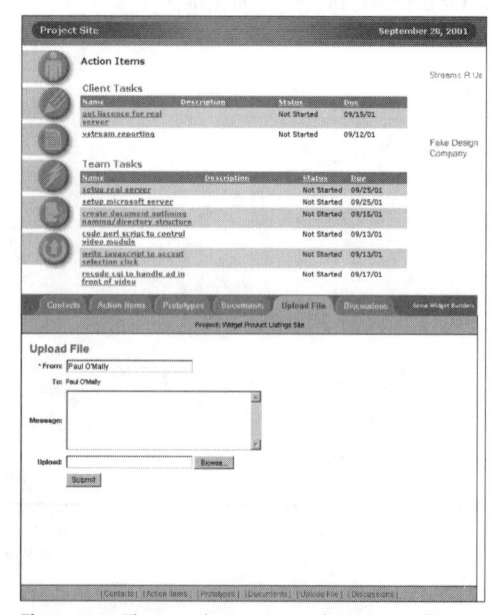

Figure 3.40 The template preview shows a small image of the template's design along with an explanation of the template.

Figure 3.41 Update the path for the project site, then click Save.

✔ **Tip**

- If you need to change the base URL for all of the project sites, the administrator can do this in the Admin area. See "Editing the Server" in Chapter 8.

Projects and Project Sites

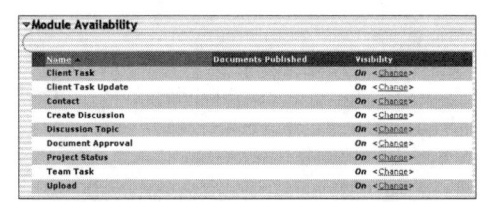

Figure 3.42 The project site shows all modules by default.

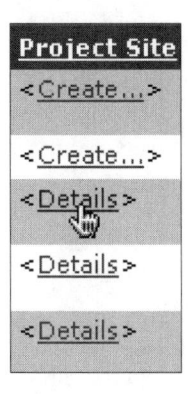

Figure 3.43 On the main Projects page, the <Details> link is in the right-most column.

Figure 3.44 On the Project page, the <Details> link is at the bottom of the Project module.

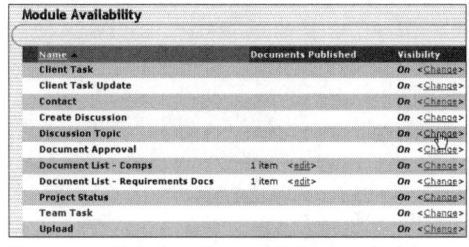

Figure 3.45 Click the <Change> link to toggle the visibility status of the project site modules.

To edit a project site and set visible modules:

1. Navigate to a place that has a <Details> link for the project site you'd like to edit. If a project site has not been created for a project, you will see a <Create...> link instead of a <Details> link. Links to Project Site details pages exist in lists of projects on your home page, on the main Projects page, and in the Project module on the Project page. Find the <Details> link in *any of the following locations:*

   ▼ If you're on your home page, you'll find the link in the Project Site column to the right of the My Projects module.

   or

   ▼ If you're on the main Projects page, you'll find the link in the Project Site column, to the right in the list of projects (**Figure 3.43**).

   or

   ▼ If you're on the Project page, you'll find the link at the bottom of the Project module at the top of the page (**Figure 3.44**).

2. Click the <Details> link. The Project Site details page opens.

3. If the Module Availability module isn't already open, open it by clicking the triangle to the left of the Module Availability heading.

   The modules listed can be either visible or hidden for the project site. If the module is shown on the project site, the word *On* appears in the Visibility column. If the module is hidden, the word *Off* appears. Toggle the visibility setting of the modules you'd like to make visible or hidden by clicking the <Change> link to the right of the module's status. The sidebar "Module Descriptions" explains each module (**Figure 3.45**).

MANAGING PROJECT SITES

61

Module Descriptions

Client Task—The Client Task module is a list of the client's tasks for the project. When you create a task, you assign it to either a team-member user or a client user. Tasks assigned to a client user appear in this module.

Client Task Update—If this module is visible, client users can update the status of tasks assigned to them. If it's not visible and the Client Task module is, client users can see tasks assigned to them but cannot change the tasks' status. If the Client Task Update module is visible, a client user can upload a file to the project when editing a task's status. For example, if a client user is assigned to get her company's logo as an EPS file, she could upload the EPS file as she marks the status Complete.

Contact—The Contact module is a contact list of the team members assigned to a project. Team-member users or client users appear on the Contact module if they have been added to it. (See Chapter 2 for information on how to add and remove users from the contact list.) The list displays each team member's name, job title, company, and email address.

Create Discussion—The Create Discussion module allows the client user to create a new discussion thread related to the project.

Discussion Topic—The Discussion Topic module displays thread topics published to the project site. Only discussion threads about the project that have been published to the project site appear, so you can still have private discussions among team members.

Document Approval—If this module is visible, client users can approve documents in the document list. If this module is not visible and a document list is visible, client users can view the documents in the document list but cannot change their approval status.

Document List—This item appears in the list of modules only if a document has been published to the document list. The Document List module organizes a group of related files into a list that the client can view. Sitespring's default Document List categories are Comps, Diagrams, Requirements Docs, Specifications, and Proposals. The administrator can edit the categories of Document Lists; see "To Edit Document List Categories" in Chapter 8. Once files are published to a Document List, click the <edit> link in the middle of the row to change items in the list.

Project Status—This module lists the project name, the project description, and the client organization name.

Team Task—This module lists team tasks that have been added to the project site. In this module the client can see tasks which have been published. Client users cannot update team tasks, regardless of the Client Task Update setting.

Upload—The Upload module lets client users upload a file to the project. When a client user uploads a file, a task that contains a link to the file is assigned to the project owner. This module is not related to a client user's ability to upload a file associated with a task. If this module is hidden and the Client Task Update module is visible, client users can still upload files associated with assigned tasks.

Projects and Project Sites

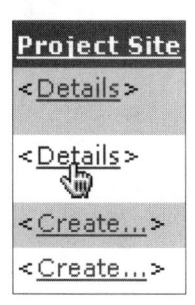

Figure 3.46 Click the project site's <Details> link.

Figure 3.47 Click the Remove icon to delete the project site.

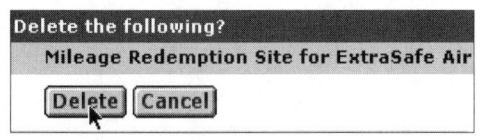

Figure 3.48 Confirm the deletion by clicking the Delete button.

To delete a project site:

1. Navigate to a place that has a <Details> link for the project site you'd like to delete. Links to Project Site details pages exist in lists of projects on your home page, on the main Projects page, and in the project details on a Project page. Find the <Details> link in *any of the following locations:*

   ▼ If you're on your home page, you'll find the link in the Project Site column to the right of the My Projects module (**Figure 3.46**).

   or

   ▼ If you're on the main Projects page, you'll find the link in the Project Site column to the right of the list of projects.

   or

   ▼ If you're on the Project page, you'll find the link at the bottom of the Project module at the top of the page.

2. Click the <Details> link.

3. The Project Site details page opens. Click the Remove icon ▬ at the top of the Project Site module (**Figure 3.47**).

4. The Delete Project Site confirmation page opens. Click the Delete button to delete the project site, or click the Cancel button to leave the project site intact (**Figure 3.48**).

   Your home page opens with a green success notice at top. The project site has been deleted.

✔ Tip

- Deleting a project site isn't as irrevocable an action as deleting a project. Still, you should think twice before deleting a project site, because if you need to re-create it for some reason, you'll have to reconfigure all the modules, give permission to all the client users, and republish any files or tasks related to the project.

MANAGING PROJECT SITES

63

Chapter 3

Exporting, Importing, and Taking Snapshots of Projects

If you're accustomed to working with Microsoft Project to keep track of project tasks, milestones, and schedules, you'll be grateful to know that you can import and export data between Sitespring and Project. While Sitespring's a great project collaboration tool, it doesn't—nor does it try to—match the project and resource scheduling capabilities of Project (**Figures 3.49** and **3.50**). By importing project plans already created in Project, you save time and avoid errors by not having to reenter the data in Sitespring. Note, however, that you can only import project information once per project. Conversely, updating your Gantt chart is much easier if you export the Sitespring data rather than reenter each task's status and completion time by hand.

Don't confuse exporting project data with taking a snapshot of a project. Exporting project data creates a single file that contains a copy of the project's tasks and deadlines. Creating a project snapshot makes a copy of all the current versions of a project's files and moves the files into a separate folder. That way you have a copy of the project's files as they existed the moment the snapshot was created. You should, disk space permitting, create a snapshot at every important project milestone. If you need to remember what the project looked like at that milestone, you can refer to the snapshot, where you have a copy of the whole project saved. It's especially important to create a snapshot at key client approvals, such as deciding on a design direction or approving a set of comps.

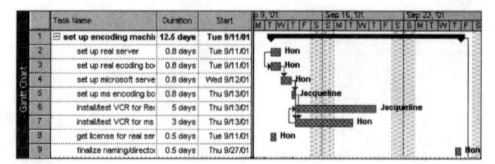

Figure 3.49 In Microsoft Project you can create Gantt charts that help you visually understand task dependencies.

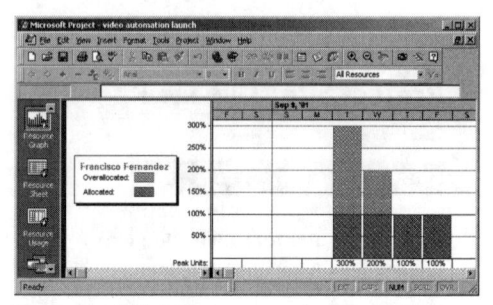

Figure 3.50 With Project you can also identify resource conflicts such as too many tasks being allocated to one person.

Sitespring can import project data that has been saved in the Microsoft Project Exchange 4.0 (MPX) format. MPX is an intermediary format for exchanging project-planning data. Microsoft Project 98 can export data in this format, as do many other project management tools. Unfortunately, Microsoft Project 2000 does not export in that format. In order to import a Project 2000 file, you must first open the file in Project 98 or use another conversion tool to convert the file. The directions below assume you've already exported the data to a file in MPX format from Project or another project-planning tool. (To export a file from Microsoft Project in MPX format, open the file in Microsoft Project 98 or earlier, then select Save As from the File menu. The Save As dialog box appears; choose MPX 4.0 from the Save As Type pull-down menu, name the file, and click Save.)

Sitespring lets you export a project in either MPX 4.0 format or Comma Separated Value (CSV) format. You should use MPX if you'll be importing the data into a project-planning tool that can import information from MPX files. If the tool you're using supports importing data from Microsoft Project, it probably supports this format. If you'll be looking at the data in Microsoft Excel, importing the data into a database, or using another tool that doesn't support MPX, you should export the data as a CSV file.

To import a project:

1. Navigate to a page in Sitespring where you can initiate importing a project. You can import a project from the Projects module on either your home page or the main Projects page. To do that, do *either of the following*:

    ▼ To navigate to your home page, click the Home button in the main navigation bar.

    ▼ To navigate to the main Projects page, click the Projects button in the main navigation bar.

2. Click the Import icon in the Projects module (**Figure 3.51**).

3. The Import Project page opens. Click the Browse button and locate the MPX file you saved with your project-planning tool. Once you've selected the file to import, click the Open button in the Open dialog box (**Figure 3.52**).

    The Open dialog box closes, and the Import File field is updated with the location of the file you'd like to import.

4. Click the Import button to import the file, or any navigation link to cancel the import process.

    The file is imported, and the Import Details Project status page opens with the results of the import and a green success notice (**Figure 3.53**).

5. Click the Continue link to go to the main Projects page. The project you just imported is listed in the main Projects page.

6. Click the link that is the name of the project you just imported.

7. The Project page opens. Verify that the data was imported correctly (**Figure 3.54**).

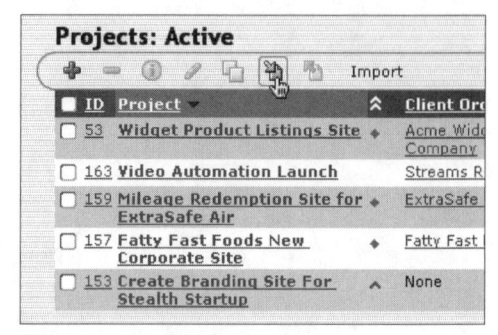

Figure 3.51 Click the Import icon.

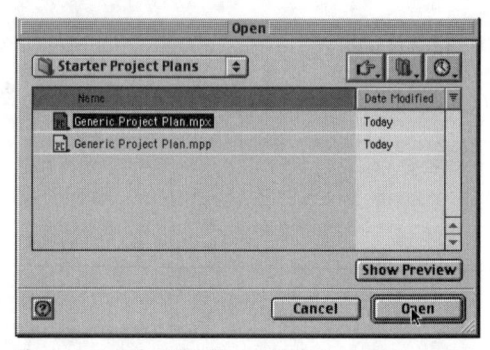

Figure 3.52 Select the file you'd like to import.

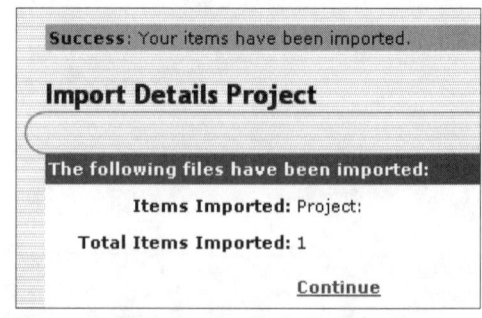

Figure 3.53 The Import Details Project page reports that the file was imported successfully.

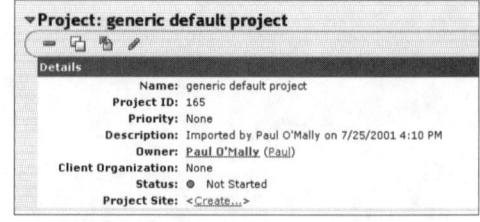

Figure 3.54 Double-check that the information was imported correctly, and assign tasks as appropriate.

Projects and Project Sites

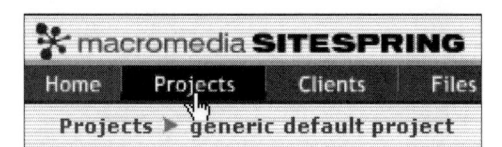

Figure 3.55 Click the Projects navigation button to go to the Projects page.

✔ **Tips**

- To get the tasks to import so that they're assigned to the right user, enter the user's Sitespring user name in the Initials field in Microsoft Project's Resource sheet. If you don't enter the appropriate user name in the Initials field, the tasks assigned to that user will import without being assigned to anyone.

- Each time you import a project, Sitespring creates a new project with its name. Before you import a file, make sure there's not already a project with the same name.

To export a project:

1. Navigate to a page that contains a project module, to the main Projects page, or to the Project page itself. To do that, *do any of the following:*

- ▼ If you're already on a page in Sitespring that has a projects module, locate the module. It will be called My Projects on your home page, or Client Projects on the Clients page.

  or

- ▼ To navigate to the main Projects page, click the Projects button in the main navigation bar (**Figure 3.55**). The main Projects page opens.

- ▼ To navigate to the Project page, click the Projects button in the main navigation bar. The Project page opens. Click the name of the project you'd like to export. The Project page opens.

continues on next page

67

Chapter 3

2. Next, you need to start the export process. To do that, *do either of the following:*

   ▼ If you're on a page with a Projects module, click the check box next to the name of the project you'd like to export. Then click the Export icon 🗎 (**Figure 3.56**).

   ▼ If you're on the Project page, click the Export icon 🗎 (**Figure 3.57**).

3. The Export Project page opens. Choose the Export Format from the pull-down menu (**Figure 3.58**). See above for information about the two format choices.

4. Click the Export button. A file download dialog box opens. On the PC, select "Save this file to disk" and click OK (**Figure 3.59**). On the Mac, click the "Save File As…" button.

5. A Save dialog box opens. Choose a location in which to save the file, replace the series of numbers in the filename field with a meaningful name, and click the Save button.

   The Save dialog box disappears.

   You can now open the file you saved with the project-planning program you've chosen.

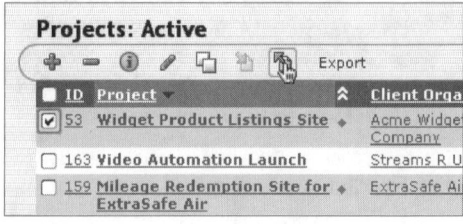

Figure 3.56 Check the name of the project you'd like to export, then click the Export icon.

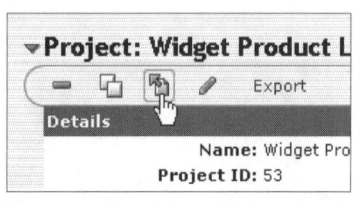

Figure 3.57 If you're on a Project page, you don't need to check anything; simply click the Export icon.

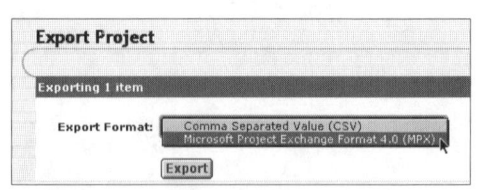

Figure 3.58 Choose the appropriate format for the file you're about to create.

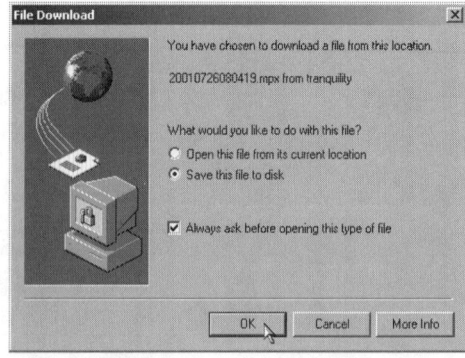

Figure 3.59 On the PC, select "Save this file to disk," then click OK to save the file to your hard drive.

Projects and Project Sites

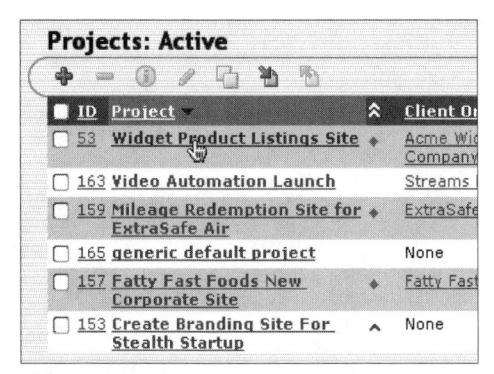

Figure 3.60 To go to the Project page, click the name of the project for which you'd like a snapshot.

Figure 3.61 Click the Create Snapshot icon.

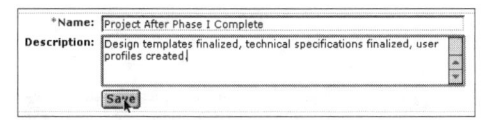

Figure 3.62 Enter a description for your snapshot.

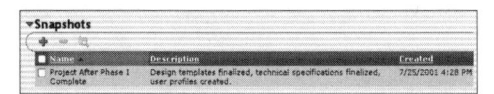

Figure 3.63 The Snapshots module lists the snapshot just created.

To create a project snapshot:

1. Navigate to the Project page for the project you'd like to take a snapshot of (**Figure 3.60**).

2. Scroll to the bottom of the page and expand the Snapshots module if it isn't expanded already.

3. Click the Create Snapshot icon ✚ (**Figure 3.61**).

4. The Create Snapshot page opens. In the Name field, enter a name for the folder that will contain the snapshot.

   Optionally, enter a description of the snapshot in the Description field. If you're taking this snapshot because the project has reached a milestone, it's a good idea to note that here. The description will show up in the Snapshots module (**Figure 3.62**).

5. Click the Save button.

   The main Projects page reloads with an updated Snapshots module at the bottom of the page (**Figure 3.63**) and a green notice at the top letting you know the snapshot has started. If the project contains a large number of files, this process may take a long time. Sitespring will email you when the snapshot is complete.

✓ Tips

- Be careful about taking snapshots of large projects, or of small projects that contain large files. Creating a snapshot duplicates all folders (and the files they contain) linked to a project, which can occupy significant disk space. Check that you have enough disk space before creating the snapshot.

- Before you close a project, consider eliminating some earlier snapshots that you don't need to keep around anymore.

Chapter 3

To view a project snapshot:

1. Navigate to the Project page for the project whose snapshot you'd like to see (**Figure 3.64**).

2. Scroll to the bottom of the page and expand the Snapshots module if it isn't expanded already.

3. Click the check box to the left of the snapshot you'd like to view (**Figure 3.65**).

4. Click the Explore icon (**Figure 3.66**).

5. If you haven't already installed the Sitespring Helper application, a warning dialog box opens instructing you to install it. Follow the directions in "To install the sitespring helper" in Chapter 4, then repeat step 4. If you have the Helper application installed, continue with step 6.

   On a PC, the Windows Explorer opens the folder containing the project snapshot. On a Mac, the Finder opens the folder.

   You can now open any folders or files contained in the project snapshot, as you would any normal file or folder. Think carefully before deleting or modifying any files or folders, for doing so will make the snapshot an inaccurate reflection of the project at the time the snapshot was taken. Instead, copy the file or folder elsewhere and work on the copy.

✔ Tip

- If you get the notice "Cannot explore the current selection. The current selection is not on a monitored share" when you try to explore a snapshot, it means that the folder in which the snapshot resides has not been shared or that Sitespring's versioning is not enabled for the folder. Your administrator will need to both share the folder and enable versioning before you can explore the snapshot.

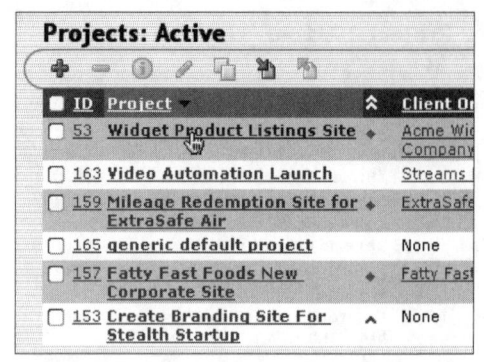

Figure 3.64 To go to the Project page, click the name of the project for which you'd like to see a snapshot.

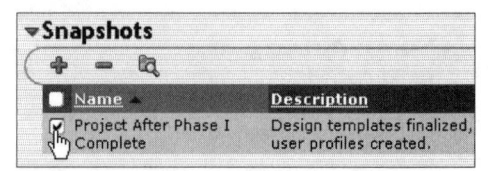

Figure 3.65 Click the check box for the snapshot you'd like to view.

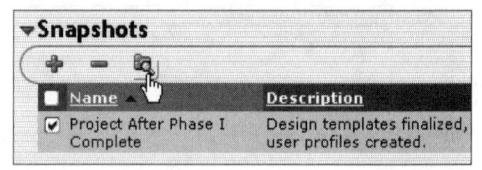

Figure 3.66 Click the Explore icon to open the project snapshot.

4

FOLDERS AND FILES

The end result of any Web project is a folder or series of folders that contains any number of files. Along the way, a file may go through many permutations. Keeping track of all the files can quickly overwhelm even a seasoned Web professional. Sitespring helps create order out of the mayhem by associating the files and folders on the production server with the projects and tasks in Sitespring. Thus any team member can easily find the latest version of a file, and project managers can easily create snapshots of entire folders related to a project. Sitespring's automatic versioning feature saves copies of interim file versions, allowing you to revert to them if needed.

As you'll learn in this chapter, folders are associated with projects, and files are associated with tasks. Chapter 3 explained how to add a folder to a project. This chapter tells you how to open a folder linked to a project, and how to remove folders from a project. This chapter also explains how to manage files—how to view and edit them; revert to an earlier version; publish them to or remove them from a project site; and move, add, or delete them. Finally, you'll learn what Sitespring Helper is and how to install and configure it.

About Versioning

If you've ever worked on a large Web project, you know what it feels like to be drowning in files as the versions multiply. It's not just the layouts that can get out of hand; the requirement documents, technical specifications, user profiles, and process diagrams also add to the swelling number of files. And since many of these documents are created by teams, each document can go through a dozen revisions in just a day as team members pass the documents back and forth for comments.

Traditional version control and document management systems try to track these changes by requiring you to follow an arduous process. To make a change, you check a document out of the system (locking out other users and preventing them from making simultaneous edits), make your changes, check the document back into the system, and enter comments about what changed. Such a formal document management process is unnecessary for many teams, and a pain even when it's needed.

Sitespring uses a less intrusive approach to tracking versions. It's so unobtrusive that if you didn't know it was happening, you wouldn't even know it was there. When your administrator configures Sitespring, he or she determines which of the server's shared folders has versioning activated.

Once versioning is turned on, every time you save changes to a file—with any program you use—the original file that is being overwritten is not lost, as it would be normally. Instead, the original file is backed up to the _revisions folder. Whenever you save, move, rename, or delete a file, a copy of the original file is placed in the _revisions folder (**Figure 4.1**).

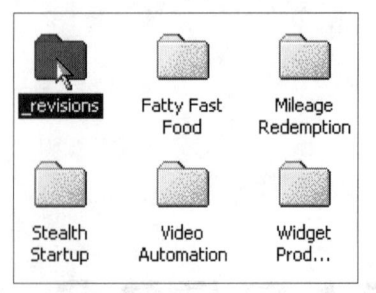

Figure 4.1 Whenever you make a change to a file, the original file moves to the _revisions folder.

Folders and Files

Figure 4.2 Three-digit sequence numbers organize the versions chronologically.

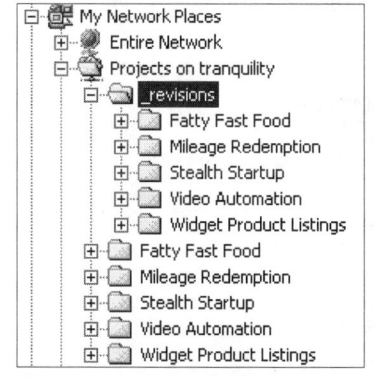

Figure 4.3 The _revisions folder, which contains the backup revisions, mirrors the structure of the folder in which it sits.

Since many files are saved multiple times, a three-digit sequence number is added to the original filename so you can tell the versions apart (**Figure 4.2**). The _revisions folder mirrors the structure of the server's folder in which it sits, so if you update a file from a nested folder, the old version of the file gets moved into the same place within the _revisions folder (**Figure 4.3**). Once the administrator has enabled versioning, you don't need to do anything in order for these versions to be created; they appear automatically no matter how the files are changed, moved, or deleted.

ABOUT VERSIONING

Managing Folders

Sitespring works with folders shared by the production server that runs Sitespring, not with local folders on your machine. When the administrator sets up Sitespring, he or she determines what top-level folders will be shared and whether version tracking will be turned on for each folder. Folders inside these top-level folders automatically inherit the characteristics of their parent folder.

When you start a new Web project, the project owner generally creates a new folder on the server, inside one of the top-level shared folders, to hold all the files that will make up the project. You should come up with a standardized folder structure for all of your projects, so that any member of the team can easily find files as needed. On any given project there will be documents about the site or project, such as technical specifications and user profiles—documents that define what you're building. Additionally there will be sample pages, document templates, logos, and navigation images—files that constitute the project itself. Create a standard folder structure and make all your projects conform to the standard (**Figures 4.4** and **4.5**). The team will more easily find files if they're located in the same place for each project.

You can also remove a folder from a project. Removing a folder does not delete the folder or its contents; rather, it breaks the association between the folder and the project. Once a folder is removed from a project, future project snapshots will not contain the folder's contents. Removing a folder from a project does not affect whether automatic versioning is turned on for the folder.

Once you've created the appropriate folders, see "To add a folder to a project" in Chapter 3 to link the folders to the project in Sitespring.

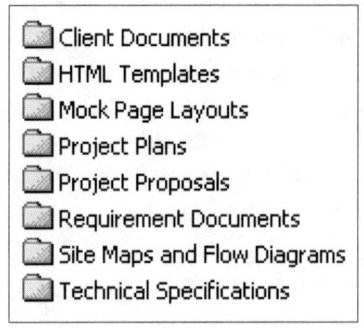

Figure 4.4 You can organize a folder structure by document type.

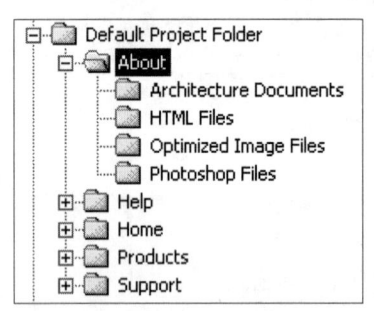

Figure 4.5 You can also organize a folder structure by site subsection and document type.

Folders and Files

Figure 4.6 Select the folder you'd like to open and click the Explore icon.

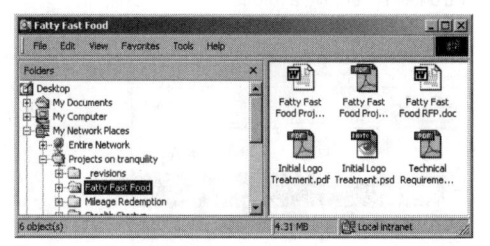

Figure 4.7 On a PC, Sitespring Helper opens the folder in Windows Explorer.

Figure 4.8 On a Mac, Sitespring Helper opens the folder in the Finder.

To explore a folder linked to a project:

1. Navigate to the Project page for the project whose folder you'd like to explore. To do that, *do either of the following*:

    ▼ If you're already on a page that has a link to the Project page you want, click the link. On your home page, these links are in the My Projects module. On either the main Projects page or a client page, they are in the Projects module.

    or

    ▼ In the main navigation bar on any page, click the Projects button. The main Projects page opens. In the Project column, click the name of the project for which you'd like to explore a folder.

2. The Project page opens. If the Folders module isn't already expanded, open the module by clicking the triangle next to the Folders heading.

3. In the list in the Folders module, find the folder you'd like to explore. Select the folder by clicking the check box to the left of the folder's name. Click the Explore icon to open it (**Figure 4.6**).

4. On a PC, Windows Explorer opens the selected folder (**Figure 4.7**). On a Mac, the folder opens in the Finder (**Figure 4.8**).

    You can work with the folders and files in Windows Explorer or the Mac Finder as you would any normal file; the versioning system—if enabled—will save a revision for each change you make.

MANAGING FOLDERS

75

Chapter 4

To remove a folder from a project:

1. Navigate to the Project page for the project from which you'd like to remove a folder. To do that, *do either of the following*:

    ▼ If you're already on a page that has a link to the Project page you want, click the link. On your home page, these links are in the My Projects module. On either the main Projects page or a client page, they are in the Projects module.

    or

    ▼ In the main navigation bar on any page, click the Projects button. The main Projects page opens. In the Project column, click the name of the project from which you'd like to remove a folder (**Figure 4.9**).

2. The Project page opens. If the Folders module isn't already expanded, open the module by clicking the triangle next to the Folders heading.

3. Find the folder or folders you would like to remove from the project in the Folders module. To select the folders, click the check box in the leftmost column next to the corresponding name. Then click the Remove icon ▬ (**Figure 4.10**).

4. The Remove Folders confirmation page opens. Click the Remove button to remove the folder from the project (**Figure 4.11**), or click the Cancel button to leave the folder linked to the project.

    The Project page reopens with a green success notice at top and the Folder module updated (**Figure 4.12**).

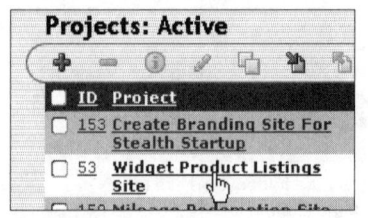

Figure 4.9 Open the main Projects page to navigate to the project from which you'd like to remove a folder.

Figure 4.10 Select the folder, then click the Remove icon.

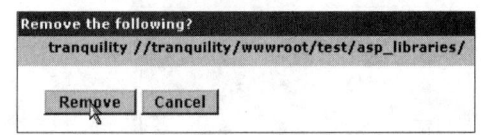

Figure 4.11 Click the Remove button to confirm the change.

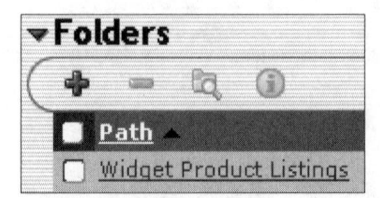

Figure 4.12 The removed folder no longer appears in the Folders module.

76

Viewing Files or File Histories

Generally speaking, you create and edit files related to your Web project with the programs you normally use. The file creation and editing process doesn't involve Sitespring directly. (See "About Versioning" earlier in this chapter for an explanation of how Sitespring creates backup files of interim file versions while you work.) What Sitespring helps you do is manage file versions and publish files to the project site.

You can view files in Sitespring's File Explorer. Alternatively, you can open folders and view files directly through Windows Explorer, the Mac Finder, or any program you choose. Generally it's easier and faster to use your operating system's normal methods to interact with files than to go through the Sitespring File Explorer. To view or open a file directly, simply navigate to the folder containing the file as you would any file on the server. Follow the directions below to view files from within Sitespring.

For folders with versioning enabled, Sitespring saves a copy of the original file into the _revisions folder each time you modify a file. You can view a list of file versions to understand a file's editing history. You might do this to find out who has worked on a file or to learn the date that a change occurred.

Chapter 4

To view or edit a current or earlier file version:

1. Click the Files button in the main navigation bar.

   The File Explorer opens.

2. Locate the file you would like to view or open. If the server running Sitespring is sharing more than one top-level folder, you can choose another top-level folder from the Root pull-down menu at the top of the File Explorer (**Figure 4.13**). You can open and close subfolders by clicking the expand ⊞ and collapse ⊟ icons (**Figure 4.14**).

3. Select the file you would like to view by clicking the check box to the left of the filename. Click the Item Information icon ⓘ at the top of the module (**Figure 4.15**).

   The file details page opens. The File module displays the file's location, the Windows user name of the person who last modified the file, the date the file was last modified, the file size, and comments (**Figure 4.16**). The Revision History module lists the same information about the backup versions of the file stored in the _revisions folder (**Figure 4.17**).

4. To view file versions, *do either of the following:*

   ▼ To view the latest version of the file in Windows Explorer or the Mac Finder, click the Explore icon at the top of the File module.

   or

   ▼ To view an earlier version of the file, click the corresponding check box to the left of the Revision column. Then click the Explore icon at the top of the Revision History module (**Figure 4.18**).

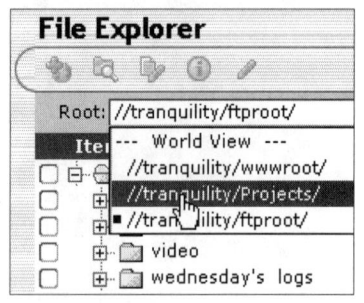

Figure 4.13 Choose another top-level folder from the Root pull-down menu.

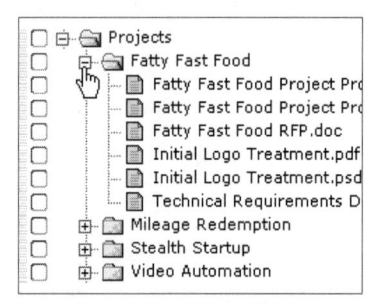

Figure 4.14 Clicking the expand icon opens the folder.

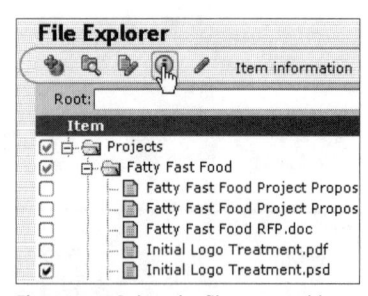

Figure 4.15 Select the file you would like to view, then click the Item Information icon.

Figure 4.16 The file details page lists information about the file.

78

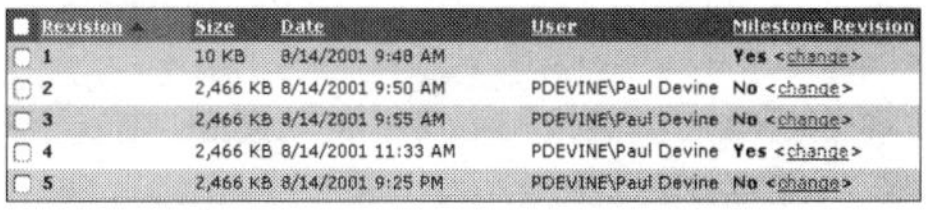

Revision	Size	Date	User	Milestone Revision
1	10 KB	8/14/2001 9:48 AM		Yes <change>
2	2,466 KB	8/14/2001 9:50 AM	PDEVINE\Paul Devine	No <change>
3	2,466 KB	8/14/2001 9:55 AM	PDEVINE\Paul Devine	No <change>
4	2,466 KB	8/14/2001 11:33 AM	PDEVINE\Paul Devine	Yes <change>
5	2,466 KB	8/14/2001 9:25 PM	PDEVINE\Paul Devine	No <change>

Figure 4.17 The Revision History module lists information about the various revisions.

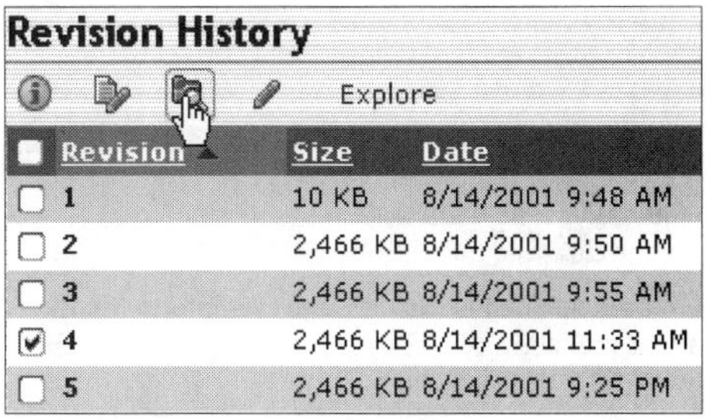

Figure 4.18 Select a revision and click the Explore icon to open the folder containing the revision.

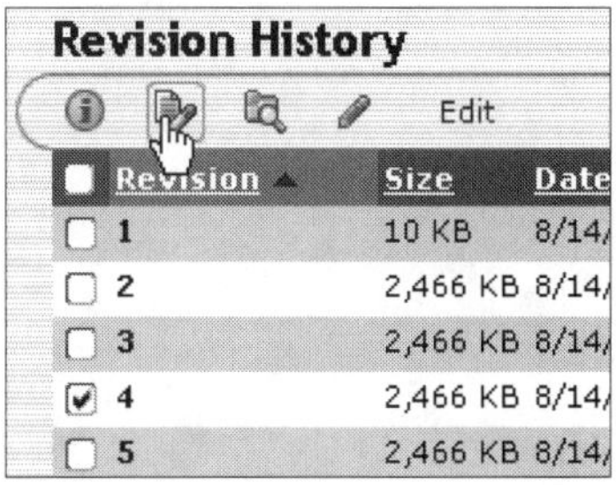

Figure 4.19 To edit a version directly from Sitespring, select the file and click the Edit icon.

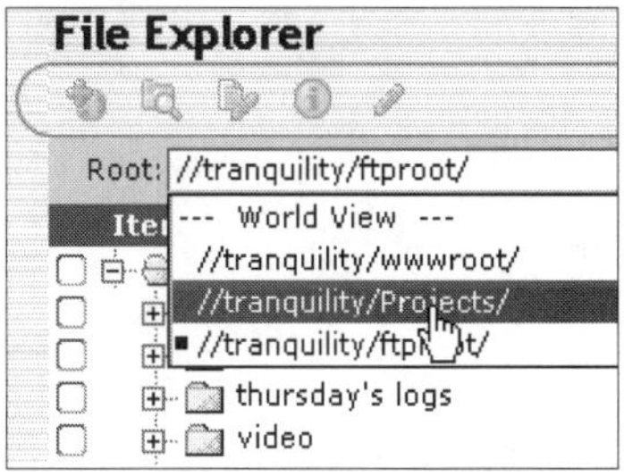

Figure 4.20 Choose another top-level folder from the pull-down menu.

The folder containing the file you want opens in either Windows Explorer or the Mac Finder.

5. To edit the file, open it as you would any file on your computer. If you want to edit a file without first opening its corresponding folder (skipping steps 6 and 7), simply select the file and click the corresponding Edit icon in Sitespring (**Figure 4.19**).

   The file you want opens in the program assigned to that file type.

✔ Tip

- If the file you'd like to view is linked to a task and you already have the Task page open, you can view the file directly by clicking the linked filename in the Linked Content module.

To view a file's revision history:

1. Click the Files button in the main navigation bar to reach the File Explorer.

   The File Explorer opens.

2. Locate the file for which you'd like to see the revision history.

   If the server running Sitespring is sharing more than one top-level folder, you can choose another top-level folder from the Root pull-down menu at the top of the File Explorer (**Figure 4.20**). You can open and close subfolders by clicking the expand ⊞ and collapse ⊟ icons. Files with a revision history have the number of revisions available in the Revisions column; files without a number listed have only their original version.

continues on next page

Chapter 4

3. Select the file you want by clicking the check box to the left of the filename.

4. Click the Item Information icon at the top of the File Explorer module (**Figure 4.21**). The file details page opens.

The File module displays the current file's location, the Windows user name of who last modified the file, the date the file was last modified, the file size, and comments (**Figure 4.22**).

The Revision History module lists information about the backup versions of the file stored in the _revisions folder (**Figure 4.23**). See notes below about each column.

Revision—A number that identifies the file's order in the sequence of revisions.

Size—The file size of the revision.

Date—The date the revision was made.

User—The file-sharing log-in identity of the user who created the version. This may be different than the user's Sitespring log-in name.

Milestone Revision—A Yes or No value that indicates whether the revision was associated with a milestone. This option helps if the administrator decides to run the Revision Cleanup Wizard, which frees disk space by removing old revisions according to specified criteria. A milestone revision will not be deleted when the wizard runs; the wizard may delete a version not marked as a milestone.

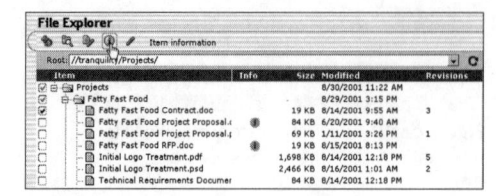

Figure 4.21 Click the Item Information icon to open the file details page.

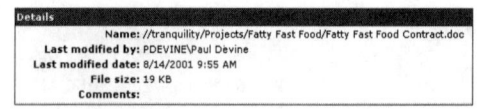

Figure 4.22 The file details page lists information about the file.

Figure 4.23 The Revision History module lists information about the various revisions.

Folders and Files

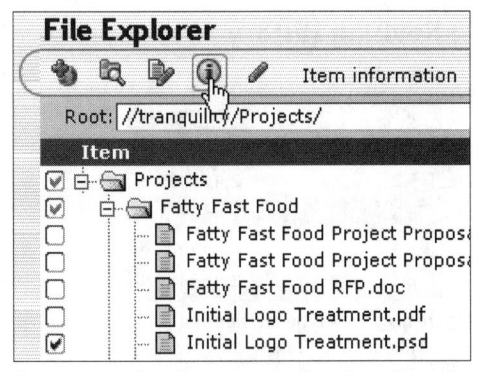

Figure 4.24 Select the current version of the file and click the Item Information icon.

Reverting to Earlier Versions of Files

You can also revert to an earlier version of a file in the File Explorer. You can use the File Explorer to access an earlier version of a file only if there is a current version of the file in the project folder or one of its subfolders. If the file has been deleted from the project folder, the file will not appear in the File Explorer, and you will need to manually copy the earlier version in the _revisions folder and put it back into the project folder.

To retrieve or revert to an earlier version:

1. Click the Files button in the main navigation bar.

   The File Explorer opens.

2. Locate the current version of the file whose earlier version you would like to revert to.

   You can open and close subfolders by clicking the expand ⊞ and collapse ⊟ icons. If the server running Sitespring is sharing more than one top-level folder, you can choose another top-level folder from the pull-down menu at the top of the File Explorer.

3. Click the check box to the left of the current version of the file. Click the Item Information icon ⓘ at the top of the module (**Figure 4.24**).

   The file details page opens. The Revision History module lists information about the backup versions of the file stored in the _revisions folder.

4. Locate the version you want to revert to.

   continues on next page

81

Chapter 4

5. Click the check box to the left of the corresponding revision number. Click the Edit icon ✏ at the top of the Revision History module (**Figure 4.25**).

   The file opens in the program assigned to that file type.

6. Select Save As from the File menu.

   The Save dialog opens.

7. Navigate to the folder that contains the current version of the file you would like to replace. In the File Name field, enter the name of the current version of the file. Click the Save button (**Figure 4.26**).

   A warning dialog opens asking if you want to replace the existing file with another that has the same name.

8. Click the OK button to replace the file (**Figure 4.27**).

   The old version is saved over the current version, and the file is restored.

✔ Tip

- Don't worry if you accidentally revert to an earlier version of the wrong file. Since each version of a file is saved, even the version you just overwrote will still be there. Simply follow the same directions to revert back to the version you just overwrote.

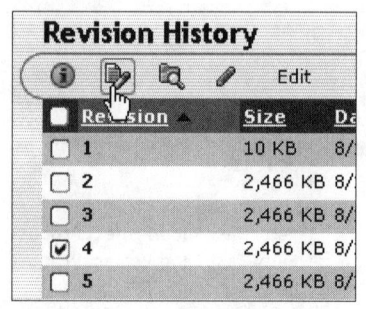

Figure 4.25 Select the revision you would like to revert to and click the Edit icon.

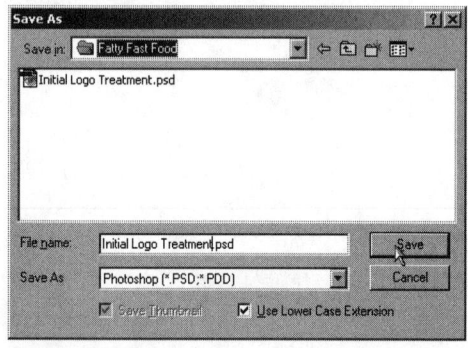

Figure 4.26 Within the program you use to edit the file, choose Save As from the File menu. Then save the file over the current version you're replacing.

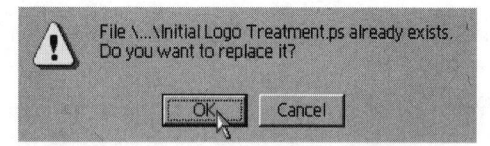

Figure 4.27 Click the OK button to confirm the file replacement.

Publishing Files

You can publish one file or a group of files to a project site for a client to review or approve. If you're publishing a single file, it can be any type, whether it's a Microsoft Excel spreadsheet or a GIF image. If you're publishing a group of files as a set, the files must be in HTML, Flash, or some other format that will allow clients to navigate through the files in their browser after clicking a single link to the set of files.

When you publish a file or a group of files to the project site, their names appear in the document list you chose. In many cases, you'll publish a file after completing a task assigned to you to prepare the file. You will often link the created file to the task assignment.

To publish a file or group of files to a project site:

1. Locate the file you'd like to publish, in *any of the following locations:*

    ▼ If the file you'd like to publish has already been linked to a task, you can find the file in the Linked Content module on the task's details page (**Figure 4.28**). Navigate to the details page for the task related to the linked file.

    ▼ If the file you'd like to publish has not been linked to a task, but the folder containing the file *has* been linked to the project, you can easily locate the file by opening the linked folder from the Project page. Do that by clicking the folder's name in the Folders module at the bottom of the page (**Figure 4.29**). The File Explorer opens to the linked folder (**Figure 4.30**). Navigate to the file you'd like to publish.

continues on next page

Figure 4.28 If the file you'd like to publish is linked to a task, you can navigate directly to the file details page from the task details page.

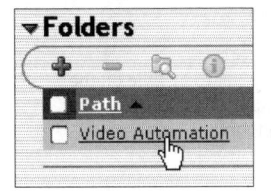

Figure 4.29 If the file you'd like to publish is inside a folder linked to a project, you can get to the file quickly by clicking the folder's link in the Folders module.

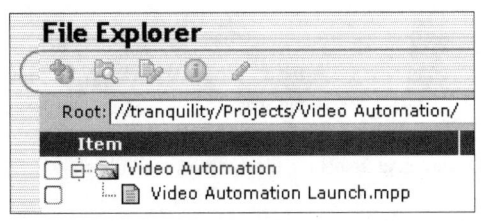

Figure 4.30 The linked folder opens in the File Explorer, where you can locate the file you'd like to publish.

Chapter 4

▼ If neither the file you'd like to publish nor the folder containing the file has been linked to a task or project, you'll need to locate the file through the File Explorer. Click the Files button in the main navigation bar. The File Explorer opens. Navigate to the file you'd like to publish (**Figure 4.31**).

2. Select the file you found in step 1 by clicking the check box to the left of the file's name.

3. From either the File Explorer or the Linked Content module, click the Publish icon 🎯 (**Figures 4.32** and **4.33**).

4. The Publish Files page opens. Enter the information about the file you are publishing. Information in the fields with an asterisk is required (**Figure 4.34**). For details about each field, read the notes below.

   *Project Site—Choose the appropriate project site from this pull-down menu of project sites when you publish the file.

   Document List—Publish your file to a category from a pull-down menu of the document list. A document list groups related files on the project site into organized lists. The default list categories are Comps, Diagrams, Requirements Docs, Specifications, and Proposals; the administrator can change these to values more suited to your organization. The file you're publishing will be listed alongside the other documents in the category you choose here.

   Expire Date—You can choose a date by which the published file will expire. After a file expires, it no longer appears on the project site.

   *Visible—Choose Yes or No to determine whether the file will be visible on the project site. A Yes value makes the file visible to client users and normal users visiting

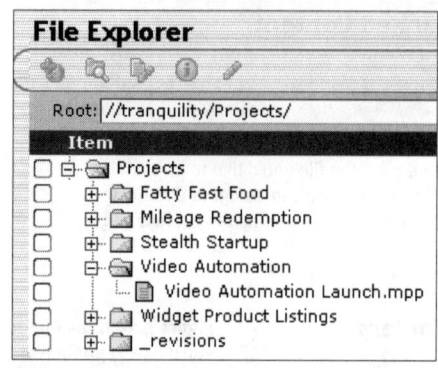

Figure 4.31 You can always get to any file on the server through the File Explorer, regardless of whether the file is linked to a task.

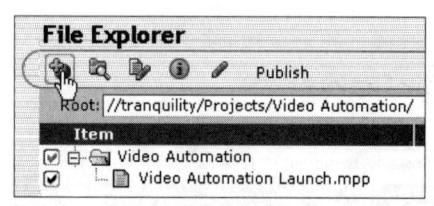

Figure 4.32 Select the file and click the Publish icon.

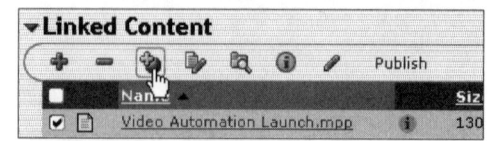

Figure 4.33 Clicking the Publish icon in the Linked Content module has the same effect as clicking the icon on the File Explorer.

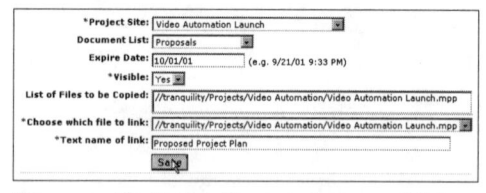

Figure 4.34 The Publish Files page lets you publish files to the project site for client review.

Folders and Files

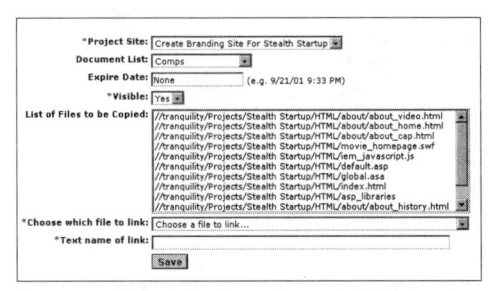

Figure 4.35 The List of Files to Be Copied displays the files you are publishing.

Figure 4.36 If you're publishing more than one file, choose the one that will be linked to from the project site.

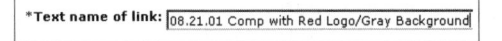

Figure 4.37 The text name you entered will show up as the link to the file on the project site.

✔ Tips

- When using the File Explorer, you can expand and collapse subfolders by clicking the expand ⊞ and collapse ⊟ icons.

- If your administrator has configured more than one top-level or root shared folder for the server, you can choose another top-level shared folder from the Root pull-down menu. Only server folders shared by your system administrator will appear in that pull-down menu.

the project site. A No value means that the file will not appear in the document list you chose above.

List of Files to Be Copied—If you're publishing just one file, the name of that file appears. If you're publishing more than one, the entire list of those files will be displayed (**Figure 4.35**).

*Choose Which File to Link—Choose the file to link to from the pull-down menu (**Figure 4.36**). If you're publishing just one file, its name will be displayed and you won't need to adjust this field. If you're publishing a set of files—usually a Web site or part of a site—you need to choose the file that opens when the client user clicks the link in the document list. Generally this should be the index or default document for the files that you are publishing. This file could be named index.html, default.asp, index.jsp, or something else, depending on how your system is configured. It's critical that the client user be able to navigate to the rest of the documents you are publishing from this file; otherwise the client user will not be able to view the related files.

*Text Name of Link—This name will be the one displayed in the document list on the project site as a hyperlink to the document to download or display. Enter a name that distinguishes this document or set of documents from others that may appear in the document list (**Figure 4.37**). Remember that this name may need to age gracefully, so don't call it something like Tuesday's Comp, which could be confusing later.

5. Click the Save button. The Project Site details page for the project to which you publish the file opens with a green success notice at top. The Document List summary in the Module Availability module updates to show the new published file count.

PUBLISHING FILES

85

Removing Files

You may want to remove files when it's no longer appropriate for them to be on the project site, or remove their names from the document list. You might, for example, remove a preliminary comp after the design has progressed. You can remove the file from the external project site and still have its name appear on the document list in the main Sitespring application, or you can remove it from both the project site and the document list altogether. You might choose to leave the file on the document list if you plan on updating the file to present to the client again.

You might also leave the file on the list if you wish to retain the file's approval history. When you remove a file from a project site, its approval history is lost—so think twice before removing files.

Document List - Comps	1 item	<edit>
Document List - Proposals	2 items	<edit>
Document List - Requirements Docs	1 item	<edit>

Figure 4.38 Click the <edit> link to open the Document List Manager page.

To remove a file from the project site or a document list:

1. Navigate to the Project Site details page for the project site that contains the document or group of documents you'd like to remove.

2. If the Module Availability module isn't already expanded, open it by clicking the expand icon ▶ next to the module heading. The module opens.

3. In the Module Availability module, locate the document list that contains the names of the documents you would like to remove. Open the Document List Manager page for that list by clicking the <edit> link in the Documents Published column (**Figure 4.38**).

4. The Document List Manager page opens. Locate the files you would like to remove in the Files module. Select the documents by clicking the corresponding check box to the left of the Link Name column.

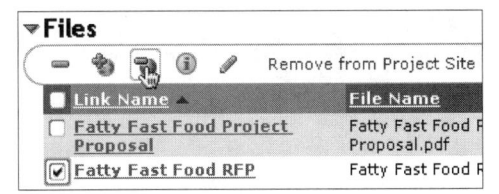

Figure 4.39 Click the Remove from Project Site icon to hide the document on the project site while still leaving its name on the document list.

Figure 4.40 Click the Remove icon to remove the document from the document list and the project site.

Figure 4.41 When you remove a document from the project site but keep its name in the document list, the Visible column updates to No.

Figure 4.42 The Files module no longer displays the file removed from the document list and project site.

5. To remove the files from the project site or the document list, *do either of the following*:

    ▼ To remove the document or document group from the project site but leave them on the document list, click the Remove from Project Site icon 🕭 (**Figure 4.39**). This prevents client users from seeing the documents.

    or

    ▼ To remove the document or document group from the project site and the document list simultaneously, click the Remove icon ▬ (**Figure 4.40**).

6. If you choose to remove the file or group of files from the project site only, the Document List Manager page reloads in your browser with the Visible column updated to No (**Figure 4.41**). The files no longer display on the project site, and step 7 will not occur.

    or

    If you choose to remove the file or group of files from the document list and project site, the Remove Documents confirmation page opens. Click the Remove button to remove the files or click Cancel to leave them.

    Removing a file from the project site also deletes its appoval history, if it had one.

7. The Document List Manager page opens with the links and filenames removed from the Files module (**Figure 4.42**).

✔ **Tip**

- Using the Visible field can be confusing at first. Once a client has seen a file and approved it, you may want to remove the file from the client's view of the project site. If you set the file's Visible field to No, the file is hidden to the client but the record of the client's approval is retained. If you remove the file, the file's approval history is lost.

Uploading Files

This procedure lets client users upload a file to the Web team through the project site. Normal users would generally not use this feature to move a file onto the server. Instead, you should simply copy the file to the appropriate folder on the production server; by using your operating system's native methods to interact with shared folders, you have more control and greater flexibility than when using Sitespring's File Explorer. Because Sitespring requires that file sharing be turned on for all folders it works with, users on the local network can always access these folders as they would other network folders. (Do not confuse uploading a file with linking a file to a task or publishing a file to a project site. If you want to link a file to a task, see "To link a file with a task" in Chapter 5. If you want to publish a file to a project site, see "To publish a file or group of files to a project site" earlier in this chapter.)

Because client users don't have access to the production server, they need to upload files through the project site. Once the client user has uploaded the file, the project owner receives an email notice saying that a file has been uploaded. Along with the email, a new task assignment is sent to the project owner with the subject line "a resource has been added."

Figure 4.43 Click the Upload File button, link, or tab, depending on the project site template.

To upload a file:

1. Log into the project site for the project to which you'd like to upload a file.

2. Click the Upload File button or link (**Figure 4.43**).

    How the Upload File button looks will depend on which template was used for the project site. There may not be an Upload File button or link if the project owner for the project site has disabled the File Upload module.

Folders and Files

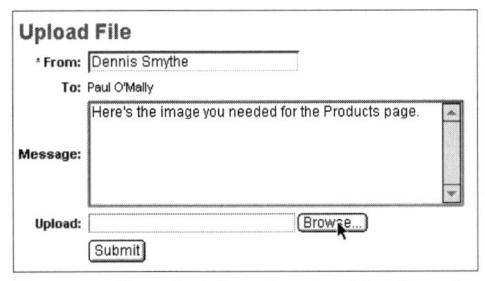

Figure 4.44 Enter the information about the file you're uploading, and click the Browse button.

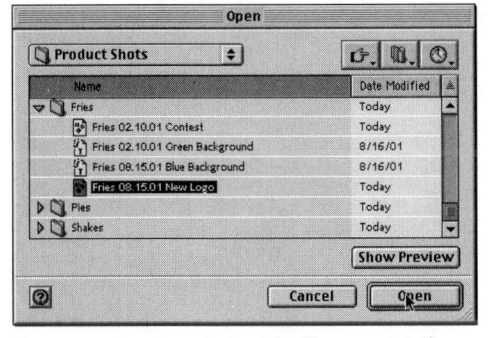

Figure 4.45 Locate and select the file you want, then click Open.

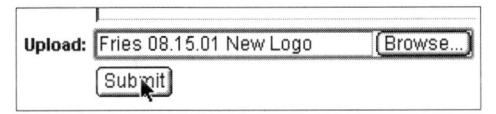

Figure 4.46 Click the Submit button to upload the file. This process may take several minutes with a slow connection, and even longer if the file is large.

3. Enter the information about the file you are uploading in the appropriate fields (**Figure 4.44**). For more information on each field, read the notes below. The required field is marked with an asterisk.

   *From—This field defaults to your full name. Enter a different name only if you'd like the file to be listed as coming from someone else.

   To—You cannot change this field; files are always uploaded to the project owner.

   Message—Enter a message to accompany the file. This should include a note about what the file is, whether it's the final version, and anything else the team may need to know about the file.

   Upload—This is the location of the file on your local system before you upload it. You will enter this value by completing step 4.

4. Click the Browse button. The Choose File dialog opens. Locate the file you would like to upload, select the file, and click Open (**Figure 4.45**).

   The dialog closes, and the Upload field lists the location of the file you'll be uploading.

5. Click the Submit button to save the information and upload the file (**Figure 4.46**). If you're uploading a large file or using a slow Internet connection, the file could take a while to upload. Your computer needs to send the entire file before the Web page updates.

6. Your file is sent, and the home page of the project site opens.

✔ Tip

- If you're a normal user visiting a client's office and want to send a file back to yourself from one of the client's computers, you can log into the project site and upload files using this method. When you get back to your office, the file you uploaded will be waiting on the server for you.

UPLOADING FILES

89

Administering Sitespring Helper

One of Sitespring's main functions is to help you work with your team's folders and files on the production server. A task may require that you edit a file in Dreamweaver or open a document in Word. Web browsers, however, cannot open files and folders on your hard drive. The same security features that safeguard your computer when you surf to a dubious Web site prevent Sitespring, a Web-based application, from interacting with your hard drive or local file servers. Sitespring needs help—hence the name, Sitespring Helper—to make the links in Sitespring open a document in the appropriate application on your machine.

In Sitespring you can link files to tasks, and link folders to tasks and projects. While working with tasks and projects that have linked items, you can click a link to open the linked file or folder. It is Sitespring Helper that causes the files and folders to open in Windows Explorer on a PC or in the Finder on a Mac. The application in which a file opens, however, is entirely up to you. You may want GIF images to open in Fireworks, or you may want them to open in ImageReady. Read on to find out how to configure Sitespring Helper to work with your favorite applications.

To install Sitespring Helper on a PC:

1. Navigate to the Help page that has a link to download the Sitespring Helper installer. Click the help tab ⓘ in the main navigation bar.

  The Help page opens in a new browser window.

Folders and Files

Figure 4.47 Click Installing Sitespring Helper in the left-hand pane.

Figure 4.48 Click the "download installer" link to begin downloading Sitespring Helper.

Figure 4.49 Double-click the Sitespring Helper installer icon to open it.

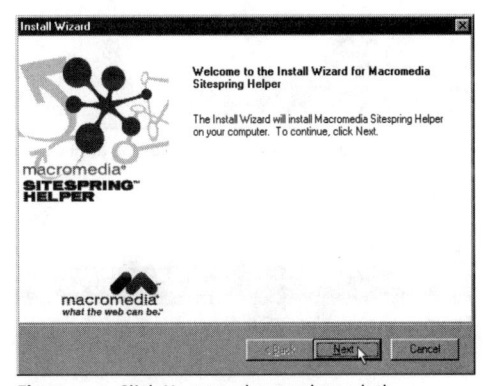

Figure 4.50 Click Next to advance through the installation wizard.

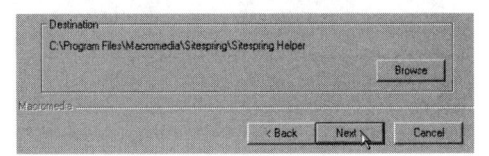

Figure 4.51 Most users can simply accept the default installation destination by clicking Next.

2. Click Installing Sitespring Helper in the left-hand navigation pane (**Figure 4.47**).

   Don't confuse this with the Installing Sitespring link above it.

   The Installing Sitespring Helper page opens on the right.

   There are two sets of instructions, one for Windows and one for Mac.

3. Locate the Windows instructions, which are listed first.

4. Click the "download installer" link near the top of the instructions (**Figure 4.48**). A File Download dialog opens. Select "Save this program to disk" and click the OK button.

5. A Save As dialog appears. Choose a location to save the installer application, and click the Save button.

6. Locate the installer you downloaded in step 5. It is called Helper_Installer.exe (depending on how your machine is configured, it may appear simply as Helper_Installer). Launch the installer application by double-clicking its icon (**Figure 4.49**).

7. The installation wizard opens. Click the Next button (**Figure 4.50**).

8. The license agreement displays. Click the Yes button to accept the license agreement.

9. The Choose Destination Path screen opens. Most users will simply click the Next button to accept the default installation destination (**Figure 4.51**). If you'd like to install the application in a different folder, click Browse, locate the folder into which you'd like to install the application, and click the Next button.

continues on next page

ADMINISTERING SITESPRING HELPER

91

Chapter 4

10. The Confirm Selections screen opens. Double-check that the application will be installed into the correct folder, and click the Next button.

   The installation process begins (**Figure 4.52**). The installation is nearly complete when the progress bar fills completely.

11. If the screen displays "The installation process is complete," click the Finish button and continue with step 12.

   On some computers you may be asked to reboot your machine before the installation process is complete. If this applies to you, select "Yes, I want to restart my computer now" and click the Finish button (**Figure 4.53**). The computer will reboot, and Sitespring Helper is now installed.

12. Launch Sitespring Helper (**Figure 4.54**).

   The first time you launch the application it will ask you if you'd like to automatically associate other previously installed Macromedia programs to file types they can open. For example, if you already have Macromedia Dreamweaver installed, clicking Yes will cause .html and .htm files to open in Dreamweaver. Most users should click the Yes button (**Figure 4.55**). If you don't have any Macromedia programs installed, clicking the Yes button has no effect.

   The installation process is now complete. See "To add a new file type" for information on how to further configure Sitespring Helper.

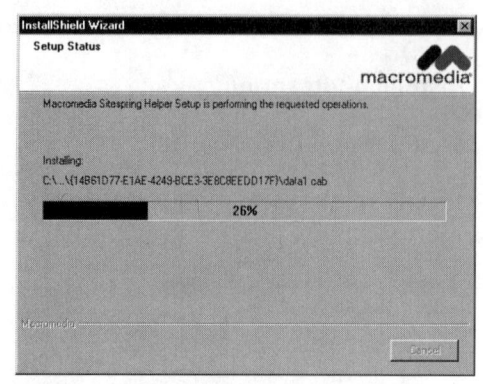

Figure 4.52 The installation process begins. The progress bar indicates how much of the installation process has been completed.

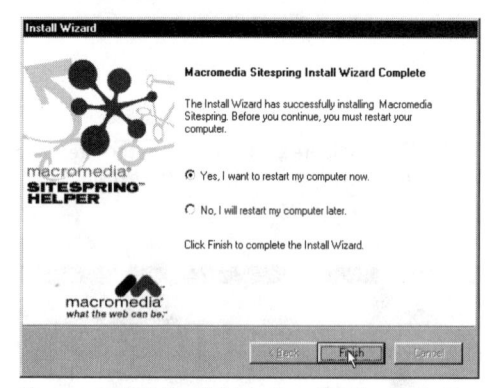

Figure 4.53 Click the Finish button after the application has been installed.

Figure 4.54 Launch the Sitespring Helper by locating it in your Start menu.

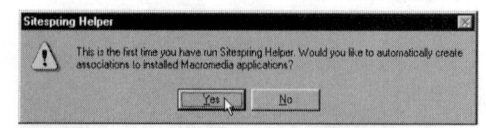

Figure 4.55 Click the Yes button to associate Macromedia programs with the file types they can edit.

Folders and Files

Figure 4.56 Click Installing Sitespring Helper in the left-hand navigation pane.

Figure 4.57 Click the "download installer" link at the top of the Mac installation instructions.

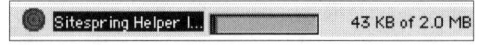

Figure 4.58 The download progress is displayed.

Figure 4.59 Launch the installer application you just downloaded.

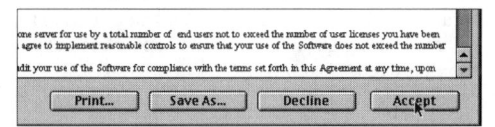

Figure 4.60 Click the Accept button to accept the license agreement.

To install Sitespring Helper on a Mac:

1. Navigate to the Help page that has a link to download the Sitespring Helper installer. Click the help tab in the main navigation bar.

   The Help page opens in a new browser window.

2. Click Installing Sitespring Helper in the left-hand navigation pane (**Figure 4.56**). Don't confuse this with the Installing Sitespring link above it.

   The Installing Sitespring Helper page opens. There are two sets of instructions, one for Windows and one for Mac.

3. Locate the Mac instructions, which are listed below the PC instructions.

4. Click the "download installer" link near the top of the Mac instructions (**Figure 4.57**).

   Sitespring Helper begins to download (**Figure 4.58**).

5. When the download completes, locate the file you just downloaded in your default download folder. The file will be called Sitespring Helper Installer.

6. Launch the installer application (**Figure 4.59**).

   The installer program launches.

7. Click the Continue button to proceed past the opening screen. The license agreement displays. Click the Accept button (**Figure 4.60**).

   continues on next page

ADMINISTERING SITESPRING HELPER

93

Chapter 4

The Sitespring Helper Installer window opens (**Figure 4.61**). The installer will default to placing the application inside the Applications folder of your system's startup disk. Most users can accept this default location and continue to step 8. If you'd like another location, choose one from the Install Location pull-down menu in the lower-left corner (**Figure 4.62**). You can select another hard drive in the list or choose Select Folder to specify a particular folder within a drive.

8. Click the Install button to proceed with the installation or click the Quit button to cancel.

   Some users may see a dialog box asking them to install CarbonLib (**Figure 4.63**), a resource file the application needs in order to run. If you are one of these users, download and install CarbonLib: At the time of this writing you could download CarbonLib from Apple at www.info.apple.com/support/downloads.html.

   The installation process begins. You will see a progress bar detailing the installation status (**Figure 4.64**). When the bar fills, the installation is complete.

9. A dialog box appears, indicating that the installation was successful. Click the Quit button to exit the installer application.

   Sitespring Helper is now installed.

Figure 4.61 From the installer window, you can choose where to install the application, or click the Install button to begin the installation.

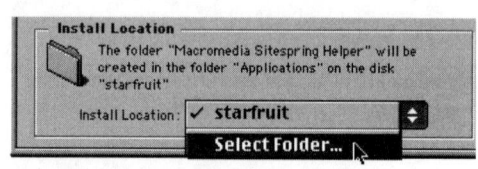

Figure 4.62 The Installation Location pull-down menu allows you to choose where to install the application.

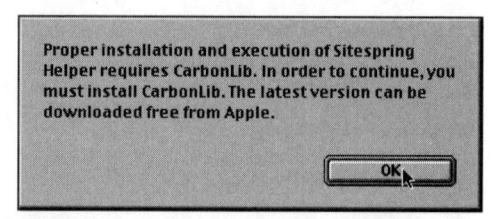

Figure 4.63 Some users of older Macs may be asked to install CarbonLib, a resource the application needs in order to run.

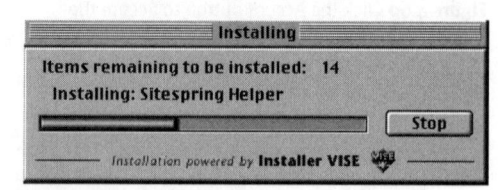

Figure 4.64 The progress bar indicates how the installation is proceeding.

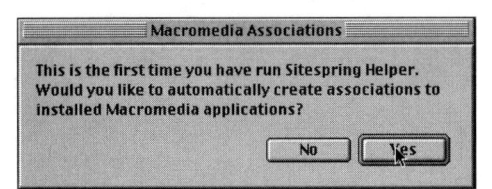

Figure 4.65 Click the Yes button to associate installed Macromedia applications with the file types they open.

10. Launch the application. You can locate it in the directory you chose in step 7; users who accepted the default location will find Sitespring Helper inside a folder named Macromedia Sitespring Helper inside the Applications folder of their startup disk.

   The first time you launch the application, it will ask you if you'd like to automatically associate other previously installed Macromedia programs to file types they can open. For example, if you already have Macromedia Dreamweaver installed, clicking Yes will cause .html and .htm files to open in Dreamweaver. Most users should click the Yes button (**Figure 4.65**). If you don't have any Macromedia programs installed, clicking the Yes button has no effect.

   The installation process is now complete. See "To add a new file type" for information on how to further configure Sitespring Helper.

Chapter 4

Configuring Sitespring Helper

Your operating system needs to tell different types of documents apart and know what applications can open them. For example, a JPEG file holds a visual image and can be opened by image editing software, while an HTML file holds formatted text and can be opened by an HTML editor. Application mapping tells Sitespring Helper what application to use to open a particular type of file. You can choose to have Sitespring Helper open a file in a specific application or in the operating system's default application for that file type.

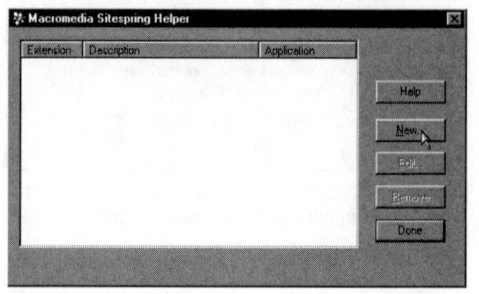

Figure 4.66 On the PC, click the New button to add a file type.

To add an application mapping:

1. Launch the Sitespring Helper application. To do that, *do either of the following:*
   - ▼ On a PC, click the Start button > Programs > Macromedia Sitespring > Sitespring Helper.
   - ▼ On a Mac, double-click the Sitespring Helper icon.

2. Sitespring Helper opens. The Mac and PC versions of Sitespring Helper function differently to accommodate how each platform works with files. *Follow the direction below for your platform:*
   - ▼ If you're on a PC, click the New button on the right side of the window (**Figure 4.66**).

   or

   - ▼ If you're on a Mac, you need to decide whether to create the file mapping to an extension or to a file type. See the sidebar "Macs and Application Mappings" that follows this section for more information.

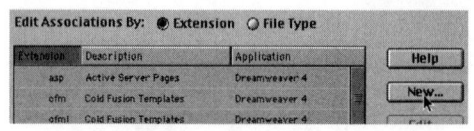

Figure 4.67 On the Mac, create a new mapping by filename extension by selecting Extension in the Edit Associations By field and then clicking the New button.

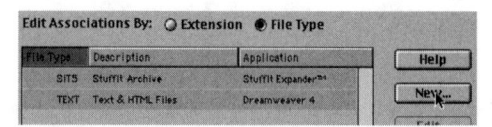

Figure 4.68 On the Mac, to create a new mapping by file type, select File Type in the Edit Associations By field and click the New button.

96

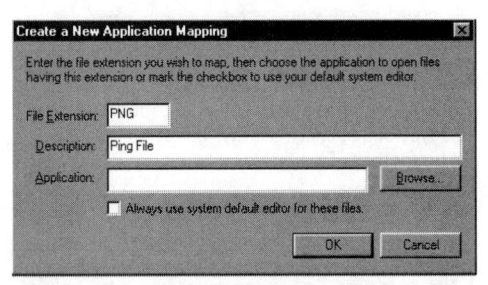

Figure 4.69 On the PC, enter the file extension and description for the application mapping you are adding.

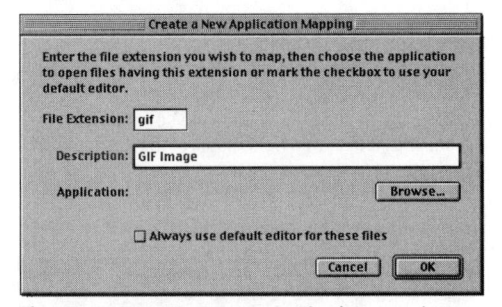

Figure 4.70 To create a new mapping by extension on the Mac, enter the extension and a description for the application mapping you are creating.

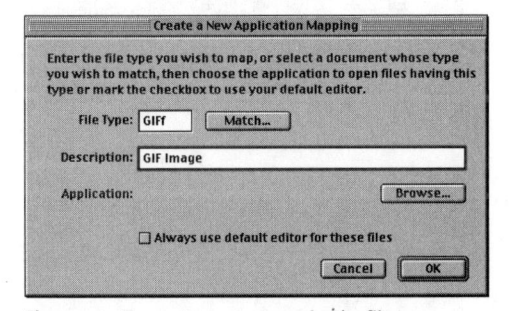

Figure 4.71 To create a new mapping by file type on the Mac, click the Match button, locate a file of the same type, and enter a description for the application mapping you are creating.

At the top of the window, use the Edit Associations By radio buttons to select whether you'd like your new mapping to be associated with an extension or file type (**Figures 4.67** and **4.68**). Click the New button.

3. The Create a New Application Mapping window opens. Enter a description and an extension or a Mac file type for the file type you are creating (**Figures 4.69**, **4.70**, and **4.71**). Read below for more information about each field.

   File Extension—All PC users and Mac users who are creating a file association by Extension will see this field. The file extension is the three-letter identifier at the end of a filename that Windows uses to identify the format of the file and the applications that can open it. For example, a JPEG image usually has an extension of .jpg and can be opened by Fireworks and ImageReady, among other applications.

   File Type—Only Mac users who are creating a file association by Mac file type will see this field. If you know it, enter the four-character abbreviation that identifies the type of file you want. If you don't know the abbreviation, you can use Sitespring Helper to find it. To find an abbreviation, click the Match button. The Select Document To Match dialog box opens. Locate a file that's of the type you want to associate. Select the file and click the Choose button. The dialog box closes, and the File Type field updates to reflect the chosen file type.

   Description—All users will see this field. Fill in a description of the type of file you are associating with the file extension. File extensions by themselves can be difficult to remember. Seeing "Photoshop Document" in the list can remind you what a .psd document is.

continues on next page

Chapter 4

4. Assign an application to open the file. You can choose to have a file open in the operating system's default editor for that file type, or you can tell Sitespring Helper to override the default by assigning the file type to a particular application. To choose an application, *do either of the following:*

▼ To use the system's default editor for the file type, click the check box next to "Always use system default editor for these files" below the Application field (**Figure 4.72**). This means that whatever program would normally launch this document if you opened it from Windows Explorer or the Mac Finder will launch the document.

or

▼ To assign a specific application, click the Browse button. On a PC, the Open dialog opens, and on a Mac, the Select Document to Match dialog box opens. Locate the application with which you'd like to associate the extension. On a PC you'll find most applications in the Program Files folder on the C drive, and on a Mac most will be located in the Applications folder of your startup disk. When you've located the application, select it. On a PC click the Open button; on a Mac click the Choose button. The window closes, and the Application field displays the path to the application (**Figures 4.73** and **4.74**).

5. Click the OK button to save the new file association (**Figure 4.75**), or click the Cancel button to discard it.

The Create a New Application Mapping window closes, and the list of file mappings updates to show your new entry.

Figure 4.72 To use the default application to launch this type of file, check "Always use system default editor for these files."

Figure 4.73 On the PC, directories are separated by a backslash. The Application field displays the path to the application.

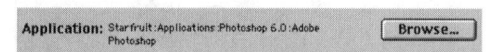

Figure 4.74 On the Mac, folders are separated by a colon. The Application field displays the path to the application.

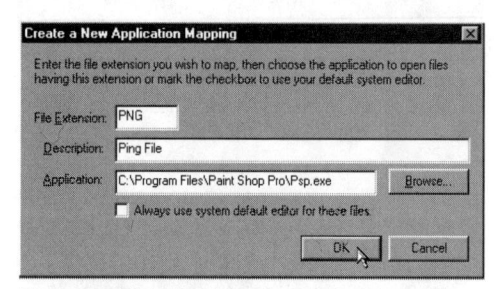

Figure 4.75 Click the OK button to save the new file-type configuration.

CONFIGURING SITESPRING HELPER

98

Folders and Files

Figure 4.76 Launch Sitespring Helper by selecting it from the Start menu.

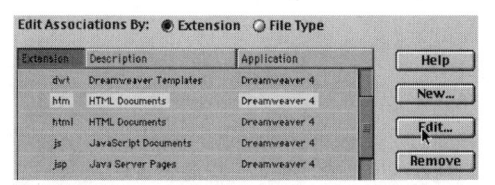

Figure 4.77 To edit a file-type application mapping on the Mac, select File Type in the Edit Associations By field, select the mapping to edit from the list, and click the Edit button.

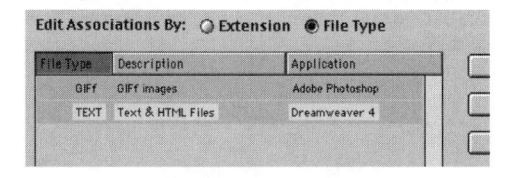

Figure 4.78 To edit an extension application mapping on the Mac, select Extension in the Edit Associations By field, select the mapping to edit from the list, and click the Edit button.

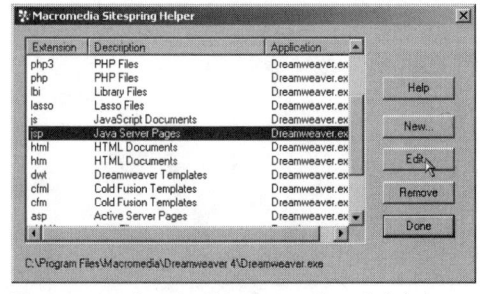

Figure 4.79 Select the file type to edit and click the Edit button.

To edit an application mapping:

1. Launch the Sitespring Helper application. To do that, *do either of the following*:

   ▼ On a PC, click the Start button > Programs > Macromedia Sitespring > Sitespring Helper (**Figure 4.76**).

   ▼ On a Mac, double-click the Sitespring Helper icon. If you accepted the default installation location, the icon will be in the Applications folder of your hard drive, inside a folder named Macromedia Sitespring Helper.

2. Sitespring Helper opens. Locate and select the application mapping you'd like to edit. To do that, *follow the directions appropriate to your platform*:

   ▼ PC users should look in the list of mappings. Select the application mapping you'd like to edit by clicking the appropriate row.

   or

   ▼ Mac users should choose to edit an association by Extension or by File Type in the Edit Associations By field. See the sidebar "Macs and Application Mappings" for more information about these choices. As you toggle the radio buttons, the list of associations changes to display either mappings by extension or mappings by file type (**Figures 4.77** and **4.78**). Select the mapping you'd like to edit from either list.

3. Select the file type you'd like to edit from the list.

4. Click the Edit button (**Figure 4.79**).

CONFIGURING SITESPRING HELPER

99

Chapter 4

5. The Edit Application Mapping window opens. Edit the description by changing the description field.

6. Choose which application will open files of this type.

   To use the system's default editor for the file type, click the check box next to "Always use system default editor for *[extension]* files" and proceed to step 7 (**Figure 4.80**). If you would like to override the system's default and choose an application, uncheck this check box and proceed to step 6.

7. Click the Browse button. On a PC the Open dialog opens; on a Mac it's the Select Document to Match dialog box. Locate the application with which you'd like to have this file type opened. On a PC, most of your applications will be in the Program Files folder on your C drive. On a Mac, your applications are likely to be in the Applications folder of your startup disk. Select the new application and click OK.

   The dialog or dialog box closes, and the Application field updates with the path to the new application (**Figures 4.81** and **4.82**).

8. Click the OK button to accept your changes, or click the Cancel button to discard them.

   The Edit Application Mapping window closes, and the list of file types updates with your newly edited information.

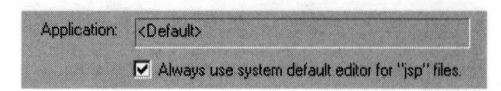

Figure 4.80 To use the default application to open this type of file, check "Always use system default editor for *[extension]* files."

Figure 4.81 On a PC, the Application field displays the path to the application with backslashes between directory names.

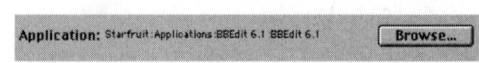

Figure 4.82 On a Mac, the Application field displays the path to the application with colons between folder names.

✔ **Tip**

- The list of file types defaults to sorting by the Extension or File Type column. You can sort the list by either the Description or Application columns by clicking the appropriate column heading.

Folders and Files

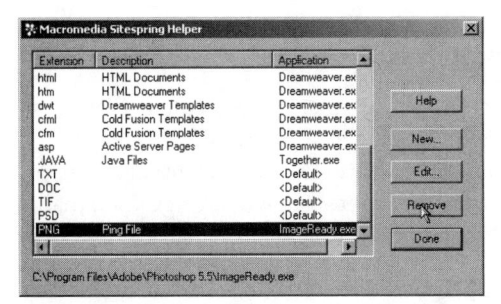

Figure 4.83 Click the Remove button to delete the file association.

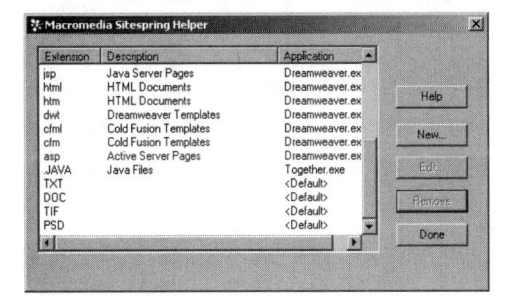

Figure 4.84 The list of file types updates, and the deleted file type is removed.

To delete a file type:

1. Launch the Sitespring Helper application. To do that, *do either of the following:*

   ▼ On a PC, click the Start button > Programs > Macromedia Sitespring > Sitespring Helper.

   ▼ On a Mac, double-click the Sitespring Helper icon. If you accepted the default installation location, the icon will be in the applications folder of your hard drive, inside a folder named Macromedia Sitespring Helper.

2. Locate and select the application mapping you'd like to delete. To do that, *follow the directions appropriate to your platform:*

   ▼ On a PC, select the file type you'd like to delete from the list by clicking the corresponding row.

   or

   ▼ Mac users should choose to delete an association by Extension or by File Type in the Edit Associations By field. See the sidebar "Macs and Application Mappings" for more information about these choices. As you toggle the radio buttons, the list of associations changes to display either mappings by extension or mappings by file type. Select the mapping you'd like to delete from either list by clicking the corresponding row.

3. Click the Remove button (**Figure 4.83**). The file type is deleted, and the list of file types updates to reflect the deletion (**Figure 4.84**).

   continues on next page

CONFIGURING SITESPRING HELPER

101

Macs and Application Mappings

Both PCs and Macs need to associate files with the applications that can open them. PCs map files to applications by using a three-digit abbreviation, or extension, at the end of a filename. A JPEG image, for example, could be named image.jpg, while an HTML document might be called document.htm. Macs, however, identify file types via a four-character abbreviation that users normally don't see. The file type isn't a requisite part of a filename on a Mac.

Because Sitespring anticipates that Mac users will be working with both Mac and PC files, the Mac version of Sitespring lets you associate a file type using either method. The PC version of Sitespring does not have this option; it determines application mapping only by using extensions. When a PC interacts with a Mac file, it can't read the Mac's hidden abbreviation, so Sitespring Helper offers no option for PC users to configure it. On a Mac, if a filename has an extension, Sitespring Helper uses the extension to determine the application mapping regardless of whether the file also has a Mac file type. (On a Mac, you can save a file with a PC-style extension; the file will then have both an extension and a Mac file type. When you save a file on a Mac, it always has a Mac file type.) If a file doesn't have a filename extension but does have a Mac file type, Sitespring Helper uses the Mac file type.

Tasks and Reports

Lose track of the tasks you and your team need to accomplish, and your project will quickly veer off course. The task management and task reporting features in Sitespring help individual team members stay on track and help project managers understand where the overall project stands.

Sitespring's task reporting features are really useful only if team members take the time to keep their task status updated. Team members should make a habit of updating their My Tasks module so the whole team can know where projects stand. The email notification feature helps with that endeavor, as users can choose to receive an email notice when they are assigned tasks.

In this chapter you'll learn how to manage tasks in Sitespring, including how to create, edit, delete, clone, reassign, and export tasks, as well as how to change their status. You'll also learn how to view tasks, link files and folders to tasks, and work with reports. Finally, you'll find out how to configure email notifications to be sent to you when certain events occur, such as when you're assigned a task.

Managing Tasks

Teams often break one large task into several smaller ones that different team members work on in sequence. Let's say, for example, you're managing a project team to create an HTML template. The functions are divided as follows: First, an information architect creates a functional mock-up of the page. Second, a graphic designer creates a visual look for the page. Third, a production person turns the visual look into an HTML document. Fourth, a programmer embeds dynamic elements that give the design functionality (**Figure 5.1**).

Depending on how your team chooses to work with tasks, the project manager might create four separate task entries and assign one to each team member, or the project manager might create only *one* main task entry. While four separate tasks are required to accomplish the main task, each of the small tasks can be started only when the task before it has been completed. If you create one task entry, you should include a note in the Comments field about the larger task's workflow on the Add Task page (**Figure 5.2**). (See "To create a task" later in this chapter.) Then, as each member of the team completes his or her portion, they reassign the main task to the next person in the queue rather than marking the task Complete. This method has the benefit of moving the work through the team efficiently and keeping the linked documents together without having to add the same documents to each task. As the task is reassigned to each team member, he or she may receive an email notification and the task will display on his or her My Tasks module.

Functional Mock-up	Visual Look	HTML Document	Dynamic Elements	Published Page
Information architect creates mock-up containing page elements and their functions.	Graphic designer creates a visual look for the page elements.	Production assistant turns visual look into HTML.	Programmer inserts code to support dynamic elements.	The completed page gets published to the site.

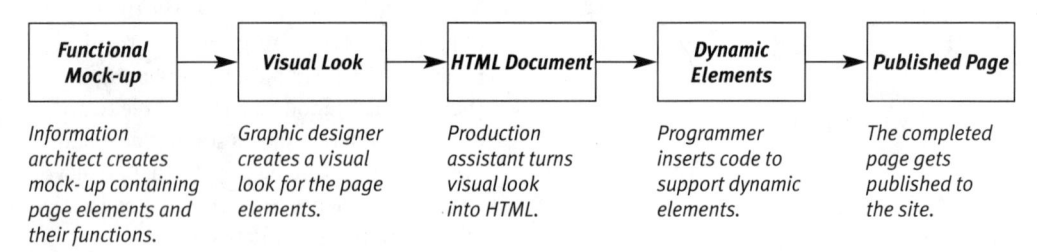

Figure 5.1 As a Web team builds an HTML template, several smaller tasks make up the larger task; each team member works on his or her task in turn.

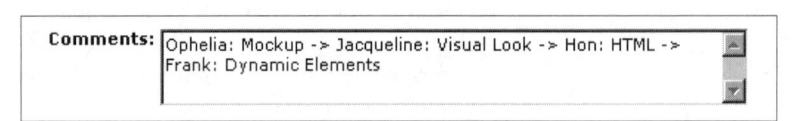

Comments: Ophelia: Mockup -> Jacqueline: Visual Look -> Hon: HTML -> Frank: Dynamic Elements

Figure 5.2 You can use the Comments field to hold information about the task's workflow.

Tasks and Reports

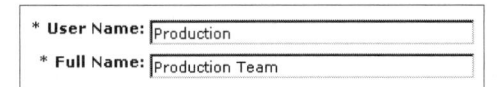

Figure 5.3 Create a user account named after the team you'd like to assign tasks to as a group.

Figure 5.4 By assigning a task to the team's user name, you assign the task to the entire team.

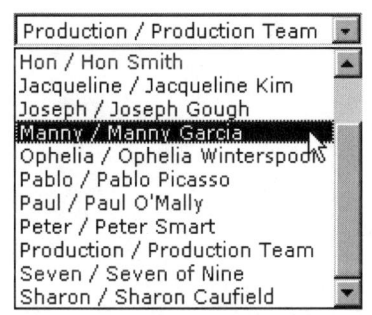

Figure 5.5 Any team members can log into the team account and assign the task to themselves.

If, however, you create a separate entry for each task at the start of the larger task, the users who have dependent tasks need to either look at the server or check with their colleague to know when the file is ready for them to do their part. Moreover, the process of tracking the task's status is more complicated, as each team member needs to check multiple task entries to learn the larger task's status. Finally, if on a large project you give each team member's tasks a separate entry, the task list could quickly grow unwieldy. There is one benefit to assigning each individual a task: The team members can more easily see upcoming tasks in their My Tasks module, as the assigned task is displayed immediately. With the one-task method, the main task displays only in the My Tasks module of the user who's currently assigned an individual task.

Now, suppose you're part of a large Web department, and you'd like to assign a specific task to anyone in a large production team. You don't care who does it; you just want to make sure it gets done. Tasks in Sitespring can be assigned to only one individual, not a whole group. You can get around this rule—if you have enough licenses—by creating a virtual user account that represents the production team. The user name on the account could be Production (**Figure 5.3**), and you could assign a task to the Production account whenever you'd like any member of the production team to accomplish the task (**Figure 5.4**). Any member of the production team could log in as the Production user, assign the next task in the My Tasks module—which effectively becomes a production queue—to themselves (**Figure 5.5**), and then log back into their own account. That way the other members of the production team know the task has been taken on, and there's a record of which team member accomplished the task.

MANAGING TASKS

105

It's important that you create a strategy for how your team deals with interdependent tasks, and that the team uses it consistently. Any seasoned Web professional knows the value of having and sticking to a file-naming convention. The same applies to task conventions.

No matter what strategy you use for managing tasks, at some point you'll need to make changes to the tasks that you've entered into the system. Any normal user can edit an individual task. But when a set of tasks needs to be updated with the same information, changing each task individually is a time-consuming—not to mention annoying—job. To avoid this hassle, you can update a set of tasks together, entering the information only once. The page from which you update multiple tasks does not let you edit as many fields as does the page for editing a single task; it wouldn't make sense for each task have the same title, for instance. The fields you can update across a group of tasks are Assigned To, Assignment Comment, Status, Priority, and Due Date.

Beyond editing, sometimes you need to just get rid of a task altogether. Think carefully before you delete a task. Once you do so, you cannot retrieve the information it contained. Project managers and the administrator may delete any task in the system, while other users may delete only the tasks they created.

When you want to create a new task that has similar properties to an existing task, you should make a duplicate of that task. Cloning the task saves you the time and hassle of entering the same information twice. Cloned tasks always retain the same Project and Client Organization information as the original task; these fields cannot be changed.

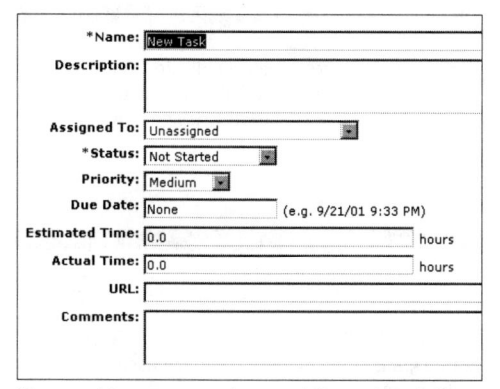

Figure 5.6 To create a task, enter information about the task in the fields.

While you can export all the tasks of a project to work with the task data in another program such as Microsoft Project, there may be times you'll want to work with a subset of a project's tasks. (For more information, see "To export a project" in Chapter 3.) Thankfully, Sitespring lets you export a single task or—even more useful—a set of tasks as a unit. You can work with Sitespring's task data in any program that can open a CSV file, such as Microsoft Excel. You might integrate the data from Sitespring with a client billing system, for example, or use the data to create a Gantt chart in Microsoft Project.

To create a task:

1. Navigate to the Project page for the project for which you'd like to create a task.

2. If the Tasks module isn't already open, open it by clicking the expand icon ▶ to the left of the Tasks heading.

3. Click the Add icon ✚ at the top of the module. The Add Task page opens. Enter the information for the task you are creating (**Figure 5.6**).

    For descriptions of each field, read the sidebar "Task Creation Fields."

4. Click Save to update your information, or click a navigation link to discard your changes. The new Task page opens with a green success notice at the top of the page.

continues on next page

Chapter 5

The success notice includes a link to add an assignment comment (**Figure 5.7**). Those comments are listed in the Assignment History module at the bottom of the Task page. Each time a task is assigned to a different user, you can give the assigned individual a comment—a message or instructions—along with the task. This is particularly useful if you use one task entry for multiple subtasks, since you can write a comment to the next user in the queue as you assign the task to him or her.

If you'd like to add an assignment comment to this task, continue with steps 5 through 7. Otherwise, you've finished creating the task.

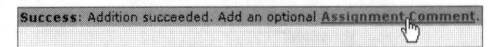

Figure 5.7 The success notice indicates that your task entry has been created. If you'd like to add an assignment comment, click the Assignment Comment link.

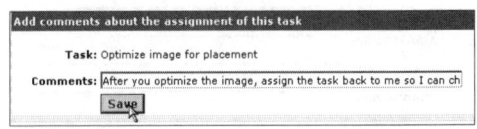

Figure 5.8 Enter your message to the assigned user in the Comments field.

5. Click the Assignment Comment link in the success notice. The Assignment Comment page opens. In the Comments field, enter the message or instructions for the assigned user (**Figure 5.8**).

6. Click the Save button.

The Task page opens with a green success notice at the top and the assignment comment listed in the Assignment History module.

✔ Tip

- You can also assign a task to a client user. Client users who work for the project's client organization are listed at the bottom of the Assigned To field.

The Add Task Fields

Whenever you create a new task, you need to provide Sitespring with detailed information. The following fields appear on the Add Task page (see step 3 in "To create a task"); information is required for fields marked with an asterisk.

*Name—Choose a descriptive name for the task. Using consistent names for similar tasks will help team members understand what's required of them and will make it easier to scan through Task modules. You should devise a task-naming convention for all team members to use.

Description—Write notes about the task, being as specific as possible. If, for example, you're creating an image, include the required dimensions, the alt text, if available, and any other details about the image you already know.

Assigned To—Using the pull-down list, assign the team member who will accomplish the task. Team members are listed alphabetically by user name or full name.

*Status—Choose the task's completion status from the pull-down menu. Sitespring's default choices are Client Completed, Completed, Not Started, Open, and Suspended. Tasks marked as Completed or Suspended do not appear on a user's My Tasks module, but display on the Tasks module of the Project page.

Priority—Indicate the task's relative importance, choosing a priority from the pull-down menu. The default choices are None, Very High, High, Medium, Low, and Very Low. Be judicious with your use of High and Very High. While all tasks are important, if you mark too many of them with a High priority, the label loses its significance. Using it sparingly will make the team members take notice.

Due Date—Key in the date and time the task is due. Enter the date in digits as month/day/year, and the time as hour:minute, with "AM" or "PM" as appropriate. For example, August 22, 2001, at 3 o'clock in the afternoon would be "08/22/01 3:00 PM." This date is used to generate email notifications as the due date nears and if the task becomes overdue.

Estimated Time—Fill in the number of hours you expect it will take to accomplish the task. Use decimal values to indicate partial hours; for example, 1 hour and 30 minutes should be entered as 1.5.

Actual Time—Enter the amount of time it took to complete the task. Leave this value blank when you create the task; update it only when you mark the task Completed. Tracking the time it took to finish a project is particularly useful if you need to export data to a project-tracking tool like Microsoft Project.

URL—Paste in the URL with which to associate the task. The URL may refer to a document, an image, or a related file on the Internet or your production server. If the task is to replace an existing file, for example, you might enter the old file's URL here.

Comments—Include any relevant details about the task. If you're using one task to refer to multiple subtasks (as discussed earlier in the chapter), enter the workflow outline here.

Chapter 5

To edit a task:

1. Navigate to a page with a Tasks module that contains the task you'd like to edit. To do that, *do either of the following*:

    ▼ If the task you'd like to edit is assigned to you, it is listed in the My Tasks module on your home page. Navigate there by clicking the Home button in the main navigation bar.

    or

    ▼ If the task you'd like to edit is assigned to another user, it is listed on the Project page for the project to which the task pertains. Navigate there by clicking the Project button in the main navigation bar. The main Projects page opens. Click the name of the project that contains the task you'd like to edit. The Project page opens.

2. If the Tasks module is closed, open it by clicking the expand icon ▶. The Tasks module opens.

3. Locate the task you'd like to edit. Since the module displays only the first ten tasks, the task you are looking for may not appear. If your task isn't listed, click the Show All link to display them all (**Figure 5.9**). The Tasks page opens.

4. Select the task you'd like to edit by clicking the check box to the left of the task name.

5. Click the Edit icon ✏ at the top of the module (**Figure 5.10**). The Edit Task page opens.

6. Update the task's information by changing field values. For more information on the fields here, see "To create a task" earlier in this chapter. You can assign the task to someone else on the team by choosing another name from the pull-down menu (**Figure 5.11**).

Figure 5.9 Click the Show All link to display all the tasks in the Tasks module.

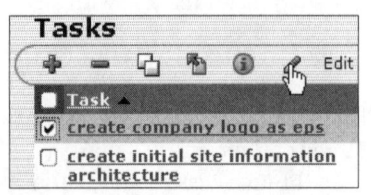

Figure 5.10 Select the task you'd like to edit and click the Edit icon.

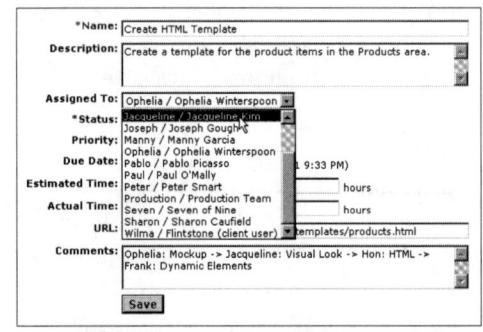

Figure 5.11 Update the information about the task. You can assign the task to somebody else by using the Assigned To pull-down list.

MANAGING TASKS

110

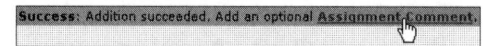

Figure 5.12 If you'd like to add a message or instructions, click the Assignment Comment link.

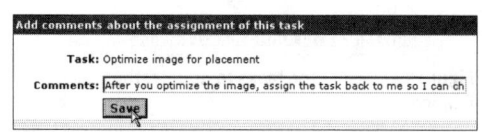

Figure 5.13 Enter your message for the assigned user in the Comments field.

7. Click the Save button to save the changes, or click any navigation link to abandon them.

   The Task page opens with a green success notice at top. If you changed the user to whom the task is assigned, the success notice includes a link to add an assignment comment (**Figure 5.12**). If you'd like to add an assignment comment, follow steps 8 and 9. Otherwise, you've finished editing the task.

8. Click the Assignment Comment link in the success notice. The Assignment Comment page opens. In the Comments field, enter the message or instructions for the assigned user (**Figure 5.13**).

9. Click the Save button.

   The Task page opens with a green success notice at the top and the assignment comment listed in the Assignment History module.

Chapter 5

To edit a group of tasks:

1. Navigate to a page with a Tasks module that displays the tasks you'd like to update. This module is called My Tasks on your home page or Tasks on a Project page. To get there, *do either of the following:*

   ▼ To navigate to your home page, click the Home button in the main navigation bar. The My Tasks module is below the My Projects module.

   or

   ▼ To navigate to a Project page, click the Projects button in the main navigation bar. The main Projects page opens. Click the name of the project that contains the tasks you'd like to edit. The Project page opens.

2. Select the tasks you'd like to update by clicking the check boxes to the left of each task's title. Click the Edit icon at the top of the module (**Figure 5.14**).

   The Edit Multiple Tasks page opens. The comment under the Details heading includes a confirmation of the number of tasks being edited (**Figure 5.15**).

3. Update the fields that you'd like to change for *all tasks* (**Figure 5.16**). If you do not want to update a field, *leave it blank or select [No Change],* and the tasks will retain their unique values for that field (**Figure 5.17**). For more information on each field, see "To create a task" earlier in this chapter.

4. Click the Update button to save your changes, or click any navigation link to cancel them (**Figure 5.18**).

   Depending on where you started from, either your home page or the Project page opens with a green success notice at top. The Tasks module displays the updated tasks.

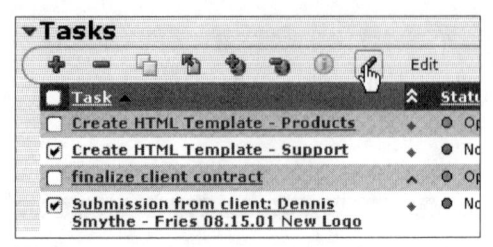

Figure 5.14 Select the tasks to update, then click the Edit icon.

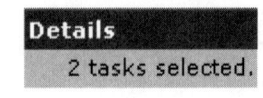

Figure 5.15 The comment under the Details header includes a confirmation of the number of tasks being edited.

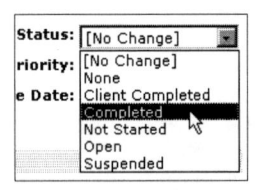

Figure 5.16 To update a field with a pull-down menu, choose a new value. Leave [No Change] selected for the fields you'd like to retain their original value.

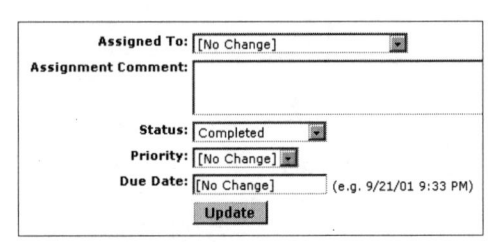

Figure 5.17 Update the fields you'd like to change for all tasks and leave the other fields empty or with [No Change] selected.

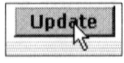

Figure 5.18 Click the Update button to save your changes.

112

Tasks and Reports

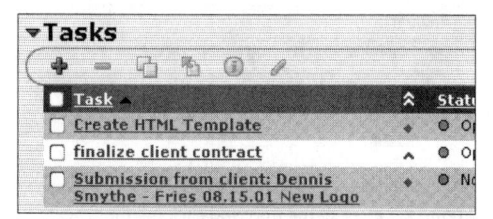

Figure 5.19 You can delete a task from the Tasks module on a Project page.

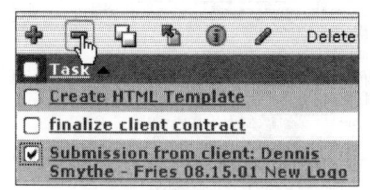

Figure 5.20 Select the task you'd like to delete, then click the Delete icon.

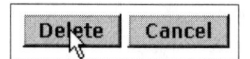

Figure 5.21 Confirm the deletion by clicking the Delete button.

To delete a task:

1. Navigate to a page from which you can delete a task. To do that, *do any of the following*:

    ▼ If you're already on the Task page for the task you'd like to delete, you can delete the task from there.

    or

    ▼ If you're on a page that contains a Tasks module, locate the module. It is called My Tasks on your home page or Tasks on a Project page (**Figure 5.19**).

    or

    ▼ To navigate to the Project page for the project that contains the task you'd like to delete, click the Projects button in the main navigation bar. The main Projects page opens. Click the name of the project that contains the task you'd like to delete. The Project page opens.

2. If the Tasks module isn't opened, open the module by clicking the Expand icon ▶. The Tasks module opens.

3. Locate the task you'd like to delete. If the module contains more than ten items, the task you are looking for may not appear, as the module displays only the first ten tasks. If your task isn't listed, click the Show All link to display all the tasks. The Tasks page opens.

4. Select the task you'd like to delete by clicking the check box to the left of the task name.

5. Click the Delete icon ━ at the top of the module (**Figure 5.20**). The Delete Task confirmation page opens.

6. Click the Delete button to delete the project (**Figure 5.21**), or click the Cancel button to leave it alone.

MANAGING TASKS

113

Chapter 5

To clone a task:

1. Navigate to a page from which you can clone a task. To do that, *do any of the following*:

    ▼ If you're already on the Task page for the task you'd like to clone, you can clone the task from there.

    or

    ▼ If you're on a page that contains a tasks module, locate the module. It will be called My Tasks on your home page or Tasks on a Project page.

    or

    ▼ To navigate to the Project page for the project that contains the task you'd like to clone, click the Projects button in the main navigation bar. The main Projects page opens. Click the name of the project that contains the task you'd like to clone. The Project page opens.

2. If you're on the Task page, click the Clone icon. If you're on a page with the Tasks module, select the task you'd like to clone by clicking the check box to the left of the task's name, then click the Clone icon (**Figure 5.22**). The Clone a Task page opens.

3. Update the information you'd like to change about the task (**Figure 5.23**). For more information about the fields listed here, see "To create a task" earlier in this chapter.

4. Click the Save button to save the new task, or click any navigation link to cancel cloning the task.

    The task details page for the new task opens with a green success notice at the top (**Figure 5.24**).

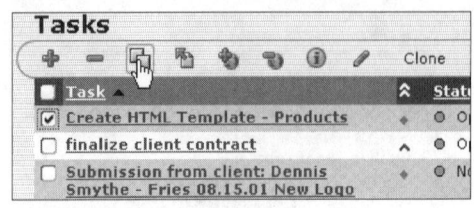

Figure 5.22 Select the task and click the Clone icon.

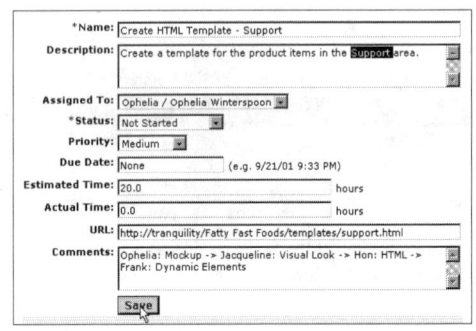

Figure 5.23 Update the information about the new task and click the Save button.

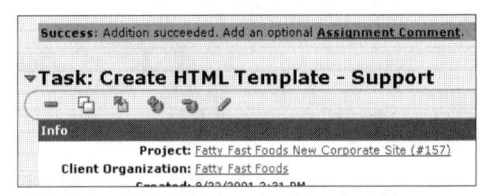

Figure 5.24 The newly cloned task opens with a success notice at the top.

✔ **Tip**

- Cloning a task resets the task's Assignment History and Linked Content modules. If you want to keep the same files linked to the new task, you need to reassociate the files with the new task (see "To link files or folders with a task" later in this chapter).

Tasks and Reports

Figure 5.25 You can export a single task from a Task page by clicking the Export icon.

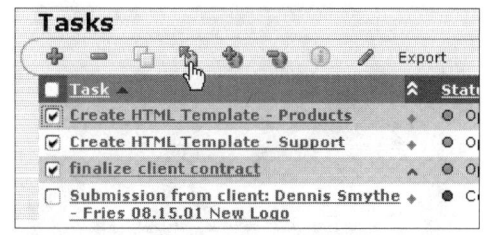

Figure 5.26 You can export one or more tasks by selecting the tasks in a Tasks module and clicking the Export icon.

Figure 5.27 Click the Export button to export the tasks you selected.

To export a task or tasks:

1. Navigate to a page from which you can export the task or tasks. To do that, *do any of the following*:

   ▼ If you're already on the Task page for the task you'd like to export, you can export the task from there.

   or

   ▼ If you're on a page that contains a tasks module, locate the module. It will be called My Tasks on your home page or Tasks on a Project page.

   or

   ▼ To navigate to the Project page for the project that contains the task or tasks you'd like to export, click the Projects button in the main navigation bar. The main Projects page opens. Click the name of the project that contains the task or tasks you'd like to export. The Project page opens.

2. If you're on the Task page, click the Export icon (**Figure 5.25**). If you're on a page with a Tasks module, select the tasks you'd like to export by clicking the check box to the left of the each task's name, then click the Export icon (**Figure 5.26**).

   Depending on how many tasks you're exporting, the Export Task or Export Tasks page opens. The Export Format field displays a pull-down menu that contains only one item, "Comma Separated Value (CSV)."

3. Click the Export button (**Figure 5.27**).

continues on next page

MANAGING TASKS

115

Chapter 5

4. Follow the procedure to download the file on your operating system. To do that, *do either of the following:*

▼ On a Mac with Internet Explorer, the Download Manager automatically begins saving the file to your default download directory (**Figure 5.28**).

or

▼ On a PC, the File Download dialog opens. Select "Save this file to disk" and click OK (**Figure 5.29**). The Save As dialog opens. Navigate to the folder in which you'd like to save the file. Enter a name for the file in the File Name field and click the Save button (**Figure 5.30**).

The file begins to download. When the process completes, locate the downloaded file. You can now open it in an application that supports the importing of CSV files. Many programs support this format. If you open the file in a project management tool such as Microsoft Project, you can create Gantt charts and resource graphs with the data (**Figure 5.31**).

To reassign a task:

Reassigning a task is the same as editing a task and updating the Assigned To field. Normal users can delete only the tasks they've created. After you've updated a task, changed the Assigned To field, and saved the task, you can add an optional Assignment Comment— a message or instructions to the assigned person. See "To edit a task" earlier in this chapter for detailed instructions.

To change a task's status:

Changing a task's status is the same as editing a task and updating the Status field. If you mark a task as Completed or Suspended, the task will no longer appear in the My Tasks module on your home page. See "To edit a task" earlier in this chapter for detailed instructions.

Figure 5.28 On a Mac using Internet Explorer, the Download Manager automatically saves the file to your default directory.

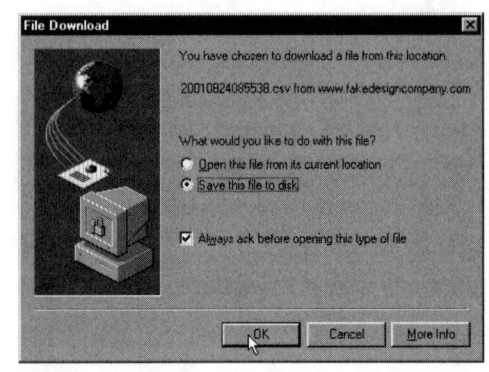

Figure 5.29 On a PC you may be prompted to open or save the file. Click the OK button.

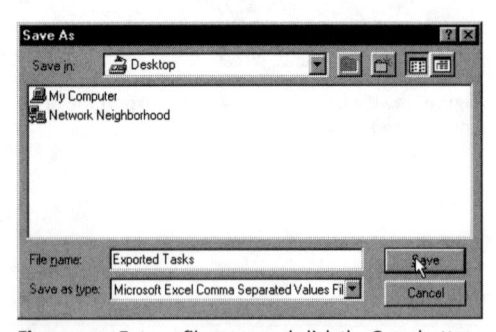

Figure 5.30 Enter a filename and click the Save button.

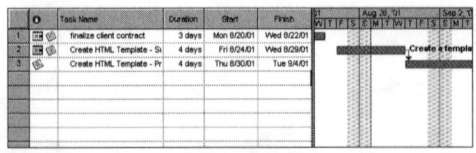

Figure 5.31 Many programs can open the exported tasks. Here the tasks have been open as a new project in Microsoft Project, where you can create a Gantt chart.

Tasks and Reports

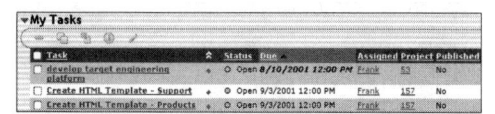

Figure 5.32 The My Tasks module on your home page lists current tasks assigned to you.

Figure 5.33 The Tasks module on each Project page lists all tasks related to that project.

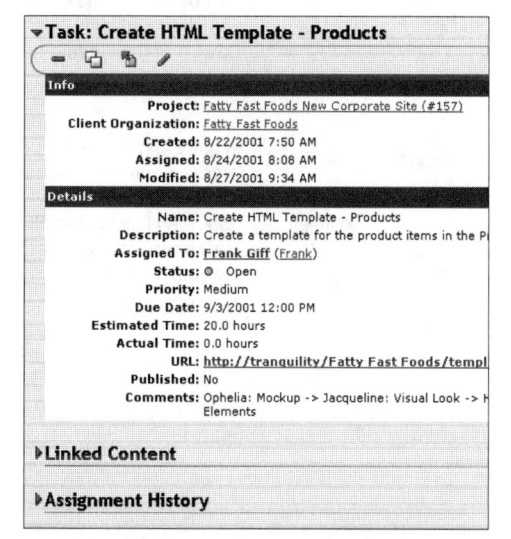

Figure 5.34 The Task page has detailed information about each task. Here the Details module is open, while the Linked Content and Assignment History modules are closed.

Viewing Tasks

Viewing tasks is one of the most common things you'll do in Sitespring. The My Tasks module on your home page gives an overview of tasks that are assigned to you (**Figure 5.32**), and the Tasks module on each Project page summarizes tasks related to a project (**Figure 5.33**). These modules give you an overview of related tasks by listing each task's name, priority, status, due date, assigned user, project, project site status, and whether the task has been published to the project site. You can view task details by simply clicking the linked task title in any module. Each task has a Task page with further details about the task, such as the date and time it was assigned, the assignment history, and a list of linked files (**Figure 5.34**).

While these task modules provide quick access to tasks, you should consider creating a report for additional task organization. On the Reports page you can create custom task reports that meet specific search criteria. See "To create a report" later in this chapter for more information.

If you want to view more detailed information about a task, you need to open its task details page. The page includes additional information related to the task such as the description, a list of linked files, the estimated and actual completion times, task-assignment comments and history, and other pertinent data.

Your My Tasks module always displays the tasks assigned to you that have an Open or Not Started status, unless the corresponding project's status has been set to Completed or Suspended. You can view completed and suspended tasks in the Tasks module of the Project page for the associated project. You may also view inactive tasks by running a report; for details, see "Working with Reports" later in this chapter.

117

Chapter 5

To view uncompleted tasks assigned to you:

1. Navigate to your home page by clicking the Home button in the main navigation bar. Your home page opens.

2. Scroll to the Tasks module, which is below the Projects module. If the module isn't open, open the module by clicking the expand icon ▶.

   The My Tasks module displays your first ten tasks with an Open or Not Started status (**Figure 5.35**). If you have more than ten tasks assigned to you, you can move through the list of tasks by clicking the page numbers at the bottom left of the module (**Figure 5.36**), or you can view all your tasks by clicking the Show All link at the bottom right (**Figure 5.37**).

   You can choose to view, edit, delete, or export any of the listed tasks. For detailed instructions, see "To view task details" below, and "To edit a task" and "To delete a task" earlier in this chapter.

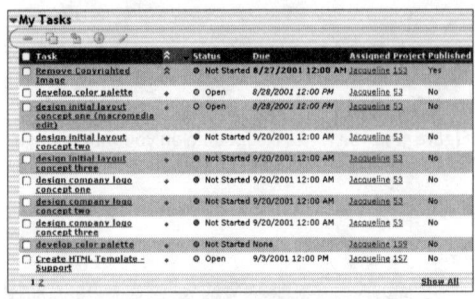

Figure 5.35 The My Tasks module lists all your tasks with a status of Open or Not Started.

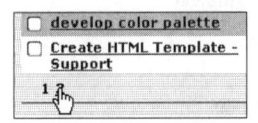

Figure 5.36 You can move through the task list by clicking the page numbers in the lower-left corner of the module.

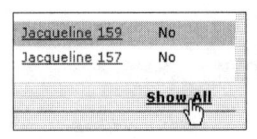

Figure 5.37 In the My Tasks module on your home page, click the Show All link to view all tasks currently assigned to you.

Tasks and Reports

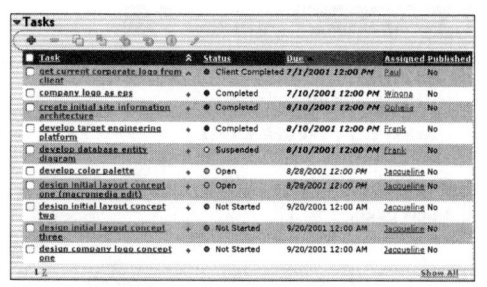

Figure 5.38 The Tasks module lists the first ten tasks for a project.

Figure 5.39 Click the Show All link to open the Tasks page, which lists all tasks for a project.

To view task details:

1. Navigate to a page containing a task's module that lists the task you would like to view. This module is called My Tasks on your home page or Tasks on a Project page. To do that, *do either of the following:*

   ▼ If the task you'd like to view is assigned to you and is current, the task is listed in the My Tasks module on your home page. If you're not on your home page, go there by clicking the Home button in the main navigation bar. Your home page opens.

   or

   ▼ If the task you'd like to view is assigned to another user, or if it's assigned to you but the status is neither Open nor Not Started, the task is listed on the Project page for the project to which the task belongs. If you're not on the Project page, navigate there by clicking the Projects button in the main navigation bar. The main Projects page opens. If the project to which the task belongs is currently open, you'll find the project listed in the Projects module. If the project has been closed or suspended, it is listed on the Inactive Projects page. To navigate there, click the Inactive Projects link in the bread crumb navigation below the main navigation bar. Once you've found the project to which the task belongs, click the linked title. The Project page opens.

2. If the task's module isn't open, open it by clicking the expand icon ▶ to the left of the module heading. The task's module expands.

3. The Tasks module displays the first ten tasks (**Figure 5.38**). If the task you'd like to view is one of the first ten tasks listed, continue with step 4. If not, open the All Tasks page by clicking the Show All link at the bottom of the Tasks module (**Figure 5.39**). The Tasks page opens.

continues on next page

VIEWING TASKS

119

Chapter 5

4. Locate the task you'd like to view in the list of tasks. You can sort the list by column heading; to do that, simply click the linked column heading. For example, to sort a list by priority, click the Priority heading. To open the task details page, *do either of the following*:

▼ Click the task's title in the Task column (**Figure 5.40**).

or

▼ Click the check box to the left of the task title, then click the View icon ⓘ at the top of the task module.

The Task page opens (**Figure 5.41**). For a detailed description of the task's fields, see "To create a task" earlier in this chapter. The Linked Content module lists files that have been linked to this task (**Figure 5.42**). The Assignment History module lists the user or users to which the task has been previously assigned, along with any assignment comments that were made by the person who assigned the task to that user (**Figure 5.43**).

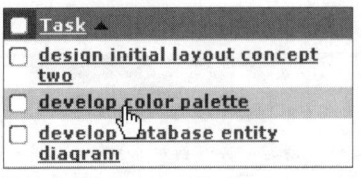

Figure 5.40 Click a task's title to open the Task page.

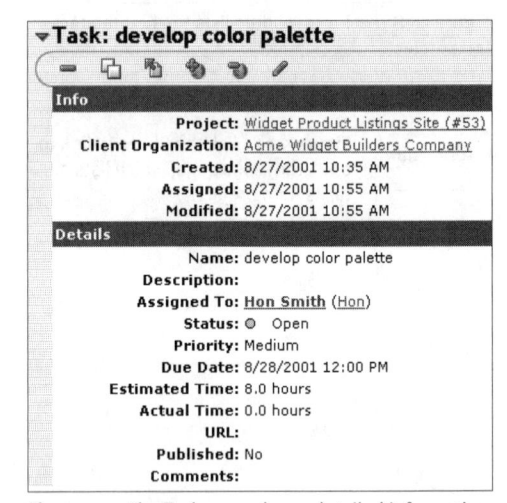

Figure 5.41 The Task page shows detailed information about the task.

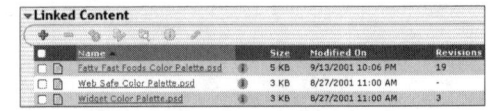

Figure 5.42 The Linked Content module displays files that are linked to the task.

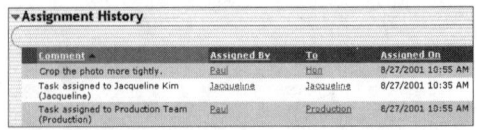

Figure 5.43 The Assignment History module lists the users who were previously assigned to the task and their assignment comment.

VIEWING TASKS

120

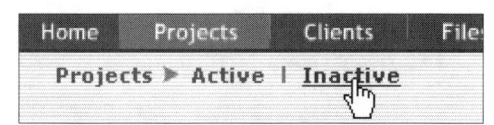

Figure 5.44 If the task you'd like to view belongs to an inactive project, click the Inactive link to see the list of those projects.

Figure 5.45 Click the title of the project to open its Project page.

To view completed or suspended tasks:

1. Navigate to the Project page for the project that contains the task you'd like to view. To do that, *do either of the following:*

    ▼ If you're a member of the project team, the project appears in the My Projects module on your home page. If you're not on your home page, go there by clicking the Home button in the main navigation bar.

    or

    ▼ If you're not a member of the project team, you'll need to navigate to the Project page via the main Projects page. Click the Projects button in the main navigation bar. The main Projects page opens. If the project to which the task belongs is still active, it is listed in the list of projects. If the project has been completed or suspended, it is no longer active and will not be listed. To view inactive projects, click the Inactive link in the bread crumb navigation below the main navigation bar (**Figure 5.44**). The Inactive Projects page opens.

2. Locate the project to which the task belongs. To do this, you can sort the list of projects by clicking any of the linked column headings. Then click the linked project title (**Figure 5.45**). The corresponding Project page opens.

3. If the Tasks module isn't already open, open it by clicking the expand icon ▶ to the left of the module heading. The module opens.

continues on next page

Chapter 5

4. Unlike the My Tasks module, which lists only current tasks, the Tasks module lists all tasks regardless of their status (**Figure 5.46**). The Tasks module lists the first ten tasks. If the task you'd like to view isn't among the first ten, navigate to the All Tasks page by clicking the Show All link at the bottom right of the Tasks module. The All Tasks page opens.

5. In the list of tasks, locate the task you'd like to view. To navigate to the Task page, *do either of the following*:

   ▼ In the Task column, click the linked task title of the task you'd like view (**Figure 5.47**).

   or

   ▼ Click the check box to the left of the task title, then click the View icon.

   The Task page opens (**Figure 5.48**). For a detailed description of the task's fields, see "To create a task" earlier in this chapter. The Linked Content module lists files that have been linked to this task. The Assignment History module lists the users to which the task has previously been assigned.

✔ **Tips**

- Don't forget that you can sort the lists of tasks by any column. Simply click the column name to sort the list by that column. Click a second time to reverse the order.

- Note that the list also provides visual indicators of a task's priority. Figure 5.46 shows circles that denote a task's status, as well as various symbols that indicate priority.

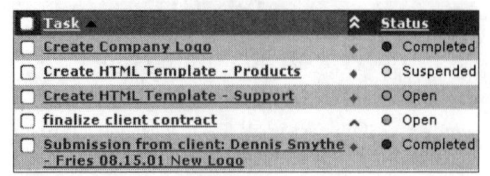

Figure 5.46 Unlike the My Tasks module on your home page, the Tasks module on the Project page lists all tasks regardless of their status.

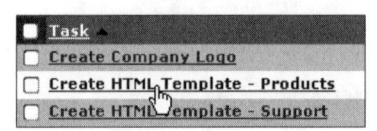

Figure 5.47 Click the task title to open the corresponding Task page.

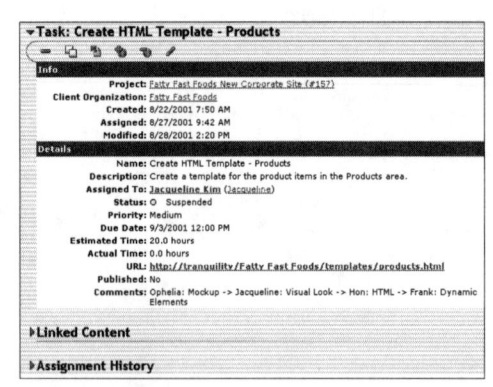

Figure 5.48 The Task page lists important information about the task.

VIEWING TASKS

122

Linking Files and Folders to Tasks

Relating files and folders to tasks is one of Sitespring's handiest features. After a healthy dose of procrastination, the last obstacle you need when you finally start to tackle your to-do items is not knowing where the files are. By linking a file or a folder to a task, you can easily open the file or folder directly from the Task page's Linked Content module without needing to go hunt something down on the server or in your email. And because Sitespring works with its versioning system, the file link always points to the latest version.

Linking files and folders to tasks turns your Web team into a virtual assembly line: As tasks are assigned to team members, the item they need to work on rides alongside each task. Train yourself and your fellow team members to link files or folders that are related to tasks or generated as a result of a task as soon as the file or folder gets created. That way you'll never be at a loss as to where a file is, and you'll always be able to open it easily as you browse through Sitespring.

Linking a file or a folder to a task doesn't mean you can't access the file as you would any other; it simply provides easier access to the task in Sitespring. Because you or other team members may also access the file directly without Sitespring, be sure to use a naming convention and folder structure when you're setting up folders and files on the development server.

If the task you're linking will relate to only one file through the course of the project, it's a good idea to link the file itself as opposed to linking the folder in which it resides. Linking the file ensures that you'll know exactly which file the task is linked to. For example, if you have a task that involves cutting up a Photoshop graphic into a template, you would want to link the task to the Photoshop file.

If, however, the task relates to a large number of files—say, to update a sitewide navigation link in hundreds of files—it's best to link the folder in which the files will reside rather than each file individually. Linking a series of files is time-consuming and may not be worth the effort. Use your best judgment to determine whether you should link a set of files or the folder in which they reside. Generally speaking, linking a handful of files is probably worth your while, although more than five would probably not be worth it. You may link to a task an individual file or folder, multiples of each, or any combination of both.

Unlinking a file or folder from a task does not delete the item from the server; it merely removes the association between the item and the Sitespring task. If a folder is linked to both a task and a project, unlinking the folder from the task does not affect the folder's association with the project.

To link files or folders with a task:

1. Navigate to a page with a tasks module that contains the task to which you would like to link files or folders. To do that, *do either of the following*:

    ▼ If the task you want to link is assigned to you, it will be listed in the My Tasks module on your home page. Navigate to your home page by clicking the Home button in the main navigation bar.

    or

    ▼ If the task you want to link is assigned to another user, it will be listed on the Project page for the project to which the task belongs. Navigate there by clicking the Project button in the main navigation bar. The main Projects page opens. Click the name of the project that contains the task you want. The Project page opens.

2. If the Tasks module isn't opened, open it by clicking the expand icon ▶. The Tasks module opens.

3. Locate the task to which you'd like to link files or folders. Since the module displays only the first ten tasks, the task you are looking for may not appear. If your task isn't listed, click the Show All link to display all the tasks. The Tasks page opens.

4. Select the task you want by clicking the corresponding title in the Task column (**Figure 5.49**). The Task page opens.

5. If the Linked Content module isn't open, open it by clicking the expand icon ▶ to the left of the module name. The Linked Content module opens.

6. Click the Link icon ✤ at the top of the module (**Figure 5.50**). The File Explorer opens.

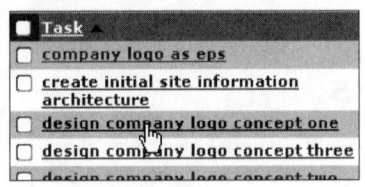

Figure 5.49 Click the title of the task to which you want to link an item.

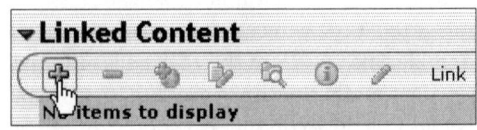

Figure 5.50 Click the Link icon to locate a file or folder.

Figure 5.51 Open subfolders by clicking the expand icon.

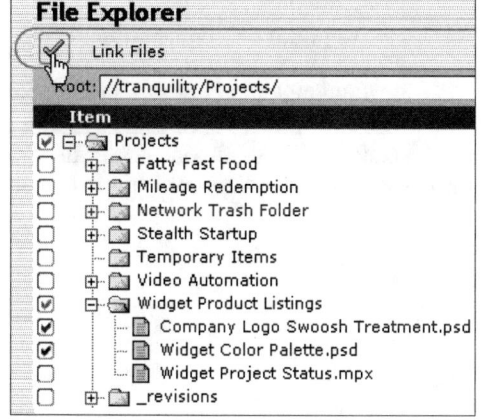

Figure 5.52 Click the Link Files icon to associate a file or folder with the task.

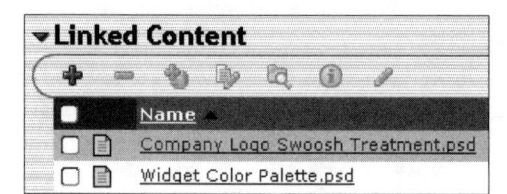

Figure 5.53 The Task page opens with the items listed in the Linked Content module.

7. Locate the file or folder you want to link to the task. If the server running Sitespring is sharing more than one top-level folder, you can choose another top-level folder from the Root pull-down menu at the top of the File Explorer. You can open and close subfolders by clicking the expand ⊞ and collapse icons ⊟ (**Figure 5.51**).

8. Select the folders or files to which you would like to link the task by clicking the check box to the left of the folder's or file's name. You may check a single file or folder, or any number of either. All checked items will be associated with the task and listed in the Linked Content module.

9. Click the Link Files icon ✔ at the top of the File Explorer (**Figure 5.52**).

   The Task page reloads with a green success notice at top and the newly linked items listed in the Linked Content module (**Figure 5.53**).

✔ **Tips**

- After you link a file to a task, you can publish the linked file to the project site, if there is one, by selecting the file and clicking the Publish icon.

- You can open a linked file in its normal application by selecting the file and clicking the Edit icon. See "To view or edit a current or earlier file version" in Chapter 4 for more details.

To unlink files or folders from a task:

1. Navigate to a page with a tasks module that contains the task from which you'd like to unlink files or folders. To do that, *do either of the following*:

    ▼ If the task you want is assigned to you, it will be listed in the My Tasks module on your home page. Navigate to your home page by clicking the Home button in the main navigation bar.

    or

    ▼ If the task you want is assigned to another user, it will be listed on the Tasks module of the Project page for the project to which the task pertains. Navigate there by clicking the Project button in the main navigation bar. The main Projects page opens. Click the name of the project that contains the task you want. The Project page opens.

2. If the Tasks module isn't open, open it by clicking the expand icon ▶. The Tasks module opens (**Figure 5.54**).

3. Locate the task from which you'd like to unlink files or folders. Since the module displays only the first ten tasks, the task you are looking for may not appear. If your task isn't listed, click the Show All link to display all the tasks. The Tasks page opens.

4. Select the task you want by clicking its title in the Task column (**Figure 5.55**). The Task page opens.

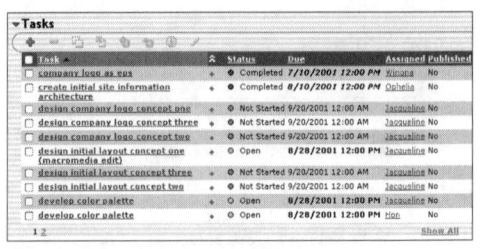

Figure 5.54 The Tasks module of the Project page lists tasks related to the project.

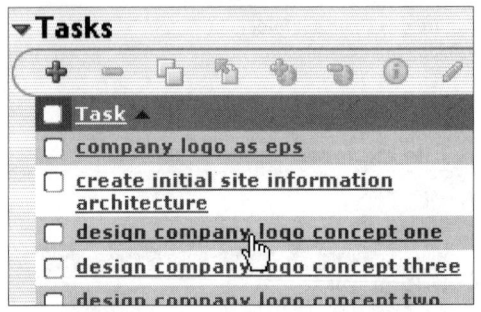

Figure 5.55 Click the title of the task from which you'd like to unlink an item.

Tasks and Reports

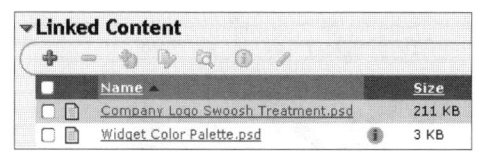

Figure 5.56 The Linked Content module lists files and folders linked to the task.

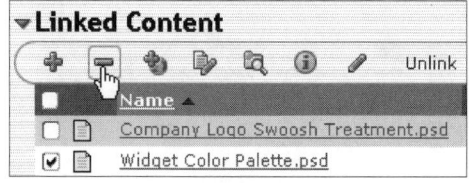

Figure 5.57 Select the item to unlink, and click the Unlink icon at the top of the module.

Figure 5.58 The Linked Content module no longer lists the unlinked item.

5. If the Linked Content module isn't open, open it by clicking the expand icon ▶ to the left of the module name. The Linked Content module opens (**Figure 5.56**).

6. In the Linked Content module, locate the folders or files you would like to unlink. Select the folders or files by clicking the check box to the left of the name of each file or folder. You may select one or more of either.

7. Click the Unlink icon ▬ at the top of the module (**Figure 5.57**). The Unlink Files confirmation page opens.

8. Click the Unlink button to unlink the files or folders, or click the Cancel button to keep the items linked to the task.

   The Task page opens with a green success notice at top and an updated Linked Content module (**Figure 5.58**).

Chapter 5

Working with Reports

Sitespring provides many organizational views into a Web team's tasks. The My Tasks module on your home page lists tasks currently assigned to you, and the Tasks module on a Project page lists project-related tasks. Additionally, you can create custom reports that list sets of tasks according to parameters you determine. These reports resemble the Tasks modules, except you choose what types of tasks get listed.

By selecting the appropriate criteria, you can generate a report that lists all high-priority tasks for the entire team or all overdue tasks for a particular project. When you create a report, you specify search parameters about the tasks that include the project, to whom the tasks are assigned, due date, status, and priority. Once you create a report, you can save it, then view it from your My Reports module.

You can save a report so that you can run the report again without having to reenter the search criteria. Each time you run a report, Sitespring regenerates the list of matching tasks based on the latest information entered. Saved reports appear in your My Reports module on your home page.

If you no longer need to access a report, you can remove it permanently from your My Reports module.

Figure 5.59 Click the New icon to create a new report.

To create a report:

1. To navigate to the Create Report page, *do either of the following:*

    ▼ If you're on your home page, click the New icon ✚ in the My Reports module at the bottom of the page (**Figure 5.59**).

    or

    ▼ If you're not on your home page, click the Reports button in the main navigation bar on any page.

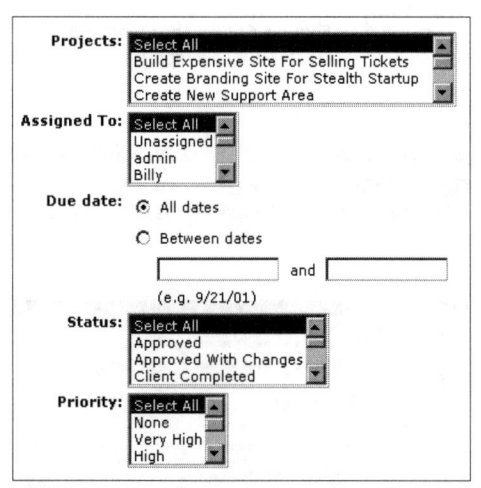

Figure 5.60 Enter information about the types of tasks you'd like your report to contain.

2. The Create Report page opens (**Figure 5.60**). Enter information about the types of tasks you would like the report to list. When the report is generated, it will list tasks that match the criteria you've entered in each of the fields.

   For example, if you wanted to see a report of all the unassigned tasks with a high or very high priority across all projects, team members, and dates, you would select Unassigned in the Assigned To field and both High and Very High in the Priority field, while leaving the default Select All selected for the other fields and the Due Date set to All Dates.

   For the fields that contain selection lists, you can highlight more than one item per field. To choose multiple items on a PC, hold down the Ctrl key as you click each item. To choose multiple items on a Mac, hold down ⌘ as you click each item. See below for notes on each field.

   Projects—Choose the project or projects to which you would like to restrict the search. All projects in the system are listed here, including inactive ones.

   Assigned To—Choose the users to whom you would like to restrict the search. You can select Unassigned to find tasks that have not yet been assigned to a team member.

   Due Date—Select All Dates, or use a date range by entering a beginning date and an ending date in the two spaces provided. The form in which you enter the dates depends on how your system administrator has configured the date setting. Users in North America will likely enter dates in the form of 08/21/01 for August 21, 2001.

   continues on next page

Status—Choose the values for the status of the tasks your report should contain. The options presented here depend on how your administrator has configured Sitespring; he or she can enter additional systemwide status choices. The system default choices are always listed, however. They are Approved, Approved with Changes, Client Completed, Completed, No Approval Needed, Needs Approval, Not Approved, Not Started, Open, and Suspended.

Priority—Choose the priority or priorities to which you would like to restrict the search. To find tasks that have not been assigned a priority, select None.

3. Click the Create button to create the report (**Figure 5.61**).

   The Report Results page opens. The number of matching tasks is listed in the gray status bar at the top of the page (**Figure 5.62**). If your report found matching tasks, the first ten tasks are listed (**Figure 5.63**). If no tasks matched your report criteria, the page lets you know (**Figure 5.64**). If your report matched more than ten tasks, you can either move through the results ten tasks at a time by clicking the page numbers at the bottom left of the module, or you can click the Show All link to display the entire list. If several hundred tasks are found, the Show All option may take a while.

   You can view, edit, and export the tasks listed as you would if the tasks were in a Tasks module. You cannot add tasks, however.

   You can save the report so that you can run it again later. See "To save a report" below for additional information.

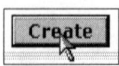

Figure 5.61 Click the Create button to create your new report.

Figure 5.62 The number of tasks included in the report is listed at the right in the gray status bar at the top.

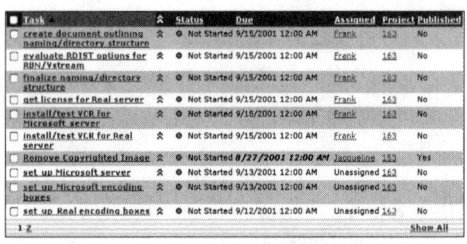

Figure 5.63 If your report found tasks that match the criteria you entered, the first ten tasks are listed on the Report Results page.

Figure 5.64 This report didn't find any tasks matching the criteria entered.

Tasks and Reports

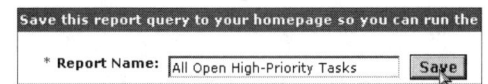

Figure 5.65 Enter a name for the report in the Report Name field, then click the Save button.

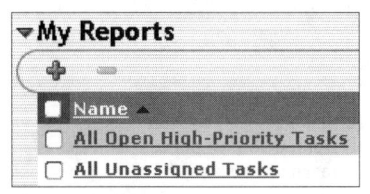

Figure 5.66 After you save a report, it appears in the My Reports module on your home page.

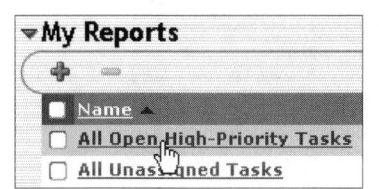

Figure 5.67 Click the report's name to generate the report again.

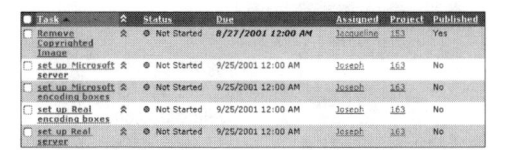

Figure 5.68 The Report Results page. lists the tasks that currently match the report's search criteria.

Figure 5.69 The status indicator at the top of the report lists how many tasks the report contains.

To save a report:

1. Create a new report by following the steps in "To create a report" above.

2. At the bottom of the Report Results page, enter a name for the report in the Report Name field (**Figure 5.65**). Each report name must be unique, so don't use a name that's already being used by another report.

3. Click the Save button.

   Your home page opens. The My Reports module at the bottom lists the newly created report (**Figure 5.66**).

To run a saved report:

1. If you're not on your home page, go there by clicking the Home button in the main navigation bar. Your home page opens.

2. Locate the report you'd like to run in the My Reports module at the bottom of the page.

3. Click the linked name of the report you'd like to run (**Figure 5.67**).

   The Report Results page opens (**Figure 5.68**). The report results are dynamic: It doesn't matter when you created the report—each time the Report Results page is opened, it updates the list of tasks based on the most recently entered information. There's no need to resave a report that's already been saved unless you change the search parameters.

   The number of matching tasks is listed in the gray status bar at the top of the page (**Figure 5.69**). If your report found matching tasks, the first ten tasks are listed. If no tasks matched your report criteria, the page lets you know. If your report matched more than ten tasks, you can either move through the results ten tasks at a time by clicking the page numbers at the bottom left of the module, or you

WORKING WITH REPORTS

131

Chapter 5

can click the Show All link to display the entire list. If several hundred tasks are found, the Show All option may take a while.

You can view, edit, and export the tasks listed as you could if the tasks were in a Tasks module (**Figure 5.70**). You cannot add tasks, however.

To delete a saved report:

1. If you're not on your home page, navigate there by clicking the Home button in the main navigation bar. Your home page opens.

2. If the My Reports module isn't open, open the module by clicking the Expand icon ▶ to the left of the module name. The module opens.

3. In the list, locate the name of the report you would like to delete. The module displays only the first ten reports. If more than ten reports constitute the list and the report you want isn't among the first ten, click the Show All link to display the remainder of them.

4. Select the reports you want to delete by clicking the check boxes next to their name.

5. Click the Delete icon ▬ at the top of the module (**Figure 5.71**). The Delete Reports confirmation page opens.

6. Click the Delete button to delete the report (**Figure 5.72**) or click the Cancel button to leave it untouched.

   Your home page reloads with a green success notice at top and an updated list of reports in the My Reports module (**Figure 5.73**).

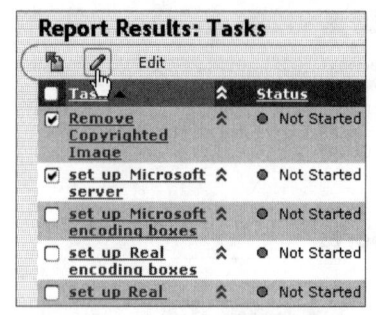

Figure 5.70 You can easily edit a group of tasks directly from the report page by selecting the tasks and clicking the Edit icon.

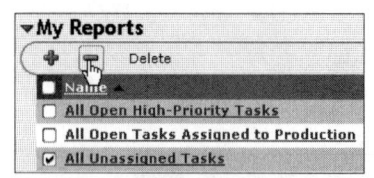

Figure 5.71 Select the report you'd like to delete, then click the Delete icon.

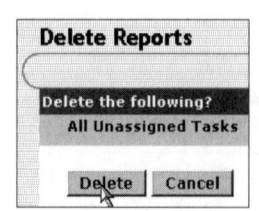

Figure 5.72 Confirm the deletion by clicking the Delete button.

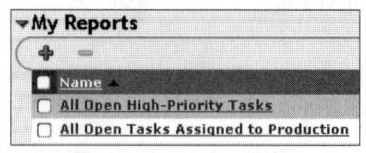

Figure 5.73 The My Reports module on your home page no longer lists the deleted report.

Using Email Notifications

By default, Sitespring sends team members email notification messages when certain key events happen, such as when you're assigned a task (**Figure 5.74**) or when a task is overdue. These emails can be helpful for team members who do not log into Sitespring every day, or if a particularly important event needs to be highlighted. However, if you're a team member who checks Sitespring periodically throughout the day, notifications flooding your in-box can be quite annoying.

When you set your notification preferences, you can choose which type of event causes an email to be sent. You can choose to have all types of events trigger email notices, or select only a few. These settings apply to every event of each type; you cannot have different settings for different projects or clients. Users with project manager permissions have an additional set of event choices under the Project Owner Notifications heading (**Figure 5.75**). These events, such as when a task becomes unassigned or a client completes a document review, apply only to project owners.

The administrator should take note that there are two system event types that are configured separately from the standard email notices. One is for normal system events, and the other is for critical system problems such as running out of disk space. See "To set the server notification email address" and "To set the notification and critical notification email address" in Chapter 8 for more information.

Users can change their own email notification preferences. By default, new accounts have all events trigger an email notice.

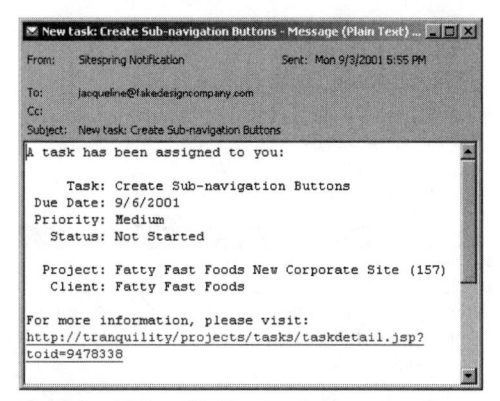

Figure 5.74 This notification email summarizes the new task assignment and includes a link to the task details page.

Figure 5.75 Users with project manager permissions have these additional choices for triggering email notices.

Chapter 5

To set email notification preferences:

1. Navigate to the Edit E-mail Notifications page. To do that, first click the Preferences tab in the main navigation bar (**Figure 5.76**). Your User Profile page opens.

2. Click the Notifications link in the bread crumb navigation area (**Figure 5.77**). Your Edit E-mail Notifications page opens (**Figure 5.78**).

   Users with project manager permissions will see additional choices (again see Figure 5.75).

3. From the list, locate the conditions for which you'd like to receive an email. Select those events by checking their corresponding check boxes. If you do not want to receive an email notice for an event, uncheck the corresponding box.

   You can toggle all the check boxes simultaneously by checking the Select/Deselect All field in the blue header near the top of the module. When you check the Select/Deselect All field, all the events will be checked; when you uncheck the field, all the events will be unchecked.

4. Click the Save button to save your changes, or click a navigation link to abandon them.

   Your Edit E-mail Notifications page reloads with a green success notice at top (**Figure 5.79**). Your notification preferences have been saved, and you may now click any navigation link to resume working in Sitespring.

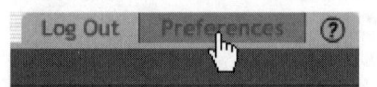

Figure 5.76 Click the Preferences tab to go to the User Profile page.

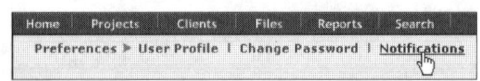

Figure 5.77 Click the Notifications link to open the Edit E-mail Notifications page.

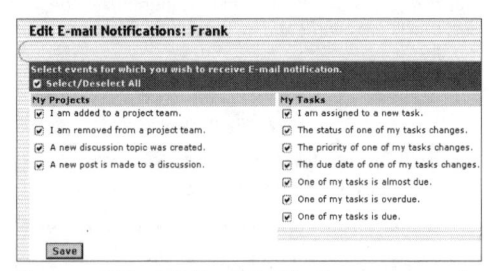

Figure 5.78 The Edit E-mail Notifications page permits you to select which types of events generate an email notice. By default, all events are selected.

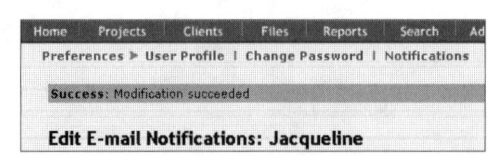

Figure 5.79 The success notice indicates that your changes were saved.

USING EMAIL NOTIFICATIONS

134

6

DISCUSSIONS

Between meetings, phones, voice mail, email, and fax machines, you could easily have doubts over whether you need yet another communication method. Before you balk and move on, however, find out how discussions—Sitespring's project-based messaging system—offer unique benefits.

Discussions are similar to message boards you may have used on the Web or America Online. Here are the three most important benefits:

- Written messages relating to a project can be kept organized in Sitespring alongside their tasks and files.

- The entire team has access to discussions and their history.

- Clients can participate in topics published to the project site, where their comments become an easily viewed written record.

In this chapter you'll learn how to start, view, and reply to discussions; how to remove individual posts; how to publish and remove discussions on the project site; and, finally, how to close a discussion to new messages and delete discussions that are no longer needed.

Working with Discussions

Discussions let your team communicate about a project and its tasks directly in Sitespring, the application that organizes them. The messages don't get lost in your in-box; they stay linked directly to a project. Users with permission can publish certain message topics, or threads, to the project site, where clients can participate and have their comments recorded publicly. Additionally, there's no chance of accidentally leaving a user out of a discussion, as can happen with email distributions; all users have access to Sitespring discussions. Finally, users who join an in-progress project don't need to nag their peers into sending them the project's email trail, as new users can log in and read the discussions on their own.

Now that you know some of the benefits of discussions, it's helpful to know their limitations. Some of the more positive features, such as ease of access, can be a drawback. If a team member makes a gaffe in a discussion, the URL can find its way around the office as quickly as an offending email. Another problem common to both email and discussions is the ease with which a client can be exposed to inappropriate information. In an email exchange, a team member could hit the Reply All button and inadvertently include a client in a tactless discussion about the client. A user could also unthinkingly publish a discussion to the project site that would best be left to the privacy of the team. Finally, you might be concerned that users won't always check the discussions and may miss important messages. While that's a possibility, you can mitigate it by setting your email notification preferences to tell you when new discussions start or new messages are posted.

A discussion generally starts when someone has a question or comment they want to present to the team or client. The user starts a new discussion—sometimes called a topic or a thread—and enters their question or comment as the first message, or post, in the discussion. An open dialogue then begins as people contribute individual posts in response to the initial message.

Each discussion, composed of numerous related messages, is tied to a particular project. If the topic is published to a project site, client users can see and participate in the discussion.

Much like face-to-face interactions, online discussions sometimes run their course and trail off, while other times they spread into new territories as the conversation builds. When a discussion has petered out, closing it can prevent a newcomer from posting a question to a month-old discussion that other users no longer read. When a discussion has evolved into a radically new topic area, closing the old discussion and starting a new one helps keep the discussions organized and can alert users that a new discussion is under way.

Finally, after a discussion has ended, sometimes it's most appropriate to simply delete the discussion. You should think carefully before you do this, however, as deleted discussions cannot be recovered. You can also delete a single post, or message, from a discussion, and leave the rest of the discussion in place. Normal users can delete only the discussions or posts they've created. Users with project manager permissions and the administrator can delete any post or discussion.

Figure 6.1 Click the name of the project to which you'd like to add a discussion.

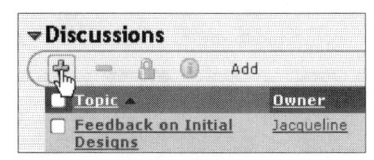

Figure 6.2 The Discussions module lists the project's discussions. Click the Add icon to create a new one.

Figure 6.3 The Info panel presents information that Sitespring enters automatically.

To start a discussion:

1. A discussion always relates to a particular project. Navigate to the Project page for the project to which you'd like to add a discussion. To do that, *do either of the following:*

    ▼ If you're already on a page that has a link to the Project page you want, click the link. On your home page, these links are in the My Projects module. On either the main Projects page or a client page, they are in the Projects module.

    or

    ▼ In the main navigation bar on any page, click the Projects button. The main Projects page opens. In the Project column, click the name of the project to which you'd like to add a discussion (**Figure 6.1**).

2. The Projects page opens. If the Discussions module is closed, open it by clicking the expand icon ⊞. The Discussions module opens.

3. Click the Add icon ✚ at the top of the module (**Figure 6.2**). The Add Discussion page opens.

    The Info panel displays information that Sitespring automatically enters for the new discussion. This information includes the project to which the discussion relates, the client organization to which the project belongs, and the name of the project owner (**Figure 6.3**).

    continues on next page

Chapter 6

4. Enter the information for the discussion you are creating (**Figure 6.4**). You must fill in both fields. They are as follows:

    *Topic—Enter the subject or focus of the discussion. Choose a clear, concisely worded topic that other members of the team—or the client, if the discussion is published to a project site—will be able to understand easily. Remember that users will scan the topic line to decide whether they should read the rest of the discussion. The topic line is also included in email notifications that tell subscribed users when a new topic begins.

    *Message—Write the main message body of the first post to the discussion. Enter the comment or question that you would like to share with the team. Remember that the tone of hastily written messages can be easily misconstrued. Keep your message brief and focused on the subject.

5. Click the Save button to save the discussion, or click any navigation link to abort it.

    The Discussion page opens and shows the newly created discussion (**Figure 6.5**).

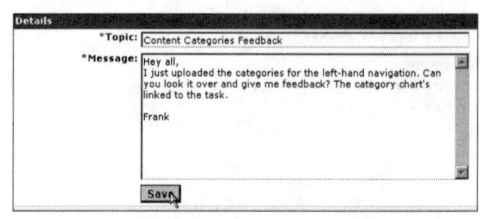

Figure 6.4 Enter the topic and message for the discussion you're creating.

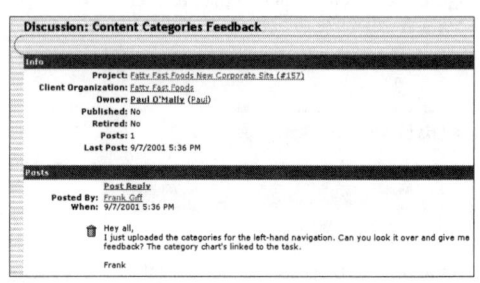

Figure 6.5 The Discussion page lists your message and allows other users to respond to it.

✔ Tips

- Before you add a new discussion, check the topics already listed in the Discussions module to see if it would be more appropriate to reply to an existing topic. If there's an ongoing discussion related to what you have in mind, reply to that discussion rather than starting a new one.

- Many people overlook the communication potential of a topic line. Your busy coworkers who won't take the time to read all the messages in every discussion are more likely to read the title of a discussion topic. Often you can convey the essence of the message body in the title itself. For example, rather than making the title "Navigation Bar," make it "Navigation Bar Is Difficult to Read."

Discussions

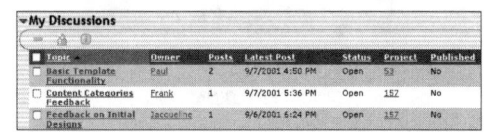

Figure 6.6 The My Discussions module lists topics linked to projects of which you're a team member.

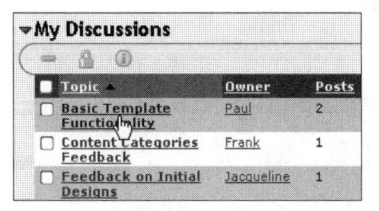

Figure 6.7 Click the linked discussion topic.

To view or reply to a discussion:

1. Navigate to a page with a Discussions module that contains the topic to which you'd like to reply. To do that, *do either of the following:*

   ▼ If the discussion you'd like to respond to is related to a project of which you're a team member, the discussion will be listed in the My Discussions module on your home page (**Figure 6.6**).

   or

   ▼ If you're on the Project page for the project to which the discussion is related, the discussion will be listed in the My Discussions module.

   or

   ▼ If you're not on a page with an appropriate Discussions module, click the Projects button in the main navigation bar. The main Projects page opens. Locate and click the linked name of the project to which your discussion pertains. The Project page opens. The discussion will be listed in the Discussions module.

2. If the Discussions module is closed, open it by clicking the expand icon ⊞. The Discussions module opens.

3. Locate the discussion topic to which you'd like to reply. Since the module displays only the first ten topics, the discussion you are looking for may not appear. If the discussion you want isn't listed, click the Show All link to display all the topics. The Discussions page opens.

4. Click the linked name of the discussion in the Topic column (**Figure 6.7**). The Discussion page opens.

continues on next page

139

Chapter 6

The Info panel at the top of the page (**Figure 6.8**) details the following information:

Project—the name of the project.

Client Organization—the name of the client organization for which the project is being done.

Owner—the name of the project's owner.

Published—a Yes or No value indicating whether this discussion has been published to the project site, so that clients can participate in the discussion.

Retired—a Yes or No value indicating whether this discussion has been closed, or retired. New posts cannot be added to retired projects.

Posts—the number of messages the discussion contains.

Last Post—the date and time the last post was added.

The Posts panel lists the individual messages in reverse chronological order, meaning the most recent post appears at the top and is followed by the preceding posts (**Figure 6.9**). In addition to the actual message, each post lists the sender of the message and the date and time it was posted.

5. If you'd like to add a post, click the Post Reply link at the top of the Posts panel (**Figure 6.10**). If there are more than five posts, another Post Reply link appears at the bottom of the list. The Post to Discussion page opens.

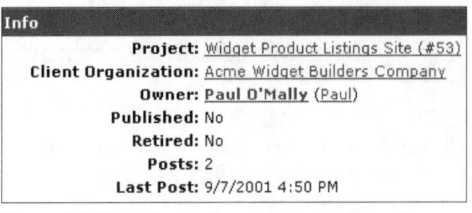

Figure 6.8 The Info panel summarizes information about the discussion.

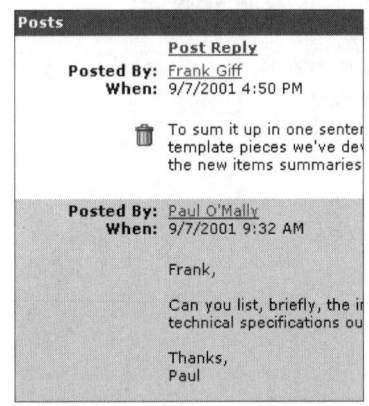

Figure 6.9 The Posts panel lists individual messages, with the most recent message at the top.

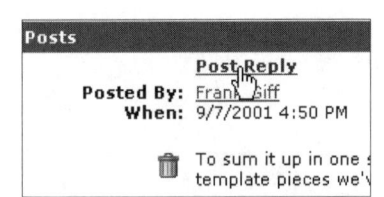

Figure 6.10 Click the Post Reply link to add another message to the discussion.

Discussions

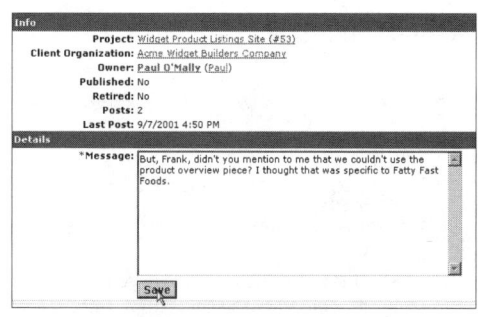

Figure 6.11 Enter the comment or question you'd like to add to the discussion, and click the Save button.

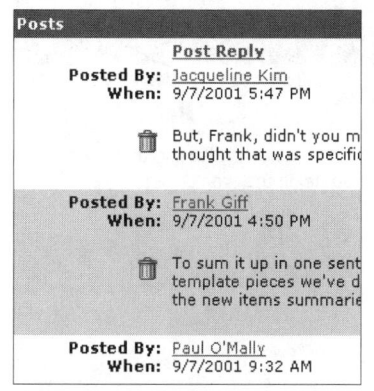

Figure 6.12 The Discussion page opens with your new message listed.

6. In the Message field, enter the comment or question you'd like to direct to the team (**Figure 6.11**). Remember that the tone of hastily written messages can be easily misconstrued. Keep your message brief and relevant to the subject of previous posts.

7. Click the Save button to save your message, or click a navigation link to abort it.

   The Discussion page opens with your newly added post at the top of the Posts panel (**Figure 6.12**).

✔ Tip

- You should start a new discussion if a new comment departs significantly from the topic of existing posts. If your discussion were a live conversation, would the new comment be taken by the other participants as a natural extension of the conversation, or would it be a jarring, off-topic remark? If the answer is the latter, a new topic is warranted.

To delete a post:

1. Navigate to a page with a Discussions module that contains the topic from which you'd like to remove a post. To do that, *do either of the following:*

    ▼ If the discussion you want is related to a project of which you're a team member, the discussion is listed in the My Discussions module on your home page (**Figure 6.13**).

    or

    ▼ If you're on the Project page for the project to which the discussion is related, the discussion will be listed in the My Discussions module.

    or

    ▼ If you're not on a page with an appropriate Discussions module, click the Projects button in the main navigation bar. The main Projects page opens. In the list of projects, locate and click the linked name of the project to which your discussion pertains. The Project page opens. The discussion will be listed in the Discussions module.

2. If the Discussions module is closed, open it by clicking the expand icon ⊞. The Discussions module opens.

3. Locate the discussion topic from which you'd like to remove a post. Since the module displays only the first ten topics, the discussion you are looking for may not appear. If the discussion you want isn't listed, click the Show All link to display all the topics. The Discussions page opens.

4. Click the linked name of the discussion in the Topic column (**Figure 6.14**).

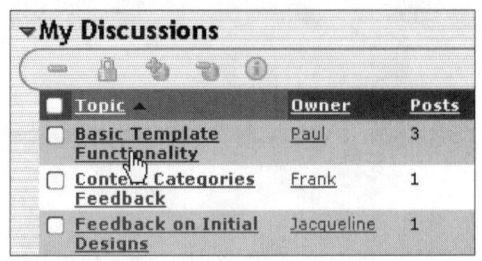

Figure 6.13 If the discussion is listed in your My Discussions module, click the linked topic title.

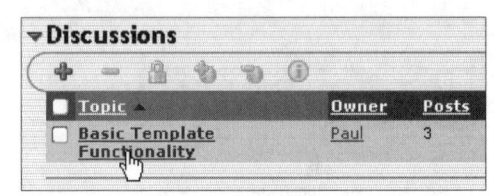

Figure 6.14 The discussion is also listed in the Discussions module on the Project page.

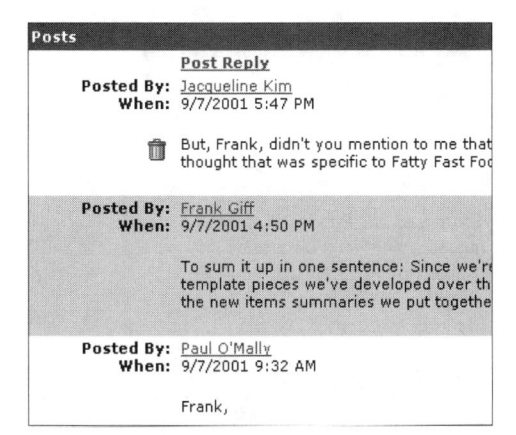

Figure 6.15 The Posts panel lists the individual messages.

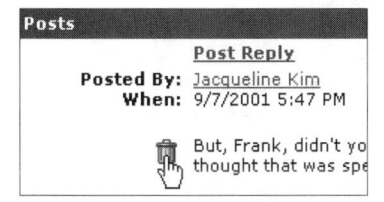

Figure 6.16 The trash can icon appears next to only those messages you have permission to delete. Click the icon to delete the message.

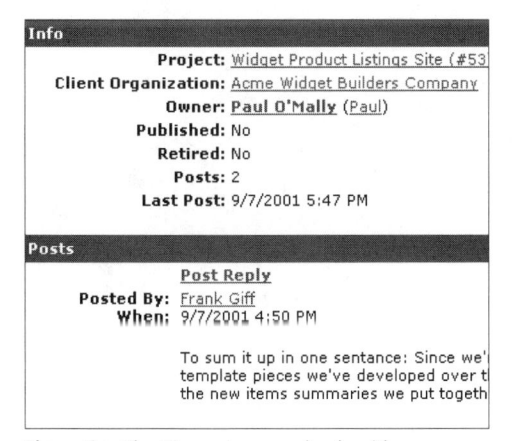

Figure 6.17 The Discussion page loads with your message deleted.

The Discussion page opens. The Posts panel lists the individual messages, or posts, in reverse chronological order, meaning the most recent post appears at the top and is followed by the preceding posts. In addition to the actual message, each post lists who the message was posted by as well as when the message was posted (**Figure 6.15**).

5. In the list of posts, locate the one you'd like to delete. Click the trash can icon to the left of the message body for the post you'd like to delete (**Figure 6.16**). The icon appears only if you have permission to delete the post. The Delete Messages confirmation page opens.

6. Click the Delete button to confirm the deletion, or click the Cancel button to abort it.

    The Discussion page opens with a green success notice at the top and an updated posts list that omits the deleted post (**Figure 6.17**).

To add or remove a discussion from a project site:

1. Navigate to a page with a Discussions module that contains the topic you'd like to either publish to or remove from a project site. To do that, *do either of the following:*

   ▼ If the discussion you want is related to a project of which you're a team member, the discussion will be listed in the My Discussions module on your home page.

   or

   ▼ If you're on the Project page for the project to which the discussion is related, the discussion will be listed in the My Discussions module.

   or

   ▼ If you're not on a page with an appropriate Discussions module, click the Projects button in the main navigation bar. The main Projects page opens. Locate and click the linked name of the project to which your discussion pertains. The Project page opens. The discussion will be listed in the Discussions module.

2. If the Discussions module is closed, open it by clicking the expand icon ⊞. The Discussions module opens.

3. Locate the discussion topic you want to add to or remove from the project site. Since the module displays only the first ten topics, the discussion you are looking for may not appear. If the discussion you want isn't listed, click the Show All link to display all the topics. The Discussions page opens. In the Discussions module, the Published column contains a Yes or No value that indicates whether a discussion is currently published to the project site (**Figure 6.18**).

4. Select the discussions that you'd like to publish or remove by clicking the check box to the left of their name (**Figure 6.19**).

Figure 6.18 The Published column indicates whether a discussion is available on the project site.

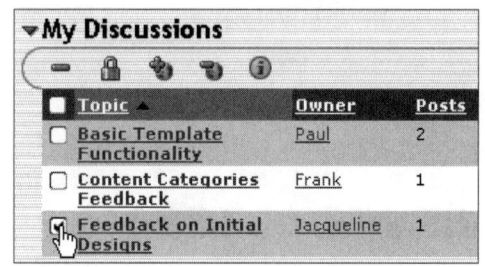

Figure 6.19 Select a discussion to work with by clicking the check box to the left of its title.

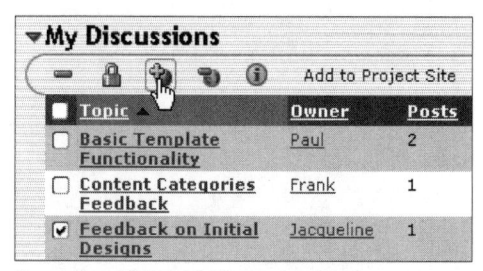

Figure 6.20 Click the Add to Project Site icon to publish the discussion on a project site, where clients can participate in the discussion.

Figure 6.21 Click the Remove from Project Site icon to remove the discussion from the project site so that clients can no longer see it.

Figure 6.22 The Published column reflects the new status of the discussions.

5. To add or remove the discussions on the project site, *do either of the following:*

    ▼ To add the selected discussions to the project site, thereby letting client users see and participate in the discussion topic, click the Add to Project Site icon (**Figure 6.20**).

    or

    ▼ To remove the selected discussions from the project site, thereby preventing client users from seeing and participating in the discussion topic, click the Remove from Project Site icon (**Figure 6.21**).

    The page reloads (this time, without a success notice at top), and the Discussions module updates the Published column to reflect the discussion's new Published status (**Figure 6.22**).

✔ Tip

- Note that if the Create Discussion module is visible on the project site then clients can also create discussions. To show or hide this module, see "To edit a project site and set visible modules" in Chapter 3.

Administering Discussions

You close, or retire, a discussion when you no longer want new messages added to the topic but you don't want to delete the messages. Often there's valuable information in the messages that you don't want to delete, yet you don't need the discussion to continue. You may reach this point after many posts are added to a topic and the conversation's focus starts to drift. If the subject changes substantially enough that it can no longer be considered coherent, it's a good idea to start a new discussion and close the old one. In addition to keeping discussions organized, starting a new thread tells team members who haven't closely followed the discussion that it has taken a different course. A team member who didn't care about the original focus of the discussion may care about the new one.

You should also close a discussion topic that duplicates an existing discussion, since having more than one discussion covering the same topic leads to confusion.

Deleting a discussion topic removes all message posts in that discussion. It also removes the discussion from the Discussions modules and, if it's published, the project site. If you'd like to delete an individual post instead of the whole discussion, see "To delete a post" earlier in this chapter.

Think carefully before deleting a discussion. You cannot restore discussions that have been deleted.

Normal users can close or delete only discussions they created. The administrator, as well as users with project manager permissions, can close or delete any discussion.

Discussions

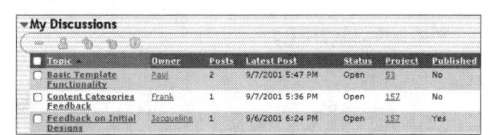

Figure 6.23 On your home page, the My Discussions module lists discussions related to projects of which you're a team member.

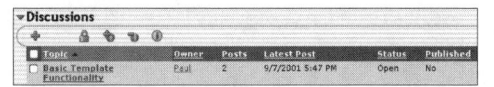

Figure 6.24 On each Project page, the Discussions module lists discussions related to the project.

To close a discussion:

1. Navigate to a page with a Discussions module that contains the topic you'd like to close. To do that, *do either of the following:*

    ▼ If the discussion you want is related to a project of which you're a team member, the discussion will be listed in the My Discussions module on your home page (**Figure 6.23**).

    or

    ▼ If you're on the Project page for the project to which the discussion is related, the discussion will be listed in the Discussions module (**Figure 6.24**).

    or

    ▼ If you're not on a page with an appropriate Discussions module, click the Projects button in the main navigation bar. The main Projects page opens. In the list of projects, locate the name of the project to which your discussion pertains. The Project page opens. The discussion will be listed in the Discussions module.

2. If the Discussions module is closed, open it by clicking the expand icon ⊞. The Discussions module opens.

3. Locate the discussion topic you want to close. Since the module displays only the first ten topics, the discussion you are looking for may not appear. If the discussion you want isn't listed, click the Show All link to display all the topics. The Discussions page opens.

4. To select the discussions you'd like to close, click the check box to the left of their name.

continues on next page

147

Chapter 6

5. Click the Close icon 🔒 at the top of the My Discussions module (**Figure 6.25**).

   The page reloads with a green success notice at top. The Discussions module updates the Status column to indicate that the discussions are closed (**Figure 6.26**).

To delete a discussion:

1. Navigate to a page with a Discussions module that contains the topic you'd like to delete. To do that, *do either of the following:*

   ▼ If the discussion you want is related to a project of which you're a team member, the discussion will be listed in the My Discussions module on your home page.

   or

   ▼ If you're on the Project page for the project to which the discussion is related, the discussion will be listed in the My Discussions module.

   or

   ▼ If you're not on a page with an appropriate Discussions module, click the Projects button in the main navigation bar. The main Projects page opens. In the list of projects, locate the name of the project to which your discussion pertains. The Project page opens. The discussion will be listed in the Discussions module.

2. If the Discussions module is closed, open it by clicking the expand icon ⊞. The Discussions module opens.

3. Locate the discussion topic you want to delete. Since the module displays only the first ten topics, the discussion you are looking for may not appear. If the discussion you want isn't listed, click the Show All link to display all the topics. The Discussions page opens.

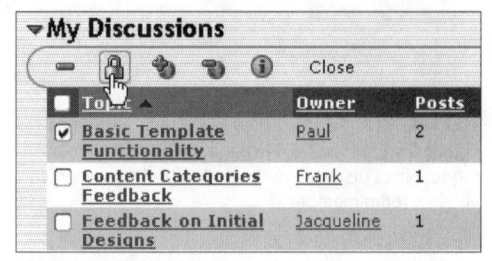

Figure 6.25 Select the discussion topic you want to close, then click the Close icon.

Figure 6.26 The Status column lists the discussion as closed.

Discussions

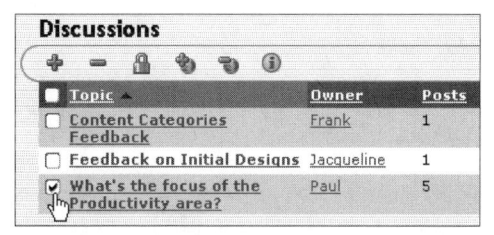

Figure 6.27 Locate the discussion you want to delete, then click the check box to the left of the topic title.

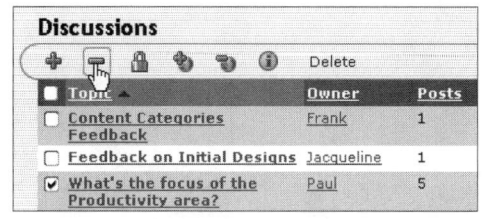

Figure 6.28 Click the Delete icon at the top of the Discussions module.

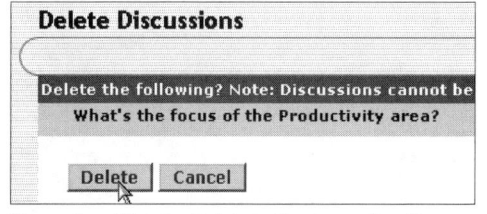

Figure 6.29 Click the Delete button to confirm the deletion.

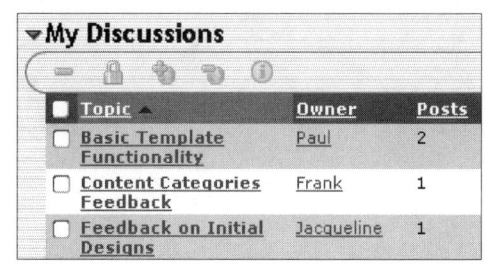

Figure 6.30 The My Discussions module no longer lists the deleted discussion.

4. To select the discussions that you'd like to delete, click the check box to the left of the topic name (**Figure 6.27**).

5. To delete the selected discussions, click the Delete icon ▬ at the top of the Discussions module (**Figure 6.28**). The Delete Discussions confirmation page opens.

6. To confirm the deletion, click the Delete button (**Figure 6.29**), or click the Cancel button to abort it.

   Your home page loads with a green success notice at the top and an updated Discussions module that no longer lists the deleted discussions (**Figure 6.30**).

ADMINISTERING DISCUSSIONS

149

Managing Version Control

7

Sitespring's automatic versioning is one of the program's most useful features. With versioning enabled, each time you modify or delete a file, a copy of the original file is made. Sitespring also lets you easily revert to an earlier version or recover a deleted file.

The one thing that can produce files faster than a Web team is a Web team that's using a system with versioning. To work effectively, this function needs to be carefully administered and managed. In this chapter you'll learn how to share folders, a prerequisite to enabling versioning; how to turn versioning on and off for particular folders; how to exclude certain file types from versioning; how to undo the exclusion of those files; and, finally, how to run the Revision Cleanup Wizard, a tool that lets you delete old versions to free disk space. To do any of these jobs, you need to log in with the administrator account.

Chapter 7

Managing Shared Folders

This chapter assumes you understand the basic dynamics of Sitespring versioning. For a detailed explanation of what versioning is and how it works, see "About Versioning" in Chapter 4.

In order to enable versioning on a folder or a drive, you must first share that folder or drive on the Windows server where Sitespring runs. Once file sharing has been enabled at the Windows 2000 server level, you can enable the folder for versioning within Sitespring. If you disable file sharing for a folder, you also disable versioning.

When you turn off versioning for a folder or drive, you do not remove old versions or stop file sharing; you merely prevent additional versions from being created. If you want to remove old versions to free up space, see "Using the Revision Cleanup Wizard" later in this chapter.

Once you remove a shared folder or drive, users cannot access the folder or its contents via the network. Before removing something shared, you should find out whether doing so will block users from gaining access to files they need for their work. You remove a shared folder from the Windows 2000 server on which Sitespring runs.

The following directions should be executed on the server, not your desktop machine. In order to add or remove a shared folder or drive, you must log onto the server using a Windows account with administrator privileges.

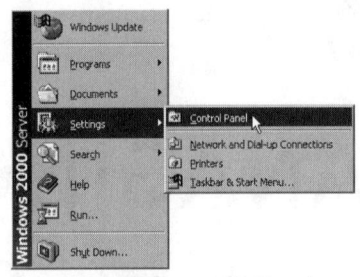

Figure 7.1 Open the server's Control Panel from the Start menu.

Figure 7.2 Launch the Computer Management console, which is located inside the Administrative Tools folder.

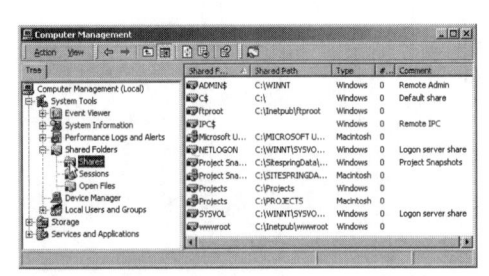

Figure 7.3 Expand System Tools and Shared Folders, then click on the Shares icon.

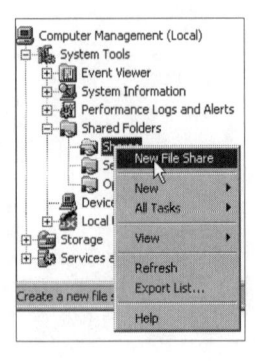

Figure 7.4 Right-click the Shares icon and select New File Share from the pop-up menu.

152

Managing Version Control

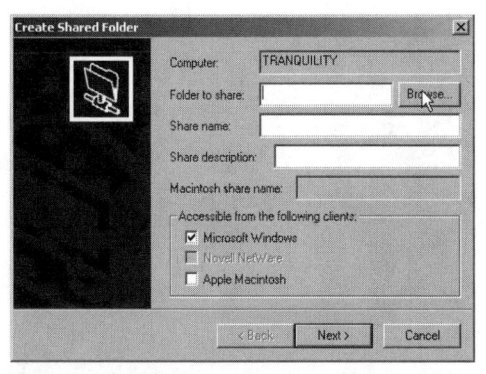

Figure 7.5 Click the Browse button to select the folder to share.

Figure 7.6 Locate the folder you'd like to share. Click the folder name to select it, then click the OK button.

Figure 7.7 Enter a descriptive name for the shared item.

To add a shared folder or drive:

1. Launch the Computer Management console. To do that, from your Start menu select Settings and then Control Panel (**Figure 7.1**). The Control Panel folder opens. Double-click the Administrative Tools icon . The Administrative Tools folder opens. Double-click the Computer Management icon (**Figure 7.2**).

2. The Computer Management console opens. If System Tools isn't already expanded in the tree pane on the left side of the window, expand it by clicking the expand icon to the left of the System Tools icon. System Tools expands. Expand Shared Folders by clicking the expand icon to the left of Shared Folders. Shared Folders expands. Click the Shares icon (**Figure 7.3**). The right pane displays the server's currently shared folders or drives.

3. Right-click the Shares icon. Select New File Share from the pop-up menu (**Figure 7.4**).

4. The Create Shared Folder Wizard opens. Click the Browse button (**Figure 7.5**). The Browse for Folder dialog opens. In the window, locate the folder or drive you would like to share. You can expand and collapse drives and folders by clicking the expand and collapse icons . Click the name of the folder or drive you want to select. The item's name appears in the Folder field. Click the OK button (**Figure 7.6**). The Browse for Folder dialog closes.

5. Enter a name for the share in the Share Name field (**Figure 7.7**). That name will appear in your Network Neighborhood when you look for the share.

continues on next page

MANAGING SHARED FOLDERS

153

Chapter 7

6. Enter a description for the share in the Share Description field. This will appear as additional information in Network Neighborhood when you select the share.

7. If you would like this share to be accessible to Macintosh clients, in the field called Accessible from the Following Clients check the Apple Macintosh check box. (If this selection is grayed out, make sure that your server has the File Server for Macintosh component installed.) The Macintosh Share Name field automatically updates to the same value you used for the Share Name field in step 5. For Sitespring to work correctly for Macintosh users, the two Share Name fields must be the same, so leave the automatically entered value alone (**Figure 7.8**).

8. Click the Next button. The wizard advances to the next screen, where you can set access permissions for the new share. Select permissions appropriate to your organization. Most users will probably select "All users have full control." That will let all network users read, add, move, and delete files in the share. If you want to apply more sophisticated permissions, first click the Custom button.

9. Click the Finish button (**Figure 7.9**). A dialog opens that indicates the share has been successfully created and asks if you would like to create an additional share. If you would like to do so, click the Yes button and repeat steps 4 through 8. Otherwise, click No (**Figure 7.10**).

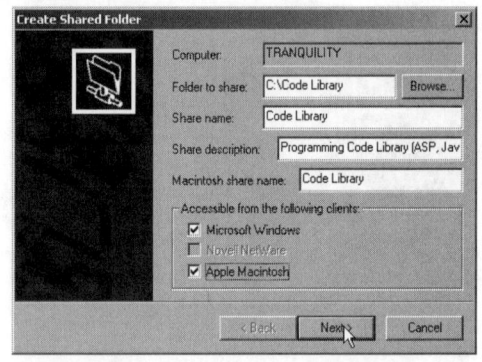

Figure 7.8 If you'd like Mac users to be able to access the share, check the Apple Macintosh option near the bottom of the window.

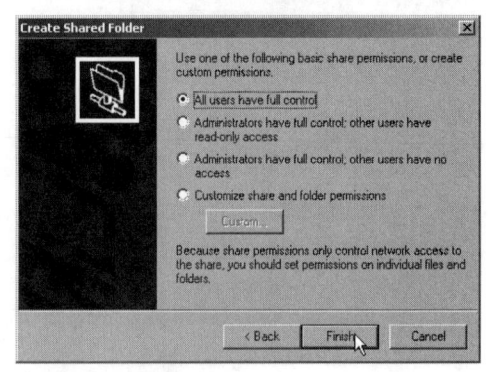

Figure 7.9 Set the permissions you'd like for the share, then click the Finish button.

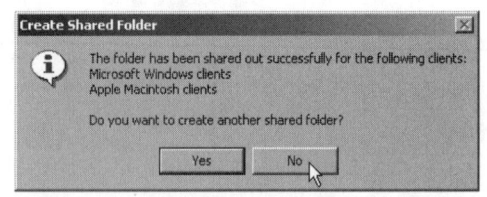

Figure 7.10 The dialog indicates the item has been shared. Click the No button to finish.

Managing Version Control

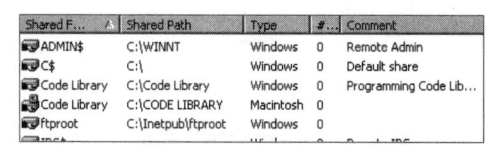

Figure 7.11 The list of shares shows the shared folder twice, once for Windows clients and once for Mac clients.

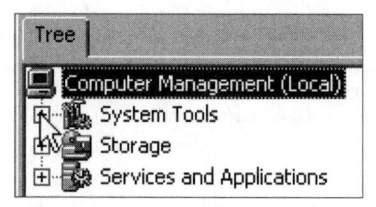

Figure 7.12 Click the expand icon to expand the System Tools entry.

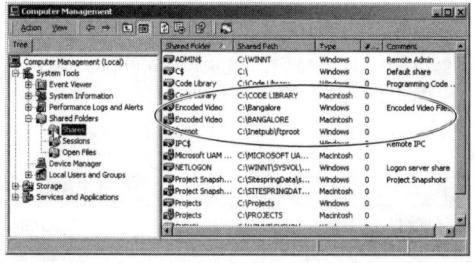

Figure 7.13 Click the Shares icon to display the list of currently shared folders, drives, and printers. Locate the shared folder you'd like to remove from the list.

10. The dialog and the wizard window close, and your share is listed in the list of shares (**Figure 7.11**).

✔ Tip

- In order to enable Sitespring's versioning on a shared folder, the folder must be on a drive that is formatted with the NTFS file system; the folder cannot be on a removable disk; and the folder cannot contain the operating system (usually c:\winnt\), a system page file (pagefile.sys), or a hibernation file (hiberfil.sys).

To remove a shared folder or drive:

1. Launch the Computer Management console. To do that, from your Start menu select Settings, then Control Panel. The Control Panel folder opens. Double-click the Administrative Tools icon. The Administrative Tools folder opens. Double-click the Computer Management icon. The Computer Management console opens.

2. If System Tools isn't already expanded in the tree pane on the left side of the window, expand it by clicking the expand icon ⊞ to the left of the System Tools icon (**Figure 7.12**); System Tools expands. Expand Shared Folders by clicking the expand icon ⊞ to the left of Shared Folders. Shared Folders expands. Click the Shares icon. The right pane displays the server's currently shared folders, drives, and printers.

3. In the list of shares, locate the share you would like to remove. Shared folders or drives that are available to both Windows and Macintosh clients are listed twice, once for each platform (**Figure 7.13**).

continues on next page

155

Chapter 7

4. Select the share that you would like to remove by right-clicking the share's name in the Shared Folder column.

5. From the pop-up menu that appears, select Stop Sharing (**Figure 7.14**).

   A dialog opens asking whether you are sure you want to stop sharing the folder.

6. Click the OK button to remove the share (**Figure 7.15**), or click Cancel to leave the folder shared.

   The dialog closes, and the list of shares updates to remove the no longer shared folder (**Figure 7.16**).

7. If your folder was shared for both Macintosh and Windows clients, repeat steps 3 through 7 on the second share for the other platform.

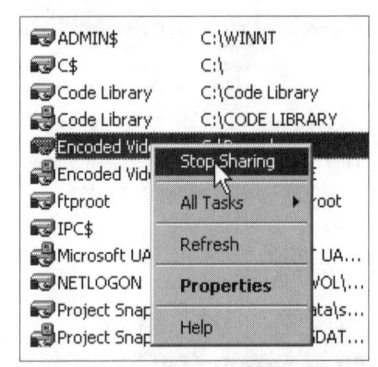

Figure 7.14 Right-click the share you'd like to remove, then select Stop Sharing.

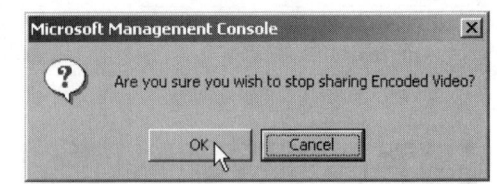

Figure 7.15 Click the OK button to confirm that you'd like to stop sharing the item.

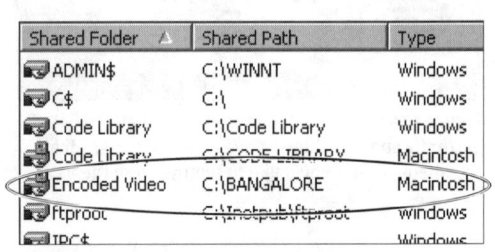

Figure 7.16 The list of shares no longer shows the folder as being shared for Windows clients. The folder is still shared for Mac clients; the steps must be repeated to remove the Mac share.

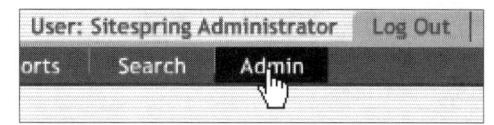

Figure 7.17 Click the Admin button in the main navigation bar.

Shared Folder Information

On the Shared Folder Management page (see step 4 in "To enable file versioning on a shared folder"), you'll find columns containing the following information:

Share Name—the name of the file share.

Macintosh Share—a Yes or No indicating whether the shared folder is available to Macintosh clients.

Share Path—the server's local file path to the shared folder or drive. This is not the path on your local machine, but the path as seen from the server's perspective.

File Versioning—an On or Off indicating whether file versioning is enabled or disabled. Clicking the <change> link toggles this value.

If the folder cannot be shared for one of the reasons mentioned above, a note indicating so is displayed in the File Versioning column.

Managing File Versioning

When your administrator installed Sitespring, he or she probably enabled file versioning on a shared folder or folders. That means every time a file is modified or deleted, a backup copy is created. If versioning needs to be enabled, whoever does so must have administrator privileges. Also, the folders or drives must be shared by the Windows server where Sitespring is installed. You cannot enable versioning on your local folders or drives.

Merely being able to share the folder or drive within Windows doesn't mean you can enable Sitespring versioning. The shared folder or drive must reside on a volume formatted with the NTFS file system, not FAT or FAT32. Additionally, versioning cannot be enabled on folders or drives that contain the operating system, a system page file, or a hibernation file.

You can disable versioning at any time. Disabling file versioning on a folder does not erase versions of files already made. (To erase old versions and free disk space, see "Using Version Control and File Extensions" later in this chapter.) Neither does disabling file versioning disable file sharing—folders with versioning turned off are still accessible to end users unless you turn off file sharing. (See "To remove a shared folder" earlier in this chapter for more information.)

To enable file versioning on a shared folder:

1. Log into Sitespring as the admin user. Only somebody using the administrator account can configure file versioning.

2. If you're not already on the Administration page, click the Admin button in the main navigation bar to go there (**Figure 7.17**). The Administration page opens.

continues on next page

Chapter 7

3. Click the Shared Folder Management link in the right column (**Figure 7.18**).

4. The Shared Folder Management page opens (**Figure 7.19**). The page displays the list of shared folders and drives on your server. For details, see the sidebar "Shared Folder Information."

5. In the list of shares, locate the row containing the share for which you would like to enable versioning. In the File Versioning column of that row, click the <change> link (**Figure 7.20**).

   The Shared Folder Management page reloads with a green success notice at the top and an updated list of shared folders that indicates versioning has been enabled (**Figure 7.21**).

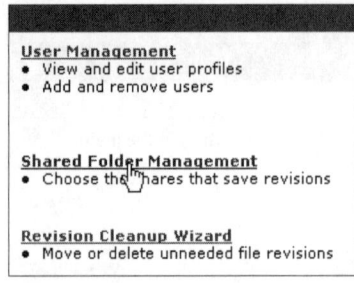

Figure 7.18 Click the Shared Folder Management link in the right column.

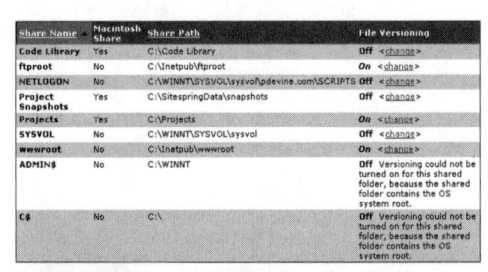

Figure 7.19 The Shared Folder Management page lists the file shares on the server and indicates whether versioning is enabled.

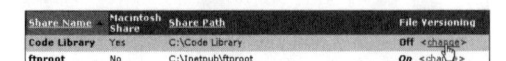

Figure 7.20 Click the <change> link for a folder or drive to toggle between disabling and enabling version control.

Figure 7.21 The Shared Folder Management page reloads with an updated list of the folders that have versioning enabled.

Managing Version Control

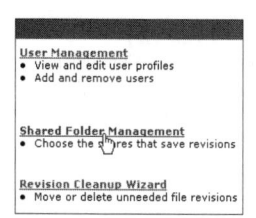

Figure 7.22 Click the Shared Folder Management link in the right column.

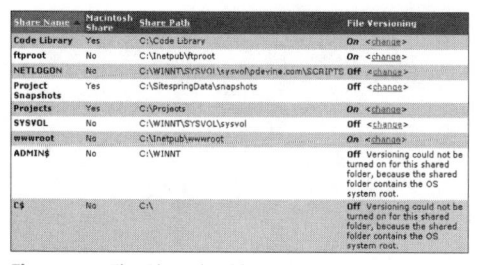

Figure 7.23 The Shared Folder Management page lists the shared folders and drives on the server and indicates which shared items have versioning enabled.

Figure 7.24 Locate the folder for which you'd like to disable versioning, then click the <change> link.

Figure 7.25 Click the Disable button to confirm that you want to disable versioning for the selected folder or drive.

Figure 7.26 The list of shared folders updates and shows that versioning has been disabled for the selected folder.

To disable file versioning on a shared folder:

1. Log into Sitespring as the admin user. Only somebody using the administrator account can configure file versioning.

2. If you're not already on the Administration page, click the Admin button in the main navigation bar to go there. The Administration page opens.

3. Click the Shared Folder Management link in the right column (**Figure 7.22**).

   The Shared Folder Management page opens. The page displays the list of shared folders and drives on your server (**Figure 7.23**). For an explanation of the columns, see "To enable file versioning on a shared Folder" above.

4. In the list of shares, locate the row containing the share for which you would like to disable versioning. In the File Versioning column of that row, click the <change> link (**Figure 7.24**). The Disable Shared Folder Versioning confirmation page opens.

5. Click the Disable button to confirm the disabling of file versioning (**Figure 7.25**), or click the Cancel button to leave it enabled.

   The Shared Folder Management page opens with a green success notice at the top and an updated list of shared folders that indicates versioning has been disabled (**Figure 7.26**).

MANAGING FILE VERSIONING

159

Version Control and File Extensions

When versioning is enabled on a folder, making a change to any file in the folder causes a backup of the original file to be made. For certain types of files, however, this can be overkill. If you configured Word, for example, to create a backup file each time it saved a document, there would be no need to enable versioning on the backup file, since the original is already being saved. Similarly, you might not want to version streaming video or database files, as these files can be quite large, and making versions of them can quickly consume disk space.

Sitespring lets you configure the versioning system to ignore files with particular extensions. By default, Sitespring ignores the extensions .bak, .ddd, .lck, .log, and .tmp. Any file named with an extension that has been configured to be excluded will not have versions created, even if it is located in a folder that has versioning enabled. This means that when a file gets modified or deleted, a copy of the original file does not get put in the _revisions folder. Since these files do not have versioning enabled, you are at risk for losing them if they are overwritten or deleted.

To exclude a file extension from versioning:

1. Log into Sitespring as the admin user. Only somebody using the administrator account can configure file versioning.

2. If you're not already on the Administration page, click the Admin button in the main navigation bar to go there. The Administration page opens.

3. Click the File Revision Management link at the bottom of the right column (**Figure 7.27**).

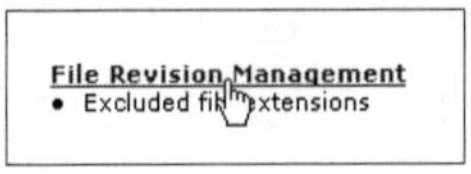

Figure 7.27
Click the File Revision Management link.

Managing Version Control

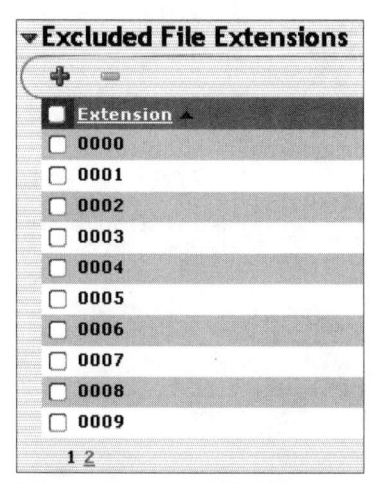

Figure 7.28 The Excluded File Extensions module lists the first ten excluded extensions.

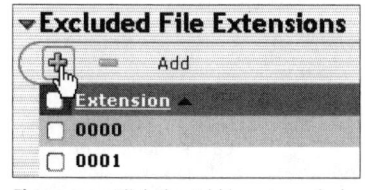

Figure 7.29 Click the Add icon to exclude an additional extension.

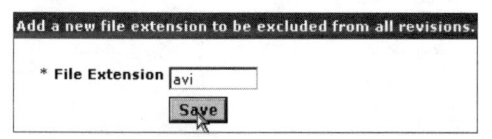

Figure 7.30 Enter the extension to be excluded and click the Save button.

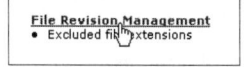

Figure 7.31 Click the File Revision Management link.

The File Revision Management page opens, and the Excluded File Extensions module lists the first ten excluded extensions (**Figure 7.28**). If you'd like to see the entire list of excluded extensions, click the Show All link.

4. Click the Add icon ✚ at the top of the module (**Figure 7.29**). The Add Excluded File Extension page opens.

5. In the File Extension field, enter the file extension you would like to exclude from versioning. You may enter the extension with or without the initial period.

6. Click the Save button to save your new extension to be excluded (**Figure 7.30**), or click a navigation link to abort it.

The File Revision Management page opens with a green success notice at the top, and an updated list of excluded extensions. If the module lists only the first ten extensions, you may have to click the Show All link to see the extension you just entered.

To undo excluding a extension from versioning:

1. Log into Sitespring as the admin user. Only somebody using the administrator account can configure file versioning.

2. If you're not already on the Administration page, click the Admin button in the main navigation bar to go there. The Administration page opens.

3. Click the File Revision Management link at the bottom of the right column (**Figure 7.31**).

continues on next page

161

The File Revision Management page opens, and the Excluded File Extensions module lists the first ten excluded extensions (**Figure 7.32**).

4. Locate the extension for which you would like to enable versioning. If the extension you want isn't listed in the first ten extensions, click the Show All link at the bottom of the module to show all the extensions (**Figure 7.33**).

5. Select the extensions for which you'd like to enable versioning.

6. Click the Delete icon — at the top of the module (**Figure 7.34**). The Delete Excluded File Extensions confirmation page opens.

7. Click the Delete button to confirm the deletion (**Figure 7.35**), or click Cancel to abort it.

   The File Revision Management page opens with an updated list of excluded extensions that no longer includes the deleted extensions. You may have to click the Show All link to see the entire list.

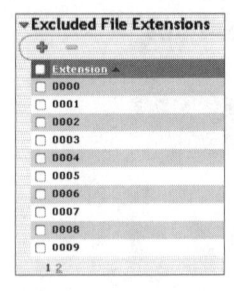

Figure 7.32 The Excluded File Extensions module lists the first ten excluded extensions. Click the Show All link to list them all.

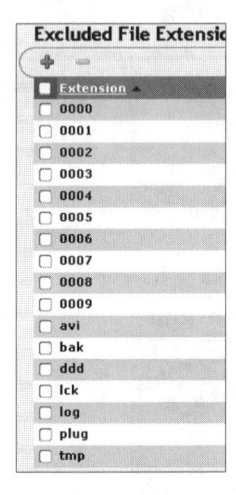

Figure 7.33 After clicking the Show All link, you can see the entire list of excluded extensions.

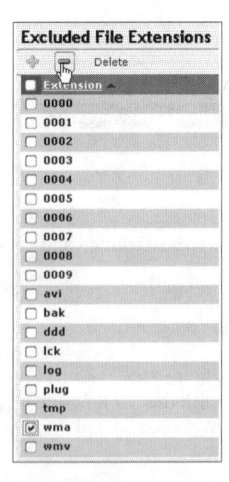

Figure 7.34 Select the extension you'd like to no longer exclude from versioning, and click the Delete icon.

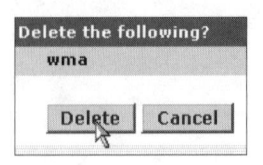

Figure 7.35 Click the Delete button to confirm removing the extension from exclusion.

Managing Version Control

Figure 7.36 At the top of the wizard, Sitespring identifies which of the wizard's six pages you're on. The current page is highlighted, while the other pages are dimmed.

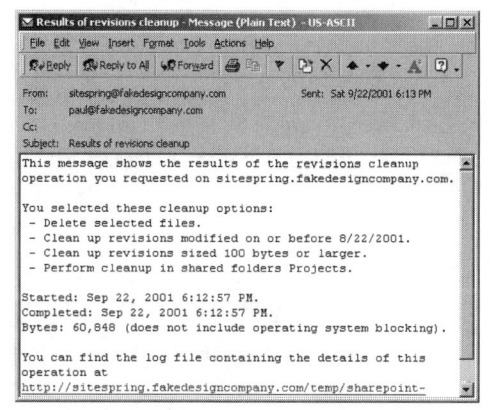

Figure 7.37 When the Revision Cleanup Wizard completes, it sends you an email with the results of the cleanup effort.

Using the Revision Cleanup Wizard

A Web team in high gear generates files quickly. A versioning system—generally a huge plus—can become a problem if versions pile up and you start to run out of disk space. Nothing's more annoying to end users than not having space to save their work, especially if the cause is simply an overabundance of file versions. Thankfully, the Revision Cleanup Wizard can help. With the wizard you can move or delete revisions from the _revisions folder according to criteria you specify.

You should also be aware that Sitespring can turn off versioning and notify the administrator when free disk space reaches critically low levels; see "To set critical notification email" in Chapter 8 for more information.

When you run the wizard, it walks you through six pages that ask you questions about what types of revisions you would like Sitespring to move or delete (**Figure 7.36**). On the first page, you select a basic strategy for the wizard. On the second, you set parameters based on the strategy you've chosen. The third page lets you choose whether to delete the files, move them to a new location, or preview the options you entered on the first two pages. When you preview the options, Sitespring sends you an email with a link to a page that lists the files that would be affected if you ran the wizard and chose to move or delete the files. Finally, on the last two pages you review and then confirm your settings. After confirming your settings, Sitespring runs the wizard in the background. When the wizard finishes, it sends you an email with the results (**Figure 7.37**).

USING THE REVISION CLEANUP WIZARD

163

To run the Revision Cleanup Wizard:

You can choose from three strategies when you run the Revision Cleanup Wizard. Each strategy identifies revisions to be moved or deleted based on criteria you set. All three strategies let you specify a file size minimum. If you enter a large minimum, the wizard handles only the largest files, which can take up a disproportionate amount of disk space. If there is a particular version of a file that you don't want the wizard to delete, you can mark that version as a milestone revision. The wizard will not delete or move milestone revisions. The three strategies are as follows.

Target revisions based on file size and disk space. This strategy removes revisions based on how many megabytes of space you'd like to reclaim; you also indicate a file size minimum that must be met for a file to be affected (**Figure 7.38**). This strategy works well if you know you need a certain amount of disk space to be freed. It also works well if you're moving the files to CD-Recordable, as you can specify the size of the CD-R disc as your target. This strategy doesn't work well, however, if you want to limit your search to files that are only older than a certain date; you might wind up moving or deleting relatively recent files.

Target revisions older than a specified date. This strategy removes revisions that have a modification date older than the date you specify and a file size larger than the amount you indicate (**Figure 7.39**). As projects move forward or reach their end, it's unlikely that you'll need to revert to earlier versions of files that have been finalized. This method works well if you don't need access to versions created before a certain date. It can also work well if you want to create a CD-R archive of the files from a certain period. However, it won't work well if most of your disk space is being consumed by more recent versions.

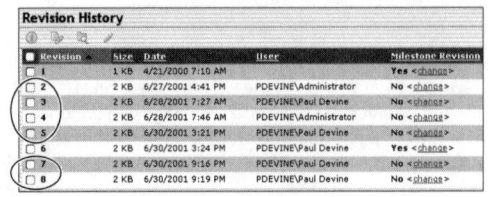

Figure 7.38 In this example of revision history for a file, each row represents a currently existing revision file. If, using the method Target Revisions Based on File Size, you specified that you'd like to delete a total of 20 MB with a minimum individual file size of 500 bytes to be eligible, six files of these files—Revisions 2, 3, 4, 5, 7, and 8—would be deleted. Revisions 1 and 6 would not be deleted because they are marked as milestone revisions.

Figure 7.39 This example uses the same revision history as in Figure 7.37, but applies the method Target Revisions Older Than a Specified Date. Here, any versions modified before June 29, 2001 would be deleted. Revisions 2, 3, and 4 would be deleted in this case, since the other revisions are either too recent or marked as milestones.

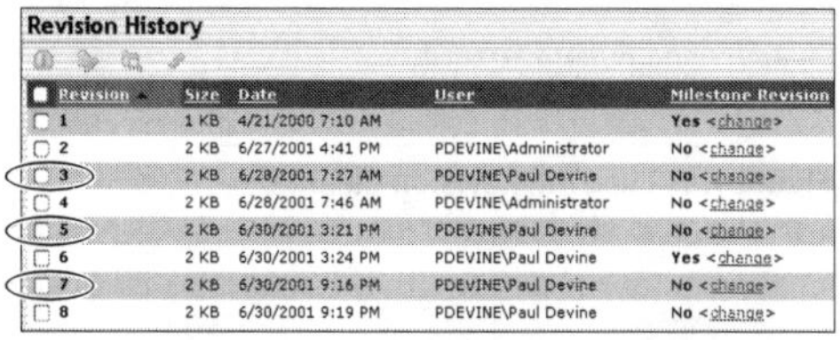

Managing Version Control

Figure 7.40 Using the same sample revision history as in Figures 7.37 and 7.38, this example applies the Target Having One Revision per Day method, with a specified date of July 30, 2001. Here, revisions 3, 5, and 7 would be deleted because they were created before the target date and they're not the final revision of the day. Revision 6 would not be deleted because it's a milestone version.

Target having one revision per day.
This strategy removes additional file versions when more than one revision exists for a given day; you also specify a minimum file size (**Figure 7.40**). Often a file changes repeatedly throughout the day. After several days, the many versions created on any one day usually aren't as important as how the file changes from day to day. With this strategy, the wizard looks at each file modified before a date you specify and removes all but the final revision for each day. Thus all intraday revisions are removed, leaving you with each day's final version of the file. If you modify many files repeatedly throughout the day over the course of several days, this strategy drastically reduces your number of revisions while still letting you see the file's chronological development day by day. Files that are modified after the date you specify are not affected. This strategy works well if you don't mind losing all interim revisions within a day. Think twice, however, if intraday changes are important to you or your team. Also, if you tend not to modify files many times in a single day, but do change them from day to day, this strategy may not significantly reduce your total number of revisions.

Now that you understand the Revision Cleanup Wizard's three basic strategies, find the one appropriate to your situation and follow the directions later in this chapter to run the wizard with that strategy. Remember that with any of the options you can always preview the files that would be affected by the settings, or move the files to a different location rather than delete them.

USING THE REVISION CLEANUP WIZARD

165

To target revisions based on file size and disk space:

1. Log into Sitespring as the admin user. Only somebody using the administrator account can run the Revision Cleanup Wizard.

2. If you're not already on the Administration page, click the Admin button in the main navigation bar to go there. The Administration page opens.

3. Click the Revision Cleanup Wizard link in the right column (**Figure 7.41**). The Revision Cleanup Wizard page opens. The first page explains how the wizard functions.

4. Click the Next button to advance to the following page. The Select Strategy page opens.

Figure 7.41 Click the Revision Cleanup Wizard link to start the process.

Megabytes	Kilobytes	Bytes
MB	KB	B
0.001	1	1024
0.005	5	5120
0.01	10	10240
0.10	100	102400
0.49	500	512000
0.98	1000	1024000
1	1024	1048576
5	5120	5242880

Figure 7.42 Use this chart to find the byte equivalent to enter for common kilobyte and megabyte amounts.

File Size and Disk Space Strategy Details

On the Configure Strategy page, you are presented with two fields (see step 6 in "To Target Revisions Based on File Size and Disk Space"). Here are the details about each one:

Number of megabytes of files you want to clean up—the number of megabytes you would like the wizard to free up on the drive. The wizard will delete the revisions whose combined file size totals an amount up to the figure you specify.

If you are planning to move these files to CD-R, you can enter the value of the disc you are using to create an archive that's the right size. Typical CDs hold 650 MB, while some extended formats hold 700 MB.

Minimum size of a file allowed for cleanup—the size in bytes of the smallest file you'd like to be cleaned up. Revision files smaller than the value you enter will not be deleted or moved. See the chart for an explanation of how bytes are related to a value with which you may be more familiar (**Figure 7.42**).

For example, if you want all files larger than 100 Kbytes to be affected, enter the number of bytes as "102400," which is 100 Kbytes. Don't use a comma in the number, as it won't be accepted.

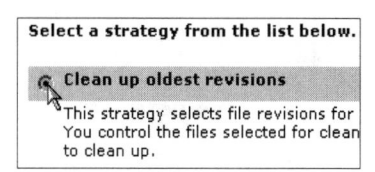

Figure 7.43 Select the first option, "Clean up oldest revisions."

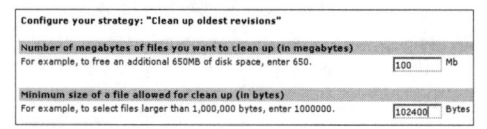

Figure 7.44 Enter the number of megabytes you'd like to free up, and the minimum file size of targeted files.

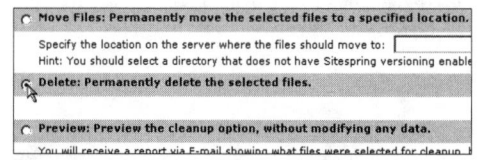

Figure 7.45 Choose whether you'd like to move the files, delete the files, or preview the list of affected files.

5. Select the first option, to clean up the oldest revisions (**Figure 7.43**), then click the Next button. The Configure Strategy page opens (**Figure 7.44**).

6. Enter the information in the two fields presented. For details on each field, see the sidebar "File Size and Disk Space Strategy Details."

7. Click the Next button. The Specify Options page opens (**Figure 7.45**). *Choose any of the following three options.*

   ▼ **Move Files: Permanently move the selected files to a specified location.** This option moves the revisions that meet your criteria to another directory on the server. If you choose this option, you need to provide the location to which the files will be moved. The location must be a directory on the Sitespring server that does not have versioning enabled. Start the location with a drive letter and include the full file path. For example, if you wanted to move them to the Old Revisions folder of the server's D drive, enter d:\Old Revisions.

   or

   ▼ **Delete: Permanently delete the selected files.** This option deletes the revisions that meet your criteria. Deleted revisions cannot be recovered, so it's a good idea to preview the settings before deleting the files.

   or

   ▼ **Preview: Preview the cleanup option, without modifying any data.** This option lets you preview the settings you've selected without touching any files. If you choose this option, Sitespring emails you a list of the files that would be affected if you chose the Move or Delete options.

continues on next page

Chapter 7

8. At the bottom of the page, select which shares should be cleaned up (**Figure 7.46**). The default is all shares selected. If you'd like to limit the wizard to a particular share, click the name of the share. To select more than one share at a time on a PC, hold down the Ctrl key as you click their names; on a Mac, hold down the Shift key.

9. Click the Next button. The Review page opens (**Figure 7.47**), summarizing the options you selected. If you want to change any of the settings, click the Previous button to back up to the appropriate page, change the value, and continue through the wizard again. If you want to cancel the wizard, click the Cancel button.

10. Click the Next button. The Confirm page opens and asks whether you are sure you want to proceed with the action (**Figure 7.48**). If you choose the preview option, this page does not appear. If this page does appear, do one of three things: Click the Next button to confirm proceeding with the wizard, click the Previous button to go back and change your settings, or click the Cancel button to abort the wizard.

    You have completed the Revision Cleanup Wizard. A page opens indicating that the cleanup process has begun (**Figure 7.49**). Depending on how many revisions are on the server, the wizard could take a long time to run. You will receive an email when the wizard completes. Click the Done button to return to the Administration page.

Figure 7.46 Choose which shares you'd like the wizard to target, or choose Select All.

Figure 7.47 The Review page summarizes the action about to be taken.

Figure 7.48 The Confirm page is your last opportunity to change your mind.

Managing Version Control

Figure 7.49 You're notified when the process has begun. If you're working with lots of revisions, the cleanup can take a while.

Figure 7.50 Choose the second option, "Clean up all revisions older than the number of days you specify."

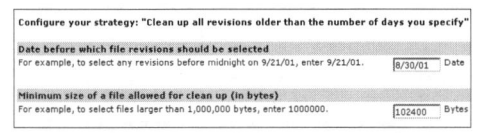

Figure 7.51 Enter your target date and minimum file size to configure the wizard to remove files modified before that date and larger than that size.

To target revisions older than a specified date:

1. Log into Sitespring as the admin user. Only somebody using the administrator account can run the Revision Cleanup Wizard.

2. If you're not already on the Administration page, click the Admin button in the main navigation bar to go there. The Administration page opens.

3. Click the Revision Cleanup Wizard link in the right column. The Revision Cleanup Wizard page opens. The first page explains how the wizard functions.

4. Click the Next button to advance to the following page. The Select Strategy page opens.

5. Select the second option, "Clean up all revisions older than the number of days you specify" (**Figure 7.50**). Then click the Next button. The Configure Strategy page opens.

6. Enter the information in the two fields presented (**Figure 7.51**). For information on those fields, see the sidebar "Date Configuration Strategy Details."

continues on next page

USING THE REVISION CLEANUP WIZARD

169

Chapter 7

7. Click the Next button. The Specify Options page opens (**Figure 7.52**). *Choose any of the following three options.*

   ▼ Move Files: Permanently move the selected files to a specified location.

   or

   ▼ Delete: Permanently delete the selected files.

   or

   ▼ Preview: Preview the cleanup option, without modifying any data.

8. At the bottom of the page, select which shares should be cleaned up (**Figure 7.53**). The default is all shares selected. If you'd like to limit the wizard to a particular share, click the name of the share. To select more than one share at a time on a PC, hold down the Ctrl key as you click their names; on a Mac, hold down the Shift key.

9. Click the Next button. The Review page opens (**Figure 7.54**). To change any of the settings, click the Previous button to back up to the appropriate page, change the value, and continue through the wizard again. If you want to cancel the wizard, click the Cancel button.

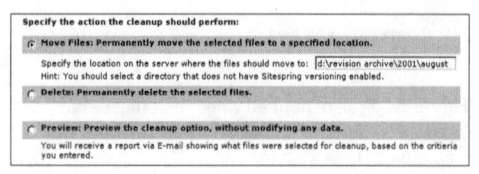

Figure 7.52 Choose whether you'd like to move the files, delete the files, or preview the files that will be affected.

Figure 7.53 Select which shares you'd like the wizard to target, or choose Select All.

Figure 7.54 The Review page summarizes your options for your review.

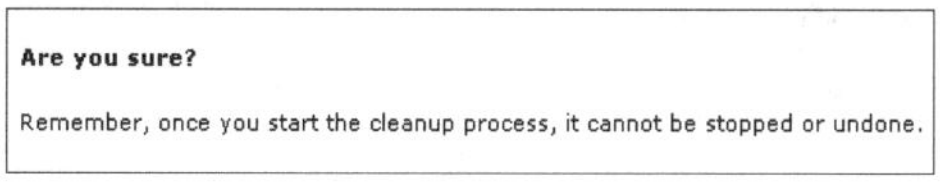

> **Are you sure?**
> Remember, once you start the cleanup process, it cannot be stopped or undone.

Figure 7.55 The Confirm page, which doesn't appear if you chose the preview option, is your last opportunity to change your mind.

> **The cleanup process has been started.**
> You will receive a notification upon completion.

Figure 7.56 You're notified when the cleanup process has started.

10. Click the Next button. The Confirm page opens and asks whether you are sure you want to proceed with the action (**Figure 7.55**). If you choose the preview option, this page does not appear. If this page does appear, do one of three things: Click the Next button to confirm proceeding with the wizard, click the Previous button to go back and change your settings, or click the Cancel button to abort the wizard.

You have completed the Revision Cleanup Wizard. A page opens indicating that the cleanup process has begun (**Figure 7.56**). Depending on how many revisions are on the server, the wizard could take a long time to run. You will receive an email when the wizard completes. Click the Done button to return to the Administration page.

Date Configuration Strategy Details

On the Configure Strategy page, you are presented with two fields (see step 6 in "To Target Revisions Older Than a Specified Date"). Here are the details about each one:

Date on or before which file revisions should be selected—the date on or before which revisions should be included. For example, if you enter 8/30/01, all files modified on or before August 30 are eligible for deletion. Files modified after that date are not affected. Because the way you enter date values in Sitespring is a configuration setting, you may need to format your date entry differently than what's shown here. The default date format is one or two digits each for the month and day, and two digits for the year, separated by forward slashes.

Minimum size of a file allowed for cleanup—the size, in bytes, of the smallest file you'd like included. Revision files smaller than the value you enter will not be deleted or moved. Entering a larger value here allows you to focus the wizard on the larger files, which take up more space per revision than smaller files do. Removing several large files can free more space than removing dozens of tiny ones. See the chart for an explanation of how bytes are related to a value with which you may be more familiar (see again Figure 7.43).

For example, if you want all files larger than 100 Kbytes to be affected, enter the number of bytes as "102400," which is 100 Kbytes. Don't use a comma in the number, as it won't be accepted.

Chapter 7

To target having one revision per day:

1. Log into Sitespring as the admin user. Only somebody using the administrator account can run the Revision Cleanup Wizard.

2. If you're not already on the Administration page, click the Admin button in the main navigation bar to go there. The Administration page opens.

3. Click the Revision Cleanup Wizard link in the right column. The Revision Cleanup Wizard page opens (**Figure 7.57**).

4. Click the Next button to advance to the following page. The Select Strategy page opens.

5. Select the third option, "Clean up all but the final revision for days with more than one file revision" (**Figure 7.58**). Then click the Next button.

6. The Configure Strategy page opens. Enter the information in the two fields presented (**Figure 7.59**). For details on those fields, see the sidebar "One Revision Per Day Strategy Details."

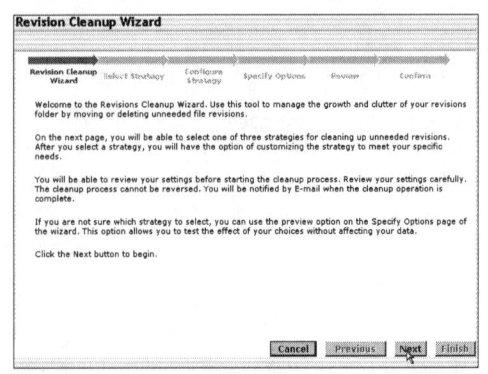

Figure 7.57 The first page of the wizard tells you how it works. Click the Next button to advance past the instructions.

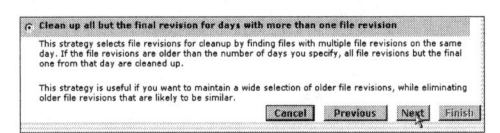

Figure 7.58 Choose the third option, "Clean up all but the final revision for days with more than one file revision," then click the Next button.

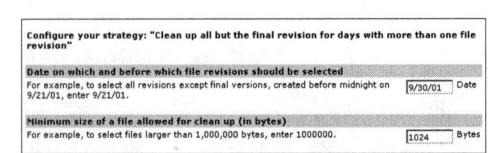

Figure 7.59 The wizard removes all files—except the final version—with modification dates on and before the date you enter here. Only files larger than the minimum you enter will be targeted.

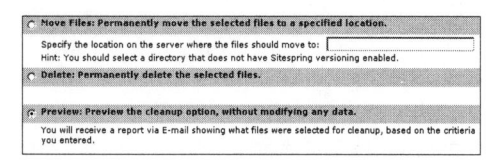

Figure 7.60 Choose whether you'd like to move the files, delete the files, or preview the files that will be affected.

Figure 7.61 Select the shares you'd like the wizard to include.

Figure 7.62 The Review page summarizes your selected options. Verify that the wizard is targeting the correct files.

7. Click the Next button. The Specify Options page opens (**Figure 7.60**). *Choose any of the following three options.*

   ▼ Move Files: Permanently move the selected files to a specified location.

   or

   ▼ Delete: Permanently delete the selected files.

   or

   ▼ Preview: Preview the cleanup option, without modifying any data.

8. At the bottom of the page, select which shares should be cleaned up (**Figure 7.61**). The default is all shares selected. If you'd like to limit the wizard to a particular share, click the name of the share. To select more than one share at a time on a PC, hold down the Ctrl key as you click their names; on a Mac, hold down the Shift key.

9. Click the Next button. The Review page opens (**Figure 7.62**). Read through the summary of the options you selected to verify that when the wizard runs, it will do what you think it will. If you want to change any of the settings, click the Previous button to back up to the appropriate page, change the value, and continue through the wizard again. If you want to cancel the wizard, click the Cancel button.

10. Click the Next button. The Confirm page opens and asks whether you are sure you want to proceed with the action (**Figure 7.63**). If you choose the preview option, this page does not appear. If this page does appear, do one of three things: Click the Next button to confirm proceeding with the wizard, click the Previous button to go back and change your settings, or click the Cancel button to abort the wizard.

You have completed the Revision Cleanup Wizard. A page opens indicating that the cleanup process has begun (**Figure 7.64**). Depending on how many revisions are on the server, the wizard could take a long time to run. You will receive an email when the wizard has completed the cleanup. Click the Done button to return to the Administration page.

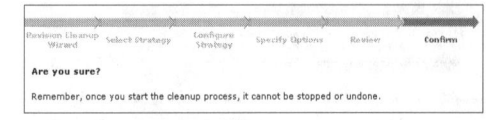

Figure 7.63 The Confirm page asks whether you'd like to proceed. This is your last chance to change your mind.

Figure 7.64 You're notified when the cleanup process has begun. You will receive an email when it is done.

One Revision Per Day Strategy Details

On the Configure Strategy page, you are presented with two fields (see step 6 in "To target having one revision per day"). Here are the details about each one:

Date on which and before which file revisions should be selected—the date on which and before which revisions should be pared down to one per day and after which the revisions should be left alone. The date is inclusive, meaning that if you enter 9/21/01, the wizard leaves only one revision per file for September 21 and all the days prior to it. Because the way you enter date values in Sitespring is a configuration setting, you may need to format your date entry differently than what's shown here. The default date format is one or two digits each for month and day, and two digits for the year, separated by forward slashes.

Minimum size of a file allowed for cleanup—the size, in bytes, of the smallest file you'd like included. Revision files smaller than the value you enter are not deleted or moved. Entering a larger value here lets the wizard focus on the larger files, which take up more space per revision than smaller files do. Removing several large files can free more space than removing dozens of tiny ones. See Figure 7.43 for an explanation of how bytes are related to a value with which you may be more familiar. Don't use a comma in the number, as it won't be accepted.

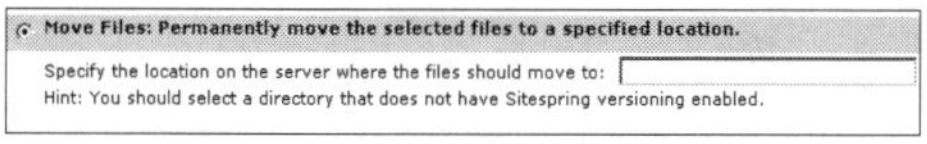

Figure 7.65 You can choose to move files rather than to delete them. This option exists with all three basic wizard strategies.

To move revisions to another drive:

When you run the Revision Cleanup Wizard, you can choose to move the files to a specified location rather than to delete them, regardless of what criteria you use to target revisions (**Figure 7.65**). This allows you to move old revisions to a spare drive, CD-R, or tape backup without having to get rid of them entirely. To do this, follow any of the directions in "To target revisions based on file size and disk space," "To target revisions older than a specified date," or "To target having one revision per day" (all earlier in this chapter), as appropriate to your situation. Also, when you're on the Specify Options page, be sure to indicate that you want to move the files rather than to delete them. If you're moving files to CD-R or another file system that has a limited size, you may find that the first method, "To target revisions based on file size and disk space," is the best approach. It lets you specify how many megabytes of data you'd like to back up, so you can target the right amount of data to fit your destination.

To preview the Revision Cleanup Wizard's effects:

When you run the Revision Cleanup Wizard, you can choose to preview the files that would be affected by running the wizard with the specified options, rather than delete or move them right away. You can do this regardless of what method you use to specify the revisions to be targeted for cleanup (**Figure 7.66**). You should definitely use the preview option before you choose to permanently delete files. Sitespring emails you a link to a page that lists the files that would be affected if you ran the wizard (**Figure 7.67**). To preview files, follow the directions "To target revisions based on file size and disk space," "To target revisions older than a specified date," or "To target having one revision per day" as appropriate to your situation, and be sure to choose the option to preview the cleanup option, rather than to move or delete the files.

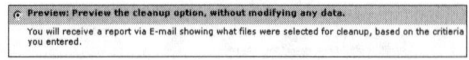

Figure 7.66 Before you run the wizard and delete files permanently, it's always a good idea to preview which files will be affected. Do this by selecting the Preview option when the wizard asks what you'd like it to do with the files.

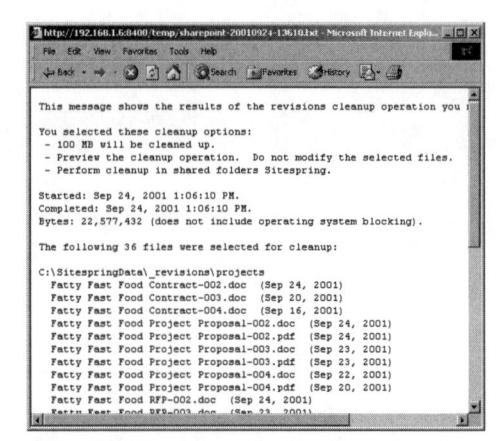

Figure 7.67 When you preview the effects of running the Revision Cleanup Wizard, Sitespring emails you a link to a page, shown here, that lists the files that would be affected.

Administering Sitespring

Sitespring has a number of tasks and configuration options that the administrator and users with project manager permissions can perform. This chapter explains the more technical and less frequently used of those tasks. If you're looking for more common administrative tasks related to everyday operations, check the chapter pertaining to the item you'd like to administer. (For example, Chapter 4, "Folders and Files," explains how to add a folder to a project and how to set up Sitespring Helper.)

In this chapter you'll learn how the administrator and users with project manager permissions can update project and task settings, and how the administrator can edit the server setup, edit the mail server configuration, update project-site settings, manage licenses, configure the log, and, finally, view detailed system information.

Updating Project and Task Settings

Sitespring users regularly update a task's status field to indicate whether the task has been completed, hasn't started, or is in some other state. When setting a task's status, the user chooses from a pull-down menu of choices (**Figure 8.1**). The system has ten predefined status values. You can add choices to the pull-down menu by creating more status values. You cannot remove or change the ten predefined choices, as the system requires them. The system-supplied values are Approved, Approved with Changes, No Approval Needed, Needs Approval, Not Approved, Client Completed, Completed, Not Started, Open, and Suspended. Some of the predefined values, such as Approved with Changes, are used for approval tracking when client users are interacting with documents; those values are not presented as choices when working with normal tasks. Status values appear to normal users and client users when they're updating a task's status. The list of task status choices includes the ones clients see when they're approving a document. When you add a status value to the system, it appears in the task status pull-down menu but not the approval status pull-down menu.

Each status value is associated with a color. When a task's status is displayed, a small circle in the corresponding color precedes the text explanation (**Figure 8.2**). The color values let users easily scan the status values in task lists, as most people can more quickly pick out colors than words. When you add a new status choice, you must assign it a color. It's a good idea to assign colors that make sense in relation to the default choices. For example, since both the Client Completed and Completed values are a shade of blue, if you were to add a Contractor Completed

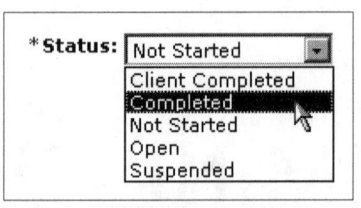

Figure 8.1 When setting a task's status, you choose the value from a pull-down list of choices, to which you can add custom menu items.

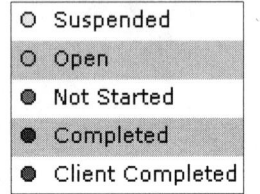

Figure 8.2 The circle to the left of the task status text is a status-associated color that lets you easily identify status while scanning the list.

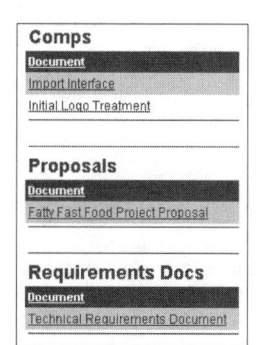

Figure 8.3 Documents published to project sites are organized into document categories.

value, another shade of blue would let you scan the task lists and more easily cull similar items.

In addition to status values and their colors, you can configure one setting for all tasks that identifies a task that's considered almost due. Almost-due tasks display differently in task modules and trigger email notices to users who choose to receive them.

Finally, documents that are published to client project sites are organized into document categories (**Figure 8.3**). This lets users and client users locate the documents more easily, as they are grouped into similar sets. The default document categories are Comps, Diagrams, Proposals, Requirements Docs, and Specifications. Unlike the default status values, which you cannot delete or change, you can delete and modify the default document categories. You can also add new ones. On a project site, a document category appears only if documents have been published in that category.

Unlike with the rest of the administrative tasks in this chapter, you don't need to log in as the administrator to update task status values, due date settings, or document categories. As long as you have project manager permissions, you can edit these values.

Chapter 8

To change task status values:

1. If you're not already on the Administration page, click the Admin button in the main navigation bar to go there. The Administration page opens.

2. Click the Project and Task Settings link at the top of the left-hand column. The Project and Task Settings page opens, and the Status Values module appears.

3. If the Status Values module isn't expanded, open it by clicking the expand icon ▶. The Status Values module opens.

4. To add, edit, or delete a status value, *do any of the following:*

   ▼ To add a status value, click the Add icon ✚ at the top of the Status Values module. The Add Status Value page opens. Enter a name for the status in the Name field. Select a color to correspond with the status by clicking on one of the colors listed in the Select Color field. The Color Selected area displays the color you choose (**Figure 8.4**). Click the Save button to save the new status, or click a navigation link to abort it.

   ▼ To edit a status value, click the check box next to the status value you'd like to edit in the Status Values module. You cannot edit the system-default status values. Click the Edit icon ✏ (**Figure 8.5**). The Edit Status Value page opens. Select a color to correspond with the status by clicking on one of the colors listed in the Select Color field. The Color Selected area displays the color you choose. Click the Save button to save your changes (**Figure 8.6**), or click a navigation link to disregard them.

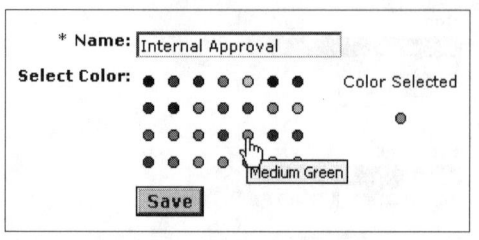

Figure 8.4 Click a color to correspond with the status, and the Color Selected value changes.

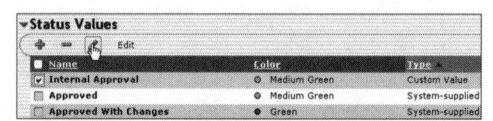

Figure 8.5 Select the status value you'd like to edit. You cannot edit system-supplied values.

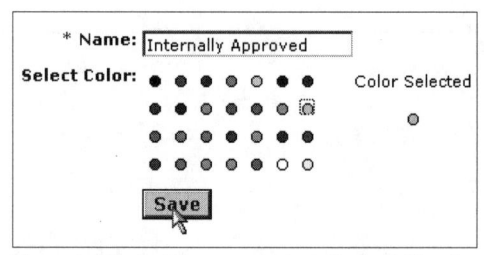

Figure 8.6 Update the status value's Name field and choose a new color for the status, then click the Save button.

Administering Sitespring

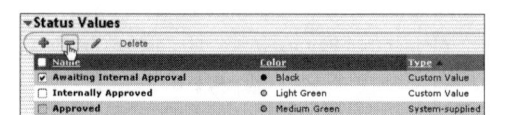

Figure 8.7 Delete a status value by selecting it and clicking the Delete icon.

Figure 8.8 Tasks that are almost due display in italics.

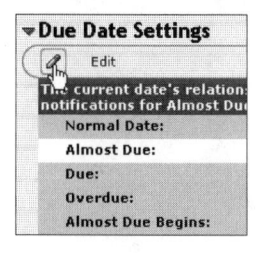

Figure 8.9 Click the Edit icon to change the number of days within which a task is considered almost due.

▼ To delete a status value, click the check box next to the status value you'd like to delete in the Status Values module. You cannot delete the system-default status values. Click the Delete icon (**Figure 8.7**). The Delete Status Values page opens. Click the Delete button to confirm the deletion, or click the Cancel button to abort it.

To change due-date settings:

1. If you're not already on the Administration page, click the Admin button in the main navigation bar to go there. The Administration page opens.

2. Click the Project and Task Settings link at the top of the left-hand column. The Project and Task Settings page opens.

    The Due Date Settings module (**Figure 8.8**) displays the format in which Normal, Almost Due, Due, and Overdue dates display; the Almost Due Begins field shows the number of days before a task's due date that a task will be considered almost due.

3. To update the Almost Due Begins field, click the Edit icon (**Figure 8.9**).

4. In the Almost Due Begins field, enter the number of days within which a task will be considered almost due. For example, if you'd like a task to be considered almost due a week before its actual due date, enter 7.

    If your team tends to have a greater number of long tasks that require several days to complete, enter a larger value, such as a week. If your team tends to have a greater number of short tasks that turn around quickly, enter a smaller value, like a day or two. Almost-due tasks are listed in modules more visibly than regular tasks are; you want to call attention only to the tasks that are starting to be in danger of missing their deadline.

continues on next page

Chapter 8

5. Click the Save button to accept your new value (**Figure 8.10**), or click any navigation link to abandon it. The Project and Task Settings page opens with a green success notice at the top and an updated Almost Due Begins value.

To change document categories:

1. If you're not already on the Administration page, click the Admin button in the main navigation bar to go there. The Administration page opens.

2. Click the Project and Task Settings link at the top of the left-hand column. The Project and Task Settings page opens, and the Document Categories module appears.

   If the Document Categories module is closed, expand it by clicking the expand icon ▶. The Document Categories module opens.

3. To add, edit, or delete a document category, *do any of the following:*

   ▼ To add a document category, click the Add icon ✚ at the top of the Document Categories module. The Add Document Category page opens. Enter a name in the Category field. If you'd like, enter a description for the document category in the description field. Click the Save button to save the new document category (**Figure 8.11**), or click a navigation link to abandon it.

Figure 8.10 Enter the new Almost Due Begins value and click the Save button.

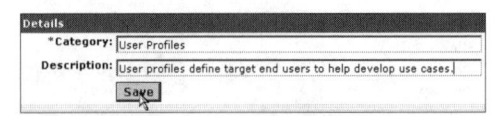

Figure 8.11 To name the document category, enter a name in the Category field; then enter a description (optional) and click the Save button.

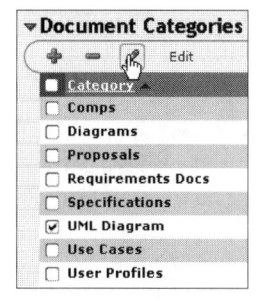

Figure 8.12 Select the document category you'd like to edit, then click the Edit icon.

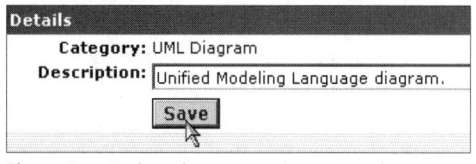

Figure 8.13 Update the category's name and description, then click the Save button.

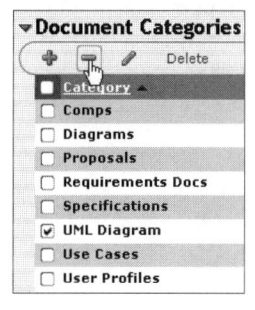

Figure 8.14 Delete a document category by selecting a category and clicking the Delete icon. You cannot delete system-defined categories.

▼ To edit a document category, click the check box next to the category you'd like to edit. You may edit the system-default document categories, but you can change only their Description field, not their name. Click the Edit icon (**Figure 8.12**). The Edit Document Category page opens. Update the name of the category in the Category field and information about the category in the Description field. Click the Save button to keep your changes (**Figure 8.13**), or click a navigation link to disregard them.

▼ To delete a document category, click the check box next to the category you'd like to get rid of. You cannot delete the system-defined document categories. Unlike the Status Values module, which identifies the values that are system-defined, the Document Categories module does not indicate those categories. The system-defined values are Comps, Diagrams, Proposals, Requirements Docs, and Specifications. Click the Delete icon (**Figure 8.14**) to delete the selected categories. The Project and Task Settings page reloads with a green success notice at the top indicating the category has been deleted.

Editing the Server Setup

For Sitespring to work correctly, you must configure values related to the server's host name or IP address and the application port number. Computers on the Internet locate each other via each machine's IP address, a unique string of 12 digits that you can think of as the computer's street address on the Internet. Since people don't like having to remember or type such a long number, the Domain Name System (DNS) relates a computer's IP address to a more human-friendly host name (**Figure 8.15**). A fully qualified host name—one that is valid on the Internet—must include the name of the machine and the domain in which it resides. For example, www.macromedia.com is the fully qualified host name of the www host in the macromedia.com domain (**Figure 8.16**). It's beyond the scope of this chapter to explain the DNS system; there are entire books dedicated to it. The bottom line is you'll need an assigned static IP address for the Sitespring server's machine or a DNS name for the machine that will work with both normal and client users' machines.

While an IP address identifies a specific computer, a port number identifies a particular application running on a computer. It's the combination of an IP address and port number that allows your Web browser to communicate with Sitespring. If you do not specify a particular port as part of an address, your Web browser assumes port 80, the default port for the HTTP protocol that Web servers use. You can, however, assign a different value. If you do so, the port number you enter will appear after the host name in the URL. For example, the URL for a Web server with a host name of www.macromedia.com running on port 80 would be `http://www.macromedia.com/`, while the URL for a Web server running on port 8088 on the same machine would be `http://www.macromedia.com:8088/`.

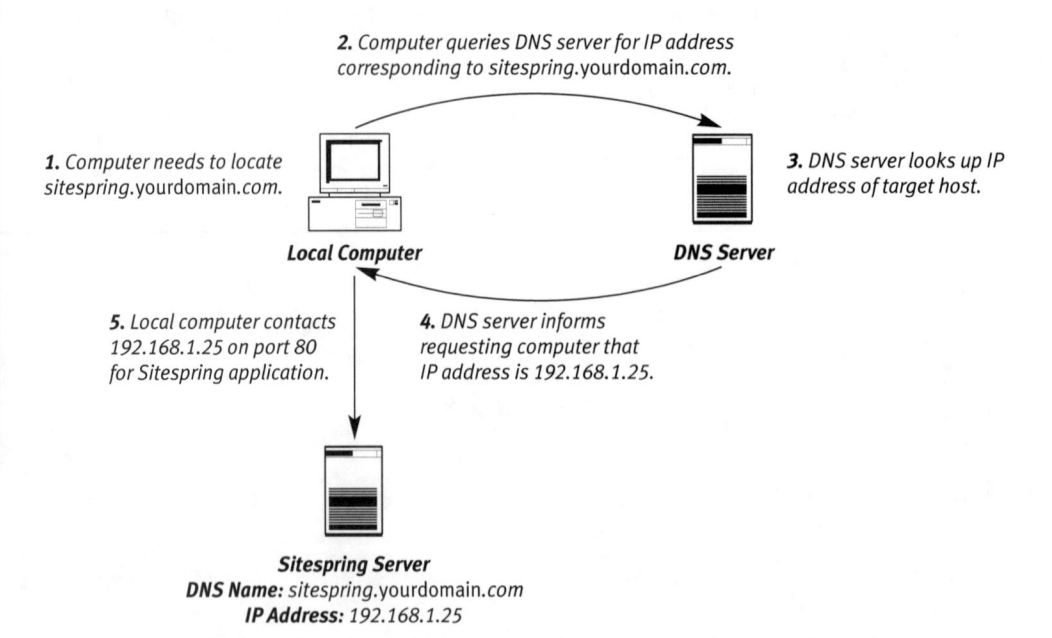

2. Computer queries DNS server for IP address corresponding to sitespring.yourdomain.com.

1. Computer needs to locate sitespring.yourdomain.com.

Local Computer

3. DNS server looks up IP address of target host.

DNS Server

5. Local computer contacts 192.168.1.25 on port 80 for Sitespring application.

4. DNS server informs requesting computer that IP address is 192.168.1.25.

Sitespring Server
DNS Name: sitespring.yourdomain.com
IP Address: 192.168.1.25

Figure 8.15 Each time your computer accesses a machine over the Internet, the IP address is determined.

Fully Qualified Host Name

www.macromedia.com

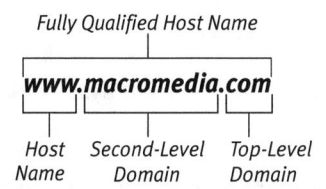

Host Name | Second-Level Domain | Top-Level Domain

Figure 8.16 A fully qualified domain name has at least three elements. Some machine names have more than two domain levels above them; for example, at universities you often see domains like machinegroup.departmentname.universityname.edu.

Port Number	Protocol Name
21	FTP
23	Telnet
25	SMTP
53	DNS
79	Finger
80	HTTP
110	POP3
119	NNTP
139	NetBios
143	IMAP
161	SNMP
162	SNMP Trap
443	Secure HTTP

Figure 8.17 Here's a list of default port numbers for commonly used applications.

Understand that different applications and communication protocols have default port values, like 21 for the File Transfer Protocol (FTP) or 25 for the Simple Mail Transfer Protocol (SMTP) (**Figure 8.17**). You cannot assign a port value that's already in use by another application or server process on your system. Common alternate values for Web servers are 8088 or 8080, after the numbers for early Intel processors. When installed, Sitespring attempts to use port 80 by default, if it's not already in use by another Web server on your machine.

You can also specify the time and date formats the server uses and the time zone in which the server resides. Setting these values lets you use the appropriate date format for your region. Americans tend to put the month before the day, while Europeans put the day before the month. You set the server's time zone so that the server knows the local time and can thus send out timely reminder notices.

To set the server host name or IP address:

1. Log into Sitespring as the admin user. Only somebody using the administrator account can edit the server host name.

2. If you're not already on the Administration page, click the Admin button in the main navigation bar to go there. The Administration page opens.

3. Click the System Configuration link in the middle of the left-hand column. The System Configuration page opens.

    The current server host name or IP address is listed at the top of the page in the Server Configuration panel, in the Server Host Name or IP field.

continues on next page

Chapter 8

4. To change the server host name, click the Edit icon ✎ at the top of the page (**Figure 8.18**). The Edit System Configuration page opens.

5. In the Server Configuration panel at the top of the page, update the Server Host Name or IP field. Enter either a fully qualified host name for your server or an assigned static IP address that client and normal users' systems will be able to recognize (**Figure 8.19**).

   If you do not know what value to enter here, speak with your network administrator or your ISP. Entering the wrong value could prevent users from operating Sitespring or cause the File Explorer or linked files or folders to function incorrectly.

6. To save your new host name or IP address, click the Save button at the bottom of the page; or click any navigation link to abandon it.

   The System Configuration page loads with a green success notice at the top.

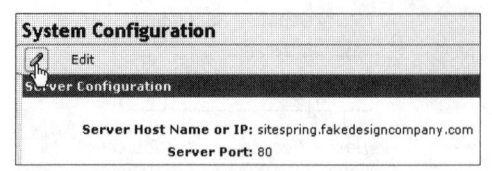

Figure 8.18 The server host name or IP address is listed at the top of the Server Configuration panel. Click the Edit button to change it.

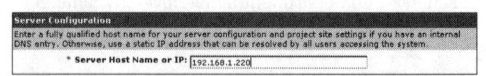

Figure 8.19 Enter either a fully qualified domain name or a static IP address for the server.

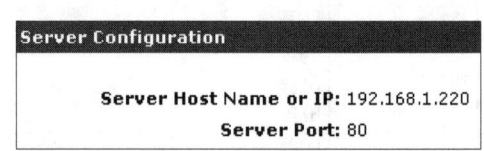

Figure 8.20 The Server Port field lists the current port used by Sitespring.

To set the Web server port:

1. Log into Sitespring as the admin user. Only somebody using the administrator account can edit the Web server port.

2. If you're not already on the Administration page, click the Admin button in the main navigation bar to go there. The Administration page opens.

3. Click the System Configuration link in the middle of the left-hand column. The System Configuration page opens.

   The current server port number is listed at the top of the page in the Server Configuration panel, in the Server Port field (**Figure 8.20**).

4. To change the server port number, click the Edit icon ✎ at the top of the page. The Edit System Configuration page opens.

Figure 8.21 In the Server Port field, enter the port number you'd like Sitespring to use.

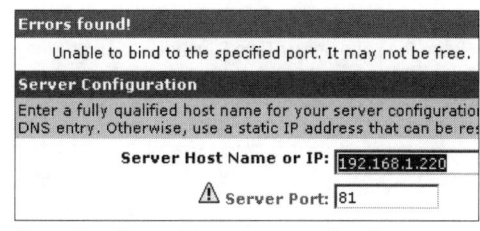

Figure 8.22 If you choose a port number that's already in use, you'll see this error message. Simply enter a different value.

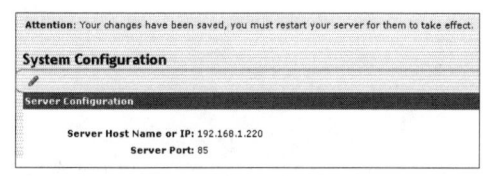

Figure 8.23 When your change has been successfully recorded, you'll see this yellow warning message indicating the change will take effect only after the system is restarted.

5. In the Server Configuration panel at the top of the page, update the Server Port field. Enter the port number you would like to use for the Web server that runs the main Sitespring application (**Figure 8.21**). Do not confuse this with the port for the project site's Web server. To set that value, see "To Change the Project-Site Port Number" later in this chapter.

6. To save your new port number, click the Save button at the bottom of the page; or click any navigation link to abandon it.

If the port you choose is in use by another application, you'll see a red error notice at the top of the page (**Figure 8.22**). Simply enter a different port number and click the Save button again. If the port you enter is available, you'll see a yellow warning message indicating that the port change will take effect only after the server is restarted (**Figure 8.23**).

After you restart the server, you'll need to include the server port you just entered in the URL you use to access Sitespring. The port number should follow a colon after the fully qualified host name.

✔ **Tip**

- If you successfully change the server port for Sitespring and—after your new Server Port value is changed but before you restart—try to change the port number back, you won't be able to. Sitespring checks to see whether the port is in use by another application, and it finds one—itself—using the port. You'll receive the same error message you would if another application were using the port.

  To get around this, simply restart the server, log into Sitespring using the port number you saved but want to change, update the port number back to the original value, and restart the server again.

187

Chapter 8

To set the server time format and time zone:

1. Log into Sitespring as the admin user. Only somebody using the administrator account can set the server time format and time zone.

2. If you're not already on the Administration page, click the Admin button in the main navigation bar to go there. The Administration page opens.

3. Click the System Configuration link in the middle of the left-hand column.
   The System Configuration page opens.
   The Server Configuration panel lists both the Server Time Format and Server Time Zone fields, among others (**Figure 8.24**).

4. To change either the server's time format or time zone, click the Edit icon ✎ at the top of the page. The Edit System Configuration page opens.

5. In the Server Configuration panel at the top of the page, choose a new value for the Server Time Format and Server Time Zone fields. For more information about each field, see the sidebar "Server Details: Time Format and Time Zone."

6. To save the new values, click the Save button at the bottom of the page; or click any navigation link to abandon them.
   The System Configuration page loads with a green success notice at the top.

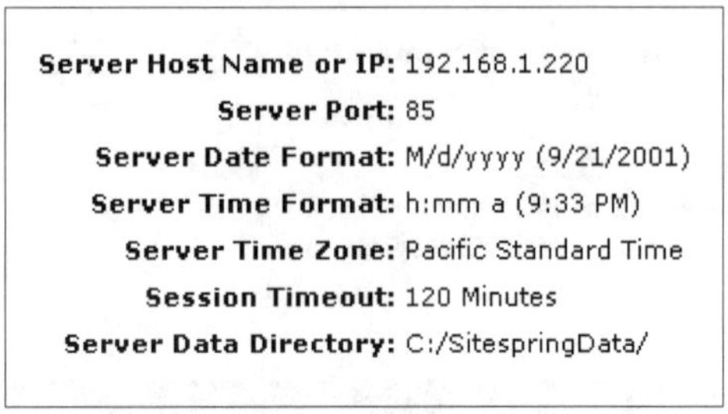

```
Server Host Name or IP: 192.168.1.220
         Server Port: 85
  Server Date Format: M/d/yyyy (9/21/2001)
  Server Time Format: h:mm a (9:33 PM)
    Server Time Zone: Pacific Standard Time
     Session Timeout: 120 Minutes
Server Data Directory: C:/SitespringData/
```

Figure 8.24 The Server Time Format and Server Time Zone fields are among those displayed in the Server Configuration panel.

Administering Sitespring

To set the server date format:

1. Log into Sitespring as the admin user. Only somebody using the administrator account can edit the server date format.

2. If you're not already on the Administration page, click the Admin button in the main navigation bar to go there. The Administration page opens.

continues on next page

Server Details: Time Format and Time Zone

Here are the choices you have when you're configuring the time on your server. (See step 6 in "To set the server time format and time zone.")

Server Time Format—Select a format for the way time will be displayed and recorded on the server (**Figure 8.25**). The pull-down menu lists four options:

h:mm a (9:33 PM)—A 12-hour format without a leading zero in the single-digit hours.

H:mm (21:33)—A 24-hour format without a leading zero in the single-digit hours.

hh:mm a (09:33 PM)—A 12-hour format with a leading zero in the single-digit hours.

HH:mm (21:33)—A 24-hour format with a leading zero in the single-digit hours.

Server Time Zone—Select the time zone in which the server resides from the pull-down menu (**Figure 8.26**). Values for U.S. time zones and those for a few other locations such as Japan Standard Time and Eastern European Standard Time are listed by their common names.

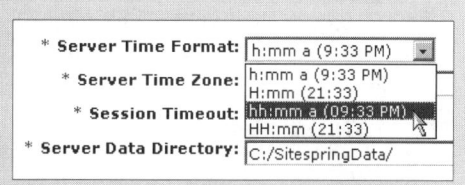

Figure 8.25 Select a display format for time values from the pull-down menu.

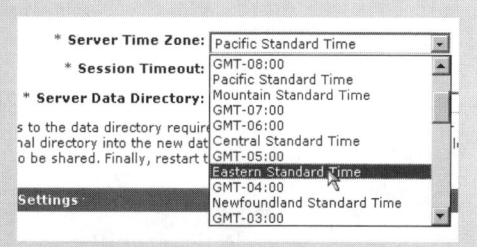

Figure 8.26 Select a time zone from the pull-down menu. Notice that uncommon values are defined in relation to Greenwich Mean Time.

In addition to the common names listed, you can choose to set the time in relation to Greenwich Mean Time (GMT), the standard by which time is defined worldwide. For example, if you were configuring a Sitespring server in Guam, which is 10 hours ahead of GMT, you'd select the entry GMT+10:00 in the pull-down menu. Likewise, if you were in Buenos Aires, which is three hours behind GMT, you'd select GMT–01:00. You'll notice that values listed by their common name can also be chosen by their GMT equivalent; there's no difference whether you choose Pacific Standard Time or GMT–08:00, as the times are the same.

EDITING THE SERVER SETUP

189

Chapter 8

3. Click the System Configuration link in the middle of the left-hand column. The System Configuration page opens.

   Among the fields listed in the Server Configuration panel is Server Date Format (**Figure 8.27**), which controls how dates are displayed and entered throughout the system.

4. To change the date format, click the Edit icon at the top of the page. The Edit System Configuration page opens.

5. In the Server Configuration panel at the top of the page, choose a new value for the Date Format field by selecting one from the pull-down menu (**Figure 8.28**). You can choose the from the following options (here, representing September 21, 2001):

   M/D/YYYY (9/21/2001)

   M/D/YY (9/21/01)

   MM/DD/YY (09/21/01)

   MM/DD/YYYY (09/21/2001)

   YY/MM/DD (01/09/21)

   YYYY-MM-DD (2001-09-21)

   DD/MM/YY (21/09/01)

   DD-MMM-YY (21-SEP-01)

   DD-MMM-YYYY (21-SEP-2001)

   YY/DD/MM (01/21/09)

6. To save your new selection, click the Save button at the bottom of the page; or click any navigation link to abandon it.

   The System Configuration page loads with a green success notice at the top.

Server Host Name or IP: 192.168.1.220
Server Port: 85
Server Date Format: M/d/yyyy (9/21/2001)
Server Time Format: h:mm a (9:33 PM)
Server Time Zone: Pacific Standard Time
Session Timeout: 120 Minutes
Server Data Directory: C:/SitespringData/

Figure 8.27 The Server Date Format field shown here determines how dates appear and how they are recorded throughout the system.

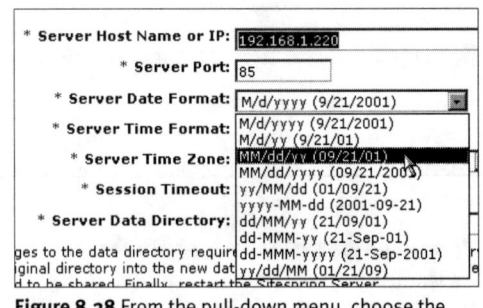

Figure 8.28 From the pull-down menu, choose the format you'd like for the display and recording of dates.

Editing the Mail Server

Sitespring sends out automatic email notices to users when significant events happen that relate to them, such as when a user is assigned a new task. In order for Sitespring to send these emails, you need to configure the application so it knows which email server and address to use.

Before editing this information, you need to know the host name or IP address of the outgoing SMTP server that Sitespring should use, the email address of the account from which Sitespring should send the email, the sender name that should be displayed, and, if needed, an account name and password to access the SMTP server.

It's a good idea to set up the mailbox used for this account so that if any end users unwittingly reply to a notice, their reply is returned with an explanation that the account is an outbound address only and that they should contact somebody in your organization for help. The other alternative is to forward the inbound mail for the account to the mailbox of another user who can respond accordingly.

You can also configure an email account to receive critical email notices when the Sitespring server's hard drives are reaching a dangerously full level.

Mail Server Setup

In the Notification Configuration panel on the Edit System Configuration page, update the values for mail-related fields (see step 6 in "To set the mail server"). Fields for required information are marked with an asterisk.

*Mail Server Host Name—Enter the name of the mail server. This will be the server that provides outbound SMTP service.

*Mail Server SMTP Port—Fill in the port number for the outbound mail server. The number for the standard port, which most users will need, is 25.

Mail Server SMTP User Name—If your outbound mail server requires you to furnish a user name, enter it here. While all inbound mail servers require a user name, many outbound mail servers do not. The account for this user name must have permission to send mail from the email address listed in the Notification E-mail field. For more information about that field, see "To set the notification and critical notification email" later in this chapter.

Mail Server SMTP Password—If your outbound mail server requires you to use a password, enter it here. While all inbound mail servers require a password, many outbound mail servers do not.

Chapter 8

To set the mail server:

1. Log into Sitespring as the admin user. Only somebody using the administrator account can set the mail server.

2. If you're not already on the Administration page, click the Admin button in the main navigation bar to go there. The Administration page opens.

3. Click the System Configuration link in the middle of the left-hand column. The System Configuration page opens.

   The Notification Configuration panel lists the current mail server's host name and port, and an optional user name and password to log into the mail server (**Figure 8.29**).

4. To change the mail server configuration, click the Edit icon at the top of the page. The Edit System Configuration page opens.

5. In the Notification Configuration panel toward the bottom of the page, update the values for mail-related fields (**Figure 8.30**). For more information about each field, see the sidebar "Mail Server Setup."

6. To save your new values, click the Save button at the bottom of the page; or click any navigation link to abandon them.

   The System Configuration page loads with a green success notice at the top and an updated list of mail server configuration values (**Figure 8.31**).

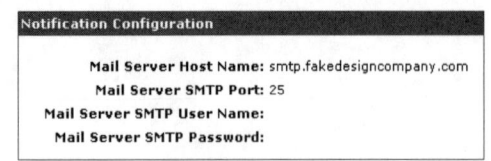

Figure 8.29 The Notification Configuration panel lists the fields related to the mail server that Sitespring uses for sending out email notifications.

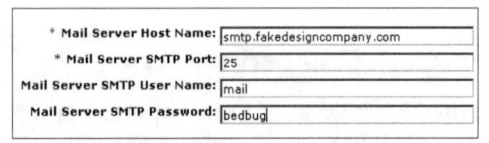

Figure 8.30 Update the mail server fields and click the Save button. The only optional fields are for the mail server SMTP user name and password.

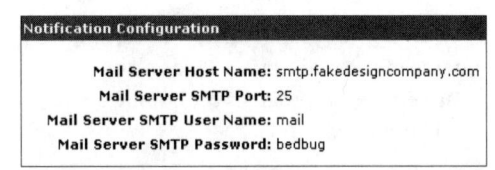

Figure 8.31 After you click the Save button, the mail server fields are updated.

Administering Sitespring

Figure 8.32 The Notification Configuration panel lists the email addresses the system is using.

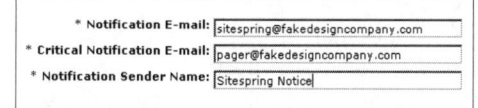

Figure 8.33 Update the notification-related email addresses.

Figure 8.34 The updated notification-related information is displayed.

To set the notification and critical notification email:

1. Log into Sitespring as the admin user. Only somebody using the administrator account can set the notification email addresses.

2. If you're not already on the Administration page, click the Admin button in the main navigation bar to go there. The Administration page opens.

3. Click the System Configuration link in the middle of the left-hand column. The System Configuration page opens.

   The Notification Configuration panel lists the current notification email address (**Figure 8.32**).

4. To change the notification email, click the Edit icon at the top of the page. The Edit System Configuration page opens.

5. In the Notification Configuration panel toward the bottom of the page, update the values for the email notification fields (**Figure 8.33**). For more information about each field, see the sidebar "Notification Email Setup."

6. To save your new values, click the Save button at the bottom of the page; or click any navigation link to abandon them.

   The System Configuration page loads with a green success notice at the top and updated email notification information (**Figure 8.34**).

EDITING THE MAIL SERVER

193

Notification Email Setup

Update the values for the email notification fields in the Notification Configuration panel toward the bottom of the Edit System Configuration page (see step 6 in "To set the notification and critical notification email"). Information for all of these fields is required.

Notification E-mail—Enter the email address of the mail account from which email notifications will be automatically sent to users. Sitespring sends email notices to inform users about pertinent events, such as being assigned a new task. All email notifications sent from the Sitespring server will have this address in the From field. Since notifications can be sent to client users as well as normal users, use an address that is appropriate for clients to see.

Filters, which people often use to sort and manage incoming email, are particularly useful for handling automatically generated email. For filters to be applied more effectively, you should set up a unique address, one that's not used by another person or application, for the mail coming from Sitespring. A good idea for an address is sitespring@[*your domain name*], or you might choose one that reflects the name of your department or organization.

Critical Notification E-mail—Enter an email address to which Sitespring will send a notice if the hard drive starts to run out of space. Since Sitespring's versioning system can use up most of a server's disk space, Sitespring has two threshold levels at which the application emails you notices indicating the server will soon run low or become critically low on free disk space. If the amount of available disk space reaches the critically low threshold, Sitespring's automatic versioning turns itself off to prevent the disk from filling. An email notice is sent to the specified address as the server approaches the low threshold, and then another is sent when it becomes critically low. Many administrators choose to have these critical notices directed to the email address for a pager, a cell phone, or another device that can notify the administrator immediately. Other, less critical system notices are sent to the email address of the administrator account.

Notification Sender Name—Type in the name that should appear as the sender of the automatically generated notices. The Notification Sender Name appears alongside the Notification E-mail address. Since client users and normal users alike will see this name listed in their in-box, type something that will allow users to quickly identify who the mail is from.

Administering Sitespring

Project-Site Settings

If you read "Editing the Server Setup" earlier in this chapter, you'll notice that the way project-site configuration works is very similar. That's no mere coincidence, as project sites are hosted by a second application server that's of the same type as the server that hosts the main Sitespring application.

One of Sitespring's most important features is that it lets you change the host name or IP address of the project-site server independently of the main Sitespring site. It's likely that the project sites will be exposed to the outside world, while the main Sitespring site will be restricted to your local area network. Being able to set a unique host name and port number for the project-site server gives you more flexibility in how you configure your server to interact with your LAN and the Internet.

You can also set a base URL for the project sites, which becomes part of the path to each project site.

Finally, you can set the maximum size, in megabytes, of files that can be uploaded through the project site. This limit prevents clients from trying to send you a large file that fills your server disk space. The limit by default is 10 MB.

To change the host name or IP address for the project site:

1. Log into Sitespring as the admin user. Only somebody using the administrator account can edit the project-site host name or IP address.

2. If you're not already on the Administration page, click the Admin button in the main navigation bar to go there. The Administration page opens.

continues on next page

195

Chapter 8

3. Click the System Configuration link in the middle of the left-hand column.
   The System Configuration page opens.
   The project-site host name or IP address is listed in the middle of the page in the Project Site Settings panel, in the Project Site Host Name or IP field (**Figure 8.35**).

4. To change the project-site host name or IP address, click the Edit icon at the top of the page. The Edit System Configuration page opens.

5. In the Project Site Settings panel at the top of the page, update the Project Site Host Name or IP field. Enter either a fully qualified host name for the project sites or an assigned static IP address that clients' and normal users' systems will be able to recognize (**Figure 8.36**).

   If you do not know what value to enter here, speak with your network administrator or ISP to find out what value you should enter. Entering the wrong value could prevent users from gaining access to the project sites.

6. To save the project site's host name or IP address, click the Save button at the bottom of the page; or click any navigation link to abandon it.

   The System Configuration page loads with a yellow warning message indicating that your changes will take effect only after the server is restarted (**Figure 8.37**). The Project Site Host Name or IP field lists the updated value.

Project Site Settings
Project Site Host Name or IP: www.fakedesigncompany.com
Project Site Port: 8500

Figure 8.35 The project-site host name or IP address is listed at the top of the Server Configuration panel. Click the Edit button to change it.

Project Site Settings
* Project Site Host Name or IP: 192.168.1.240
* Project Site Port: 8500

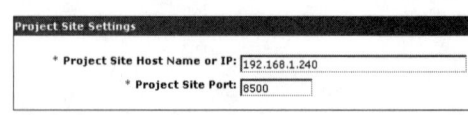

Figure 8.36 Enter either a fully qualified domain name or a static IP address for the server.

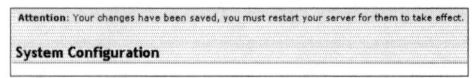

Attention: Your changes have been saved, you must restart your server for them to take effect.
System Configuration

Figure 8.37 A yellow warning message indicates that the new host name or IP address will take effect only after the server is restarted.

PROJECT-SITE SETTINGS

196

Administering Sitespring

Figure 8.38 The Project Site Port field lists the current port used by the project sites.

Figure 8.39 In the Project Site Port field, enter the port number you'd like Sitespring to use for project sites.

To change the project-site port number:

1. Log into Sitespring as the admin user. Only somebody using the administrator account can edit the project-site port.

2. If you're not already on the Administration page, click the Admin button in the main navigation bar to go there. The Administration page opens.

3. Click the System Configuration link in the middle of the left-hand column. The System Configuration page opens.

   The project-site server port is listed in the middle of the page in the Project Site Settings panel in the Project Site Port field (**Figure 8.38**).

4. To change the project-site port, click the Edit icon at the top of the page. The Edit System Configuration page opens.

5. In the Project Site Settings panel in the middle of the page, update the Project Site Port field. Enter the number of the port you would like to use for the Web server that runs the project sites (**Figure 8.39**). Do not confuse this with the port for the main Sitespring Web server; to set that value, see "To set the web server port" earlier in this chapter.

6. To save your new port number, click the Save button at the bottom of the page; or click any navigation link to abandon it.

continues on next page

PROJECT-SITE SETTINGS

197

Chapter 8

If the port you choose is in use by another application, you'll see a red error notice at the top of the page (**Figure 8.40**); simply enter a different port number and click the Save button again. If the port you enter is available, you'll see a yellow warning message indicating that the port change will take effect only after the server is restarted (**Figure 8.41**). Your new port value will be listed in the Project Site Port field.

After you restart the server, you'll need to include the port number in the URLs to each project site when you access the sites. The port number should follow a colon after the fully qualified host name. (For details on the format for project-site URLs, see step 6 in the section "To change the project-site base URL" later in this chapter.) Sitespring's references to the project sites inside the main Sitespring application will automatically update to point to the new port; any bookmarks or manually created links, however, will need to be updated.

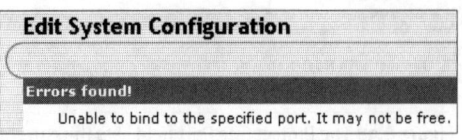

Figure 8.40 If you choose a port number that's already in use, you'll see this error message. Simply enter a different value.

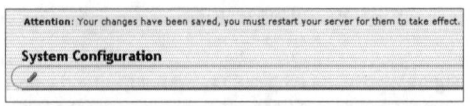

Figure 8.41 When your change has been recorded successfully, you'll see this yellow warning message indicating the change will take effect only after the system is restarted.

✔ Tip

- If you successfully change the project-site port for Sitespring and—after your new Project Site Port value is changed but before you restart—try to change the port number back, you won't be able to. Sitespring checks to see whether the port is in use by another application, and it finds the current project sites using the port. You'll receive the same error message you would if another application were using the port.

  To get around this, simply restart the server, log into Sitespring, and update the port number back to the original value, then restart the server again.

Administering Sitespring

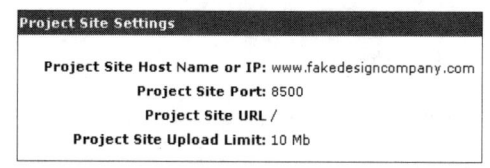

Figure 8.42 The Project Site URL field lists the base URL for the project sites.

Figure 8.43 Enter the new base URL you'd like to use for all your project sites.

Figure 8.44 Here are two example URLs for two project sites on the same server. Both contain the base URL of /projects.

To change the project-site base URL:

1. Log into Sitespring as the admin user. Only somebody using the administrator account can edit the project-site port.

2. If you're not already on the Administration page, click the Admin button in the main navigation bar to go there. The Administration page opens.

3. Click the System Configuration link in the middle of the left-hand column. The System Configuration page opens.

   The project-site base URL is listed in the middle of the page in the Project Site Settings panel in the Project Site URL field (**Figure 8.42**).

4. To change the project-site base URL, click the Edit icon at the top of the page. The Edit System Configuration page opens.

5. In the Project Site Settings panel in the middle of the page, update the Project Site URL field (**Figure 8.43**). The value in this field is used in the URL used to create the project sites' URLs.

   The format for the URLs is http://[Project Site Host Name or IP]:[Project Site Port number]/[Project Site URL]/[Name of Client Organization]/[Name of Individual Project]/ (**Figure 8.44**). As you can see, the project-site URL becomes the beginning of the path to the project sites after the port number. The project-site URL entered here is used only for the URL construction and does not relate to the path to the documents for the project sites on the server's hard drive.

   continues on next page

PROJECT-SITE SETTINGS

199

Chapter 8

6. To save your base URL, click the Save button at the bottom of the page; or click any navigation link to abandon it.

The System Configuration page loads with a yellow warning message at the top indicating that your changes will take effect only after the server is restarted (**Figure 8.45**). The Project Site Host Name or IP field lists the updated value.

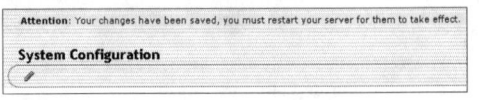

Figure 8.45 A warning message indicates that your changes will take effect only after the server is restarted.

To change the project-site file size upload limit:

1. Log into Sitespring as the admin user. Only somebody using the administrator account can edit the project-site file size upload limit.

2. If you're not already on the Administration page, click the Admin button in the main navigation bar to go there. The Administration page opens.

3. Click the System Configuration link in the middle of the left-hand column. The System Configuration page opens.

   The maximum upload file size is listed in the middle of the page in the Project Site Settings panel, in the Project Site Upload Limit field (**Figure 8.46**).

4. To change the maximum size of a file that can be uploaded through the project sites, click the Edit icon ✎ at the top of the page. The Edit System Configuration page opens.

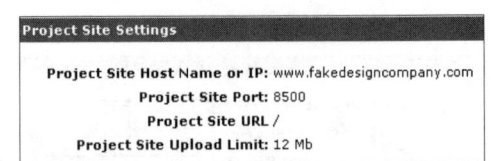

Figure 8.46 The Project Site Upload Limit field is listed in the Project Site Settings panel. Click the Edit button to change it.

Administering Sitespring

Figure 8.47 Enter the limit, in megabytes, within which a client's uploaded file size should be restricted.

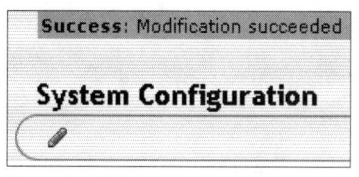

Figure 8.48 The green success message indicates your file size limit has been implemented.

5. In the Project Site Settings panel in the middle of the page, update the Project Site Upload Limit field. Enter the size, in megabytes, of the largest file a client can upload through a project site. Choose a value that seems appropriate based on available disk space and the size of files your clients normally send (**Figure 8.47**). Entering a value that's too big will let clients upload files that could use substantial disk space; a value that's too small could prevent clients from uploading files you may need.

6. To save the maximum upload file size you entered, click the Save button at the bottom of the page; or click any navigation link to abandon it.

   The System Configuration page loads with a green success notice (**Figure 8.48**), and the Project Site Upload Limit field lists the updated value.

PROJECT-SITE SETTINGS

201

Chapter 8

Managing Licenses

The basic Sitespring Server comes with a license that allows for three, five, or ten normal users and an unlimited number of client users. You cannot add more users than your license permits. If you'd like to add normal users, you need to buy additional licenses in one-user or five-user increments.

The directions below explain how to add licenses to your existing server after you have purchased them. Each license gives you the additional number of users granted by that license. You can also remove licenses you no longer need.

To add a license:

1. Log into Sitespring as the admin user.

2. If you're not already on the Administration page, click the Admin button in the main navigation bar to go there. The Administration page opens.

3. Click the License Management link toward the top of the left-hand column. The License Management page opens.

4. If the Additional User Licenses module isn't expanded, expand it by clicking the expand icon ▶. The Additional User Licenses module opens.

5. Click the Add icon ✚ (**Figure 8.49**). The Add License Key page opens. Type or paste the new license number into the License Key field (**Figure 8.50**).

6. Click the Save button to save your new license, or click any navigation link to cancel it.

7. The License Management page opens with an updated list of licenses. The number of users provided by each license is listed in the Additional User Licenses page (**Figure 8.51**).

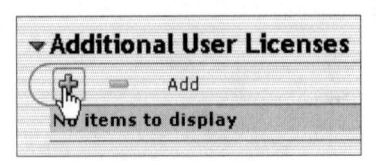

Figure 8.49 Click the Add icon to add a new user license.

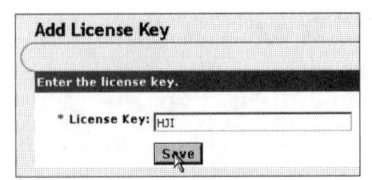

Figure 8.50 Enter the new license into the License Key field.

Figure 8.51 The License Management page displays the new license information.

✔ Tip

- License key and license number refer to the same thing: the 21-character sequence of letters and numbers that identify your license.

202

Administering Sitespring

Figure 8.52 Click the Delete icon to remove the selected licenses.

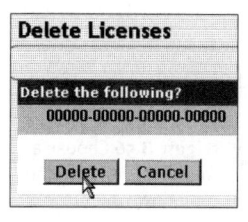

Figure 8.53 Click the Delete button to confirm the deletion.

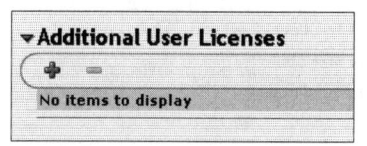

Figure 8.54 The License Management page reflects the deleted licenses.

To remove a license:

1. Log into Sitespring as the admin user. Only somebody using the administrator account can remove licenses.

2. If you're not already on the Administration page, click the Admin button in the main navigation bar to go there. The Administration page opens.

3. Click the License Management link toward the top of the left-hand column. The License Management page opens.

4. If the Additional User Licenses module isn't expanded, expand it by clicking the expand icon ▶. The Additional User Licenses module opens.

5. From the list of licenses in the Additional User Licenses list, locate the licenses you'd like to remove. Select them by clicking the check box to the left of each license number.

6. Click the Delete icon ▬ (**Figure 8.52**). The Delete Additional User Licenses confirmation page opens. Click the Delete button to confirm the deletion (**Figure 8.53**), or click the Cancel button to abort it.

    The License Management page opens with a green success notice at the top and an updated set of licenses (**Figure 8.54**).

✔ Tip

- Removing a license also removes the right to maintain the number of user accounts that license allows. If deleting a license will cause the number of current users to exceed the number of users allowed by your remaining licenses, Sitespring won't let you delete that license. You'll first need to delete the individual user accounts allowed by that license.

MANAGING LICENSES

203

Chapter 8

Configuring the Log

As Sitespring functions, it creates a log file that contains information about certain events. You can configure Sitespring to note in the log the level of detail that's useful to you. Sitespring can note nothing, note only errors, note errors and normal system operations, or note other diagnostic information as well as errors and normal operations. These log files can help advanced users diagnose system problems. For example, if you create your own project-site templates, you'll need access to the logs during the debugging process in order to read the error messages about the problems in your code. In this situation you'd want to set the log level to Debug.

In addition to the log level, you can specify the maximum file size to which a log can grow. Once the log has reached its maximum size, Sitespring starts a new one. You can also specify how many logs Sitespring keeps before it starts to delete the oldest ones. This prevents the log files from consuming too much disk space, which can occur when the settings are configured to track a large amount of information.

Finally, you can view the current log and look for errors or specific activities in the system.

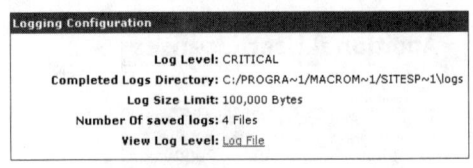

Figure 8.55 The current logging information is displayed in the Logging Configuration panel.

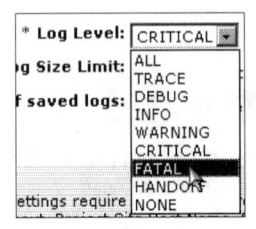

Figure 8.56 Choose a new log level from the pull-down menu.

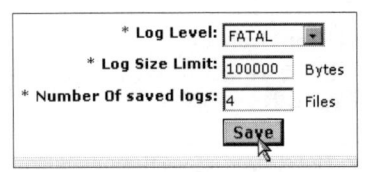

Figure 8.57 Click the Save button to save the log level.

To set the log level:

1. Log into Sitespring as the admin user. Only somebody using the administrator account can change the log level.

2. If you're not already on the Administration page, click the Admin button in the main navigation bar to go there. The Administration page opens.

3. Click the System Configuration link in the middle of the left-hand column. The System Configuration page opens.

4. In the Logging Configuration panel at the bottom of the page, the Log Level field displays the current log level (**Figure 8.55**).

204

Administering Sitespring

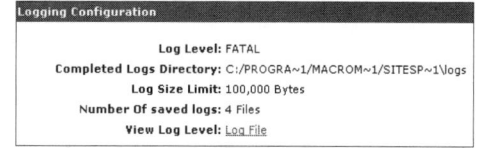

Figure 8.58 The new log level is displayed.

5. To change the log level, click the Edit icon ✎ at the top of the page. The Edit System Configuration page opens.

6. From the Log Level pull-down menu, choose a new log level (**Figure 8.56**). The levels are listed in decreasing level of detail. For information on what the log level includes, see the sidebar "Log Level Details."

7. To save your new log level, click the Save button at the bottom of the page (**Figure 8.57**); or click any navigation link to abandon it.

   The System Configuration page loads with a green success notice at the top and an updated log level listed (**Figure 8.58**).

Log Level Details

Here are the options Sitespring gives you when you're choosing a new log level on the Edit System Configuration page (see step 6 in "To set the log level").

All—All possible items (listed below) will be logged.

Trace—In addition to the items listed below, stack traces, which help identify programming errors, will also be included. Stack traces can add significantly to the size of a log entry, as each trace is usually many lines long.

Debug—In addition to the items listed below, information that's useful for debugging project-site templates will be included.

Info—In addition to the items listed below, informational messages will be included.

Warning—In addition to the items listed below, messages warning of possible problems will be included.

Critical—In addition to the information listed below, critical messages will be included. Critical messages are less serious than fatal messages, and include key system events like when the versioning system starts.

Fatal—In addition to the information listed below, fatal error messages will be included.

Handoff—A handoff log entry is made when a milestone is revised. For example, when a file is "handed off" from one team member to the next, the milestone should be updated and a handoff log entry would be made.

None—Nothing will be logged at all.

To set the log size limit:

1. Log into Sitespring as the admin user. Only somebody using the administrator account can change the log size limit.

2. If you're not already on the Administration page, click the Admin button in the main navigation bar to go there. The Administration page opens.

3. Click the System Configuration link in the middle of the left-hand column. The System Configuration page opens.

   In the Logging Configuration panel at the bottom of the page, the Log Size Limit field displays the current maximum size the log can grow, in bytes (**Figure 8.59**).

4. To change the log size limit, click the Edit icon at the top of the page. The Edit System Configuration page opens.

5. Update the Log Size Limit field to the maximum number of bytes any one log should contain (**Figure 8.60**).

6. To save your new log size limit, click the Save button at the bottom of the page; or click any navigation link to abandon it.

   The System Configuration page loads with a yellow warning message at the top indicating that your changes will take effect only after the server is restarted (**Figure 8.61**). The Log Size Limit field displays your updated value.

   If you've set a log level that includes more detail, the logs will reach the size limit more quickly. You should think about setting a larger limit if your log level includes more detail.

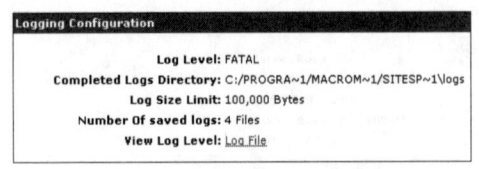

Figure 8.59 The current size to which logs are restricted is listed in the Log Size Limit field.

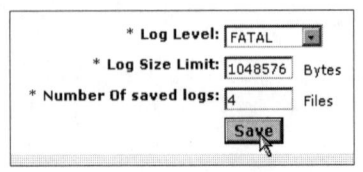

Figure 8.60 Enter the maximum number of bytes a log file should contain.

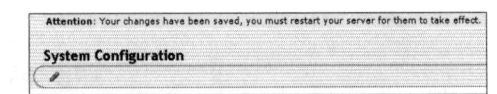

Figure 8.61 The yellow warning message indicates the new log size limit will take effect only after the server is restarted.

✔ Tip

- Remember that there are 1,024 bytes in a kilobyte (see the chart in Figure 7.43). So if you want the maximum log size to be 1 MB, enter the number of bytes as "1048576" (without commas).

Administering Sitespring

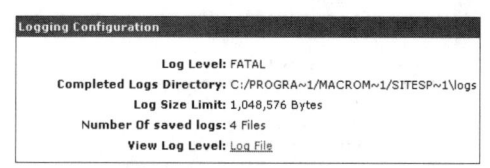

Figure 8.62 The Number of Saved Logs field lists the maximum number of log files that are saved.

Figure 8.63 Enter the new maximum number of log files you'd like to retain at any one time, then click the Save button.

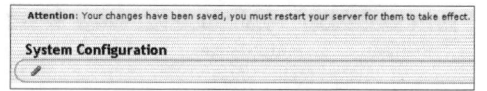

Figure 8.64 The warning message at the top indicates that your changes will take effect only after the server is restarted.

✔ Tips

- The total amount of disk space used by the log files is the number of saved logs multiplied by the log size limit.

- By setting a lower number in the Number of Saved Logs field, you conserve disk space, but you'll have a shorter history in your available logs. This could make it more difficult to identify a problem, but you'll save on space.

To set the number of logs saved:

1. Log into Sitespring as the admin user.

2. If you're not already on the Administration page, click the Admin button in the main navigation bar. The Administration page opens.

3. Click the System Configuration link in the middle of the left-hand column. The System Configuration page opens.

   In the Logging Configuration panel at the bottom of the page, the Number of Saved Logs field displays the number of logs that are saved before the oldest log is deleted (**Figure 8.62**).

4. Click the Edit icon ✏ at the top of the page. The Edit System Configuration page opens.

5. Update the Number of Saved Logs field to the number you'd like.

   Sitespring will write to a log until the file size reaches the limit set in the Log Size Limit field. At that time Sitespring starts a new log, and when the total number of logs exceeds the amount specified in the Number of Saved Logs field, it deletes the oldest one.

6. To save your new log level, click the Save button at the bottom of the page (**Figure 8.63**); or click any navigation link to abandon it.

   The System Configuration page loads with a yellow warning message at the top indicating that your changes will take effect only after the server is restarted (**Figure 8.64**). The Number of Saved Logs field displays your updated information.

207

Chapter 8

To view the server log file:

1. Log into Sitespring as the admin user.

2. If you're not already on the Administration page, click the Admin button in the main navigation bar to go there. The Administration page opens.

3. Click the System Configuration link in the middle of the left-hand column. The System Configuration page opens.

   At the bottom of the page, the Logging Configuration panel lists information about the logs (**Figure 8.65**).

4. You can view either the most recent entries in the current log or any of the log files.

   ▼ To view the most recent log file, click the Log File link in the View Log Level field (**Figure 8.66**). The Log File page opens and displays the most recent log file (**Figure 8.67**).

   ▼ To view any of the log files, you'll need to access the Sitespring server's local disk that contains the logs. Notice the path to the log directory listed in the Completed Logs Directory field, in the Logging Configuration panel (**Figure 8.68**). Navigate to that directory on the Sitespring server and you'll see the log files are simple text files that you can open in Notepad or another text editor.

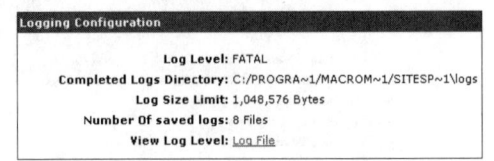

Figure 8.65 The Logging Configuration panel lists information about the log files.

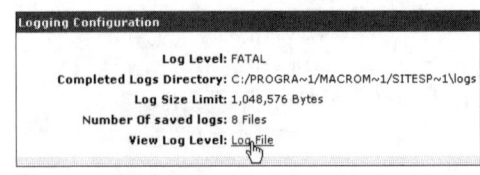

Figure 8.66 Click the Log File link to view the most recent log file contents.

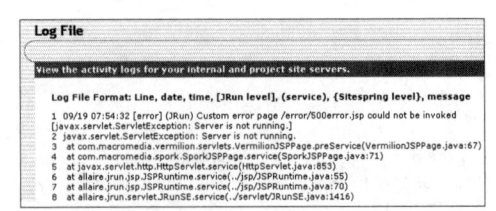

Figure 8.67 The log file displays information about the functioning of the system.

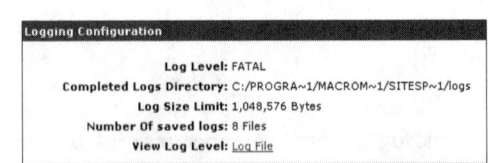

Figure 8.68 The Completed Logs Directory lists the path to the log files' directory. Because of the way Windows represents long file names, this is the shortened version of the path to C:\ Program Files\ Macromedia\Sitespring\logs\.

Viewing Detailed System Information

If you'd like to view detailed information about Sitespring and its environment, you can access the System Information page, which you can reach from the Administration page. The System Information page lists details such as which build of Sitespring you are running, how much free memory the server has, and other more detailed information about the Java environment on which Sitespring depends. You can read about which version of the Java Virtual Machine the server is running in and what version of the Java language is supported. This can be helpful if you are creating your own project-site templates and writing your own JavaServer Pages (JSP) tags. This information can also be helpful if you're trying to diagnose memory-related problems, as you can easily view how much system memory is available.

To view detailed system information:

1. Log into Sitespring as the admin user. Only somebody using the administrator account can view the detailed system information.

2. If you're not already on the Administration page, click the Admin button in the main navigation bar to go there. The Administration page opens.

3. Click the System Information link toward the bottom of the left-hand column. The System Information page opens.

continues on next page

4. The Product Information panel lists Sitespring's version number and build information (**Figure 8.69**). The Memory Information panel lists the server's free memory and total memory in bytes and the percentage of free memory (**Figure 8.70**). The System Properties panel lists detailed information about the Java environment in which Sitespring runs (**Figure 8.71**). Sitespring is based on the JRun application server, another Macromedia product. You can view information about the Java version and the virtual machine version in use.

Figure 8.69 The Product Information panel lists Sitespring's version and build numbers.

Figure 8.70 In the Memory Information panel, you can see how much free and installed memory is on the server.

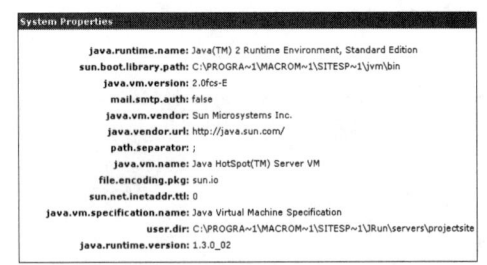

Figure 8.71 The System Properties panel lists information about the Java environment in which Sitespring runs.

Index

12/24-hour time formats, 189
+ icon, 49
? icon, 14

A

accounts
    for client organizations, 33–36
    for client users, 37–42
    limitation on number of, 21
    for normal users, 22–29
Add Discussion page, 137
Add Document Category page, 182
Add Excluded File Extension page, 161
Add icon, 22
Add License Key page, 202
Add Project page, 44
Add Task page, 104, 107, 109
Add Team Members page, 55
Add to Project Site icon, 57
Add User page, 22
Additional User Licenses module, 202, 203
Admin button, 14
Administration page, 14, 22, 209
Administrative Tools folder, 152, 153, 155
administrators
    and Document List categories, 62
    and file versioning, 151, 157
    and project/task settings, 177, 179
    and shared folders, 152
    what they can/cannot do, 20, 21
application mapping, 96–102
approval history, file, 86, 87
approval tracking, task, 178
Assignment Comment page, 108, 111
Assignment History module, 108, 111, 114, 120

B

backup files, 160
base URL, 60, 199–200
bread crumb trail, 12
Browse for Folder dialog, 153
bytes, 166, 206

C

CarbonLib file, 94
Cleanup Wizard. *See* Revision Cleanup Wizard
client communications, 9, 10, 58
Client Completed status, 109
client organization accounts, 33–36
    adding/editing, 33–34
    associating clients/projects with, 34
    deleting, 35–36
    purpose of, 33
client organizations
    adding/editing accounts for, 33–34
    contrasted with client users, 21
    defined, 21
    viewing phone/URL list for, 13
Client Organizations page, 13, 34
client problems, 4–5
Client Task module, 62
Client Task Update module, 62
client user accounts, 37–40
    adding, 38
    deleting, 40
    editing, 39
    fields associated with, 37
client users
    adding to/removing from contact lists, 42
    assigning tasks to, 55, 62, 108

Index

client users, *continued*
    associating with client organizations, 34
    contrasted with client organizations, 21
    defined, 20
    granting/revoking permissions for, 40–41
    what they can/cannot do, 20, 21, 37
    working with accounts for, 37–42
Clients button, 13
Clone a Task page, 114
Clone icon, 48
Clone Projects page, 48
cloning
    projects, 45, 47, 48
    tasks, 106, 114
Closed status, 51
collaboration tools, 64
collapse icon, 16
color-coding, status value, 178–179
Comma Separated Value. *See* CSV format
communication protocols, 185
communications, client, 9, 10, 58
Complete/Completed status
    for projects, 51
    for tasks, 109, 116, 121–122
Completed Logs Directory field, 208
Comps document category, 62, 179, 183
Computer Management console, 152, 153, 155
Computer Management icon, 153
Configure Strategy page, 166, 171, 174
contact list
    adding/removing names, 32, 42, 54, 57
    purpose of, 30
    sorting, 30
    viewing, 30–31
Contact module, 62
Contacts page, 42
Control Panel folder, 153, 155
Create Discussion module, 62, 145
Create Report page, 13, 128–129
Create Shared Folder Wizard, 153
Create Snapshot icon, 69
Critical log level, 205
critical notification email, 194
CSV format, 65, 115
CVS version-management system, 11

D

date, cleaning up files based on, 164, 169–174
date-due setting, task, 181–182

date format, server, 185, 189–190
Debug log level, 204, 205
Delete Client Organizations page, 35, 36
Delete Client Users page, 40
Delete Discussions page, 149
Delete icon, 26
Delete Project Site page, 63
Delete Projects page, 53
Delete Reports page, 132
Delete Status Values page, 181
Delete Task page, 113
Delete User Accounts page, 26
diagnostic information, 204, 209
Diagrams document category, 62, 179, 183
Discussion page, 138, 141
Discussion Topic module, 62
discussions, 135–149
    adding to/removing from project sites, 144–145
    closing, 146–148
    deleting, 136, 146, 148–149
    pros and cons of, 135–136
    removing posts from, 136, 142–143
    replying to, 139–141
    saving, 138
    starting, 137–138, 141
    viewing, 139–141
Discussions module, 137, 139, 142, 147–148
disk space
    cleaning up files based on, 164, 166–168
    and file-versioning feature, 163
    for log files, 207
    notification of critically low, 194
    and project snapshots, 64
DNS, 184
Document Approval module, 62
document categories
    adding, 182
    default values for, 62, 179, 183
    deleting, 183
    editing, 183
    purpose of, 179
Document Categories module, 182–183
document list
    changing document categories, 62, 182–183
    organizing files into, 62
    removing files from, 86–87
Document List Manager page, 86–87
Document List module, 62
document-management systems, 72

Index

Domain Name System, 184
Download Manager, 116
Dreamweaver, 92, 95
Due Date Settings module, 181

E

Edit Document Category page, 183
Edit E-mail Notifications page, 134
Edit icon, 24
Edit Project page, 52
Edit System Configuration page
   and date format, 190
   and host name, 186
   and log file, 205, 206, 207
   and mail server, 191, 192
   and time format/zone, 188
Edit Task page, 110
email filters, 194
email notification feature
   configuring Sitespring for, 191–194
   and project-team assignments, 55
   purpose of, 10, 133
   setting preferences for, 27, 29, 133–134
   and task management, 103, 104
error messages, 204, 205
Excluded File Extensions module, 161, 162
expand icon, 16
Explore icon, 70
Export icon, 68
Export Project page, 68
Export Task page, 115
exporting
   contrasted with taking snapshots, 64
   projects, 67–68
   supported file formats, 65
   tasks, 107, 115–116
extensions. *See* file extensions

F

FAT/FAT32 file system, 157
Fatal log level, 205
fields
   application mapping, 97
   client user account, 37
   discussion, 138
   normal user account, 23
   project, 45
   publishing, 84–85
   task, 109

File Download dialog, 116
File Explorer
   accessing, 13
   alternatives to, 77
   and file publishing, 83–85
   finding/selecting folders with, 49–50
   and linking of files/folders to tasks, 124–125
   purpose of, 13
   reverting to earlier versions of files with, 81–82
   viewing/editing files with, 77, 78–80
file extensions
   and application mapping, 97, 99, 100, 101
   defined, 97
   deleting files by, 101
   excluding from versioning, 160–162
file formats
   for importing/exporting, 65
   for publishing to project site, 83
file mapping, 96–102
File Revision Management page, 161
file sharing, 70, 74, 88, 152–159
file size
   cleaning up files based on, 164, 166–168
   limiting uploads based on, 195, 200
file systems
   FAT/FAT32, 157
   NTFS, 155, 157
File Transfer Protocol, 185
File Upload module, 88–89
file-versioning feature, 151–176
   contrasted with version-management systems, 11, 72
   disk-space considerations, 163
   enabling/disabling, 152, 155, 157–159
   excluding file extension from, 160–162
   how it works, 9, 72–73, 77
   purpose of, 71, 151
files, 77–89
   associating with applications, 96–98, 102
   backing up, 160
   creating/editing, 77, 79
   downloading, 116
   keeping track of, 7, 9, 71, 72–73
   linking to tasks, 123–127
   publishing, 83–85, 125
   removing, 86–87
   reverting to earlier versions, 81–82, 151
   uploading, 62, 88–89
   viewing, 77–80
   viewing revision history, 79–80

213

Index

Files button, 13
filters, email, 194
Finder. *See* Mac Finder
Flash, 83
folders. *See also* specific folders
   accessing from server, 47
   adding to projects, 47, 49–50
   expanding/collapsing, 16, 49, 78, 85
   linking to tasks, 123–127
   managing, 74–76
   removing from projects, 74, 76
   sharing, 70, 74, 88, 152–159
   standardizing structure of, 74
Folders module, 50, 75, 76
FTP, 185
fully qualified host name, 184, 185

G

Gantt charts, 107, 116
GIF format, 83
GMT time zone, 189
Greenwich Mean Time, 189

H

Handoff log level, 205
hard disk. *See* disk space
Help button, 14
Helper application. *See* Sitespring Helper
Home button, 13
home page, 12
host name
   fully qualified, 184, 185
   for mail server, 191
   for project site, 195–196
   saving, 186
   setting, 185–186
HTML format, 83
HTTP protocol, 184

I

Import Details Project page, 66
Import icon, 66
importing, 64–67
   from Microsoft Project, 64, 65
   project-name considerations, 67
   supported file formats, 65
Inactive Projects page, 51, 119
Info panel, 140

Install Wizard, 91–92
interface elements, 12–18
IP address
   for project site, 195–196
   purpose of, 184
   saving, 186
   setting, 185–186
Item Information icon, 78

J

Java, 209, 210
Java Virtual Machine, 209
JavaServer Pages, 58, 209
JRun application server, 210
JSP tags, 58, 209

K

kilobytes, 166, 206

L

License Key field, 202
License Management page, 202, 203
licenses
   adding/removing, 202–203
   restrictions on number of users, 21, 202
Link Files icon, 125
Link icon, 124
Linked Content module
   and file publishing, 83, 84
   and file viewing, 79
   and linking of files/folders to tasks, 124, 127
   and task cloning, 114
   and task viewing, 120
linking/unlinking
   projects and users, 54–57
   tasks and files/folders, 123–127
log file, 204–208
   purpose of, 204
   setting log level, 204–205
   setting number of logs saved, 207
   setting size limit, 206
   viewing, 208
Log Out button, 14
Log Size Limit field, 206, 207
Logging Configuration panel, 204, 206, 207, 208

214

Index

M

Mac Finder, 75, 77, 78, 90
Macintosh
   and application mapping, 96–102
   choosing multiple items on, 129
   Download Manager, 116
   and file extensions, 102
   installing Sitespring Helper on, 93–95
   and shared folders, 154, 155, 156, 157
Macromedia programs, 92, 95
mail. *See* email
mail server, 191–194
mapping, application, 96–102
megabytes, 166
memory, viewing available, 209, 210
Memory Information panel, 210
messages, discussion, 138
messaging system, 135. *See also* discussions
Microsoft Excel, 65, 83
Microsoft Project, 64, 65, 107
Microsoft Project Exchange, 65
Milestone Revision option, 80
milestone revisions, 80, 164, 205
Module Availability module, 61, 86
modules, 16–18, 62. *See also* specific modules
MPX format, 65
My Discussions module, 16, 139, 142, 147–148
My Projects module, 16, 48, 59, 137
My Reports module, 16, 128
My Tasks module, 16, 103, 105, 117–119

N

navigation bar, 12–13
New File Share command, 152
normal users
   defined, 20
   viewing information about, 30–31
   what they can/cannot do, 20, 27
   working with accounts for, 22–29 (*See also* user accounts)
Not Started status
   for projects, 45, 47, 48
   for tasks, 109
Notification Configuration panel, 191, 192, 194
notification preferences, 133–134
NTFS file system, 155, 157
Number of Saved Logs field, 207

O

Open status
   for projects, 45
   for tasks, 109
organization charts, Web team, 2
owner, project, 45

P

passwords
   for client users, 37, 39
   for mail servers, 191
   for normal users, 22, 23, 27–28
path, project, 60
PC. *See also* Windows
   and application mapping, 96–102
   choosing multiple items on, 129
   File Download dialog, 116
   and file extensions, 102
   installing Sitespring Helper on, 90–92
permissions
   administrator, 20
   granting/revoking, 40–41
   project manager, 20, 23, 43, 177
   user, 23
Permitted Client Users module, 41, 42
plus-sign icon, 49
port numbers
   for commonly used applications, 185
   for mail servers, 191
   for project sites, 197–198
   purpose of, 184
   for Web servers, 186–187
Post Reply link, 140
Posts panel, 140, 143
Preferences button, 14, 28
priority options
   for projects, 45
   for tasks, 109, 122, 129, 130
problems, 4–8
   client-related, 4–5
   lost files, 7
   project planning, 8
   team member, 5–6
Product Information panel, 210
Project. *See* Microsoft Project
project-collaboration tools, 64
project fields, 45
project manager permissions, 177

215

Index

project managers, 20, 23, 43
project owners, 45
project paths, 60
project-site contact list. *See* contact list
Project Site page, 40–41
Project Site Port field, 197, 198
Project Site Settings panel, 196, 197, 201
Project Site Upload Limit field, 200, 201
project sites, 58–63
    adding/removing discussions, 144–145
    configuring servers for, 195–201
    creating, 58, 59–60
    customizing, 58–59
    defined, 43, 58
    deleting, 63
    editing, 61
    granting/revoking permissions for, 40–41
    publishing files to, 83–85, 125
    removing files from, 86–87
    setting visible modules for, 61–62
    templates for, 58, 60
    uploading files to, 62, 88–89
project snapshots, 64, 69–70
Project Status module, 62
projects, 43–70
    adding/removing folders, 47, 49–50, 74, 76
    cloning, 45, 47, 48
    completing, 51–52
    creating, 44–45
    defined, 24, 43
    deleting, 51, 53
    editing, 46
    importing/exporting, 66–68
    linking/unlinking users, 54–57
    managing, 47–50, 58, 64
    naming, 45
    prioritizing, 45
    suspending, 51–52
Projects button, 13
Projects page, 13, 15, 59
Proposals document category, 62, 179, 183
Publish Files page, 84
Publish icon, 84
publishing files, 83–85, 125

Q

question mark icon, 14

R

Remove Folders page, 76
Remove from Project Site icon, 87
Remove Team Members page, 56
Report Results page, 130
reports, 128–132
    creating, 13, 128–130
    deleting, 132
    running, 131–132
    saving, 128, 131
Reports button, 13
Requirements Docs document category, 62, 179, 183
Revision Cleanup Wizard, 163–176
    and administrator permissions, 20
    how it works, 163
    and milestone revisions, 80
    moving revisions to another drive, 175
    previewing effects of, 176
    purpose of, 163
    strategies for using, 164–174
Revision History module, 78–80, 81–82
_revisions folder
    cleaning up, 163
    and file versioning, 72–73, 77, 81, 160

S

Saved Logs field, Number of, 207
Search button, 13
Search page, 13
Server Configuration panel, 188, 190
server setup
    mail server, 191–194
    project-site server, 195–201
    Sitespring server, 184–190
Shared Folder Management page, 157, 158, 159
shared folders/drives, 152–159
    adding, 153–155
    enabling/disabling versioning on, 152, 155, 157–159
    and Macintosh clients, 154, 155, 156, 157
    removing, 152, 155–156
Shares icon, 152
Simple Mail Transfer Protocol, 185. *See also* SMTP
Sitespring
    accessing, 8
    configuring, 14
        log file, 204–208

Index

mail server, 191–194
Web server, 184–190
interface, 12–18
major features, 8–11
purpose of, 1
viewing detailed information about, 209–210
Sitespring Helper, 90–102
and application mapping, 96–102
configuring, 96–100
installing, 90–95
launching, 92, 95, 96
and project snapshots, 70
purpose of, 90
SMTP, 185, 191
snapshots, project, 64, 69–70
Snapshots module, 69
SourceSafe, 11
Specifications document category, 62, 179, 183
status field
for projects, 45
for tasks, 109, 116, 130, 178–181
Status Values module, 180
Suspended status
for projects, 51
for tasks, 109, 116, 121–122, 178
System Configuration page, 185–186, 188, 190, 206
System Information page, 209
System Properties panel, 210
System Tools icon, 155

T

task list, 15–16, 122. *See also* tasks
task management features, 10, 103
Task page, 117, 120
task reporting features, 103. *See also* reports
tasks, 104–127
assigning to users, 55, 62, 105–106, 108, 116
attaching comments, 109, 111
changing due date, 181–182
changing status, 109, 116, 178–181
cloning, 106, 114
creating, 106, 107–109
deleting, 106, 113
describing, 109
editing, 106, 110–112
exporting, 115–116
linking/unlinking files and folders, 123–127
managing, 104–106
naming, 109
organizing into reports, 117, 128
(*See also* reports)
prioritizing, 109
saving, 111, 114
sorting, 122
viewing, 117–122
Tasks module, 110, 112, 117
Team Members page, 31
Team module, 54
Team Task module, 62
teams. *See* Web teams
templates, project-site, 58, 60
threads, discussion, 62
time formats, 185, 188, 189
time zones, 189
top-level domains, 185
topics, discussion, 138, 139, 141, 146, 148–149
Trace log level, 205
troubleshooting, 204, 209

U

Unlink icon, 127
unlinking. *See* linking/unlinking
Upload File button, 88
Upload Limit field, Project Site, 200, 201
Upload module, 62, 88–89
URL
associating task with, 109
components of, 185
for project sites, 60, 199–200
for Web servers, 184
user accounts, 22–29. *See also* client user accounts
adding, 22–24
changing email notification preferences, 29
changing passwords, 27–28
changing user profiles, 28
deleting, 25–26
editing user information, 24–25
fields associated with, 23
limitation on quantity of, 21
user licenses. *See* licenses
User Management page, 22, 24, 30
user profiles, 27, 28
users. *See also* specific types
adding to project teams, 54
assigning tasks to, 55, 62, 105–106, 108
linking to projects, 54–57
types of, 20
viewing information about, 30–31

217

Index

V

version control systems, 9, 11, 72
versioning feature, 151–176
    contrasted with version control systems, 11, 72
    disk-space considerations, 163
    enabling/disabling, 152, 155, 157–159
    excluding file extension from, 160–162
    how it works, 9, 72–73, 77
    purpose of, 71, 151
visibility settings, module, 61

W

Warning log level, 205
Web development process, 4
Web projects, 4–8. *See also* projects
Web servers
    default port for, 184, 185
    setting up, 185–190
    time/date formats for, 185, 188–190
    URL for, 184
Web teams
    adding/removing users, 54, 56
    creating/viewing contact lists for, 30–32
    how Sitespring helps, 8–11
    problems faced by, 4–8
    role of, 2–3
    sample organization charts, 2
    small vs. large, 2
Windows. *See also* PC
    and application mapping, 96–102
    and file extensions, 102
    installing Sitespring Helper under, 90–92
    and long file names, 208
    opening/viewing files and folders under, 75, 77, 78, 90
Windows Explorer, 75, 77, 78, 90
wizards
    Create Shared Folder Wizard, 153
    Install Wizard, 91–92
    Revision Cleanup Wizard, 20, 80, 163–176
workflow, 10

New from Peachpit Press!

FREE TRIAL OFFER

VISUAL QUICKSTART ONLINE LIBRARY
Quick Search, Quick Find, QuickStart

Over 25 top Web and Graphics Visual QuickStarts, just $49.95* a year!

Over 25 Books! a $450 value for $49.95*

Our new **Visual QuickStart Online Library** offers you

- Easy access to the most current information on Web design and graphics via the Web—wherever you are, 24 hours a day, 7 days a week
- Powerful, advanced search features that enable you to find just the topics you want across multiple books, ranked by relevance
- Updates to new editions of the books as they become available
- Easy ways to bookmark, make notes, and send email alerts to colleagues
- Complete access to over 25 of the bestselling books for only $49.95* a year (that's more than $450 worth of books for less than the price of three *Visual QuickStart Guides*!)

You'll find all your favorite *Visual QuickStart Guides,* as well as those you want to read next, including:

HTML for the World Wide Web
Photoshop for Windows and Macintosh
Illustrator for Windows and Macintosh
Perl and CGI for the World Wide Web
Flash for Windows and Macintosh

Free Trial Offer!

Give it a try, it's on us. We invite you to test Peachpit's new Visual QuickStart Online Library, FREE for one week. Just visit **www.quickstartonline.com** and sign up for your free trial today!

*Charter price of $49.95 a year is available for a limited time to early subscribers.

www.quickstartonline.com

Peachpit Press

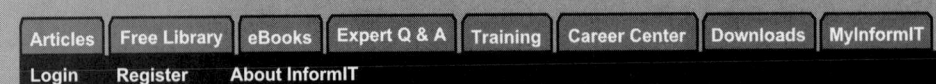

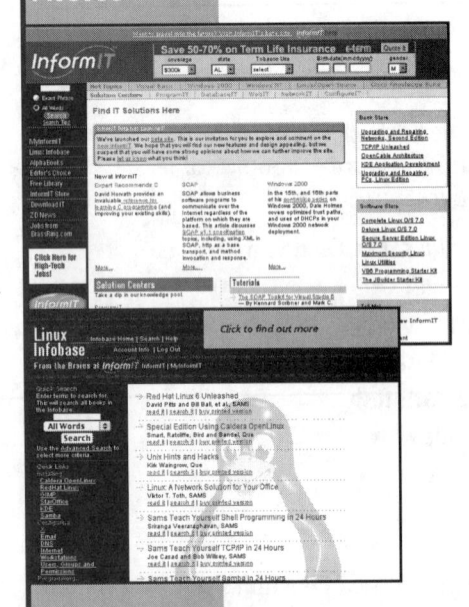